MOUNT EVEREST

THE RECONNAISSANCE, 1921

MOUNT EVEREST

THE RECONNAISSANCE, 1921

BY

Lieut.-Col. C. K. HOWARD-BURY, D.S.O.
AND OTHER MEMBERS OF THE
MOUNT EVEREST EXPEDITION

WITH ILLUSTRATIONS AND MAPS

GYAN

Published by

Gyan Publishing House
5, Ansari Road
Daryaganj, New Delhi-110002
Phone: 011-47034999, 9811692060
E-mail: books@gyanbooks.com

Distribution Network
gyanbooks.com
India, USA, Canada, UK, Australia, France

ISBN : 978-81-212-2893-0 (PB)
First Published, 1922

2nd Impression 2021

Printed at: Gyan Press, Delhi.

Mount Everest
The Reconnaissance, 1921
Author: C. K. Howard-Bury

MOUNT EVEREST
THE RECONNAISSANCE, 1921

By

Lieut.-Col. C. K. HOWARD-BURY, D.S.O.

AND OTHER MEMBERS OF THE
MOUNT EVEREST EXPEDITION

WITH ILLUSTRATIONS AND MAPS

LONGMANS, GREEN AND CO.

55 FIFTH AVENUE, NEW YORK

LONDON: EDWARD ARNOLD & CO.

1922

PREFACE

The Mount Everest Committee of the Royal Geographical Society and the Alpine Club desire to express their thanks to Colonel Howard-Bury, Mr. Wollaston, Mr. Mallory, Major Morshead, Major Wheeler and Dr. Heron for the trouble they have taken to write so soon after their return an account of their several parts in the joint work of the Expedition. They have thereby enabled the present Expedition to start with full knowledge of the results of the reconnaissance, and the public to follow the progress of the attempt to reach the summit with full information at hand.

The Committee also wish to take this opportunity of thanking the Imperial Dry Plate Company for having generously presented photographic plates to the Expedition and so contributed to the production of the excellent photographs that have been brought back.

They also desire to thank the Peninsular and Oriental Steam Navigation Company for their liberality in allowing the members to travel at reduced fares ; and the Government of India for allowing the stores and equipment of the Expedition to enter India free of duty.

J. E. C. Eaton, A. R. Hinks — *Hon. Secretaries.*

CONTENTS

NATURAL HISTORY

By A. F. R. WOLLASTON

APPENDICES

LIST OF ILLUSTRATIONS

LIST OF MAPS

LIST OF MAPS

INTRODUCTION

By Sir FRANCIS YOUNGHUSBAND, K.C.S.I., K.C.I.E.

The idea of climbing Mount Everest has been vaguely in men's mind for thirty or forty years past. Certainly that veteran mountain-climber and mountain-lover, Douglas Freshfield, had it persistently rising within him as he broke away from the Swiss Alps and subdued the giants of the Caucasus and then sought still higher peaks to conquer. Lord Curzon also had had it in his mind, and when Viceroy of India had written suggesting that the Royal Geographical Society and the Alpine Club should make a joint exploration of the mountain. Bruce, Longstaff and Mumm would have made this exploration in 1905 if the permission of the Nepalese and Tibetan Governments had been available. So also would Rawling a few years later. All these, and doubtless others, had contemplated at least a preliminary reconnaissance of Mount Everest.

But, so far as I know, the first man to propose a definite expedition to Mount Everest was the then Captain Bruce, who, when he and I were together in Chitral in 1893, proposed to me that we should make a glorious termination to a journey from Chinese Turkestan across Tibet by ascending Mount Everest. And it is Bruce who has held to the idea ever since and sought any opportunity that offered of getting at the mountain.

It stands to reason that men with any zest for mountaineering could not possibly allow Mount Everest to remain untouched. The time, the opportunity, the money, the ability to make the necessary preliminary preparation might be lacking, but the wish and the will to stand on the summit of the world's highest mountain must have been in the heart of many a mountaineer since the Alps have been so firmly trampled under foot. The higher climbers climb, the higher they want to climb. It is certain that they will never rest content till the proudest peaks of the Himalaya are as subdued and tamed as the once dreaded summits of the Alps now are.

Men simply cannot resist exercising and stretching to their fullest tether the faculties and aptitudes with which they each happen to be specially endowed. One born with an aptitude for painting is dull and morose and fidgety until he can get colours and a brush into his hand and commence painting. Another is itching to make things—to use his hands and fashion wood or stone or metal into forms which he is continually creating in his mind. Another is restless until he can sing. Another is ever pining to be on a public platform swaying the audience with his oratory and playing on their feelings as on a musical instrument. Each has his own inner aptitude which he aches to give vent to and bring into play. And more than this, he secretly owns within himself an exceedingly high standard—the highest standard—of what he wants to attain to along his own particular line, and he is never really content in his mind and at peace with himself when he is not stretching himself out to the full towards this high pinnacle which he has set before him.

Now fortunately all men are not born with the same aptitudes. We do not all want to sing or all want to orate or all want to paint. Some few want to climb mountains. These men love to pit themselves against what most others would consider an insuperable obstacle. They enjoy measuring themselves against it and being forced to exercise all their energies and faculties to overcome it. The Duke of the Abruzzi is as good an example of this type as I know. He was never happy until he had discovered some inaccessible and impracticable mountain and then thrown himself against it and come to grips with it in dead earnest and either conquered it or been thrown back from it utterly and completely exhausted, but with the satisfaction that anyhow he had exercised every nerve and muscle and faculty to the full. His native mountains he had early conquered over and over again, so he had to look further afield to Mount Elias in Alaska and Ruwenzori in East Africa; and having vanquished these he would doubtless have turned his eyes to Mount Everest if for political reasons the way to that mountain had not been barred, and he was compelled therefore to look to the next highest mountain, namely, the peak K2 in the Karakoram Himalaya in the neighbourhood of which he attained to a greater height, 24,600 feet, than has yet been attained by any man on foot.

The Duke no doubt is human and would like his name to go down to posterity as having conquered some conspicuously lofty and difficult peak. But undoubtedly the ruling passion with him would be this love of pitting himself against a great mountain and feeling that he was being forced to exert himself to the full. To such men a tussle with a mountain is a real tonic—something bracing and refreshing. And even if they are laid out flat by the mountain instead of standing triumphant on its summit they have enjoyed the struggle and would go back for another if they ever had the chance.

Others—like Bruce—climb from sheer exuberance of spirits. Blessed with boundless energy they revel in its exercise. It is only on the mountain side, breathing its pure air, buffeting against its storms, testing their nerve, running hair-breadth risks, exercising their intelligence and judgment, feeling their manhood and looking on Nature face to face and with open heart and mind that they are truly happy. For these men days on the mountain are days when they really live. And as the cobwebs in their brains get blown away, as the blood begins to course refreshingly through their veins, as all their faculties become tuned up and their whole being becomes more sensitive, they detect appeals from Nature they had never heard before and see beauties which are revealed only to those who win them. They may not at the moment be aware of the deepest impressions they are receiving. But to those who have struggled with them the mountains reveal beauties they will not disclose to those who make no effort. That is the reward the mountains give to effort. And it is because they have much to give and give it so lavishly to those who will wrestle with them that men love the mountains and go back to them again and again.

And naturally the mountains reserve their choicest gifts for those who stand upon their summits. The climber's vision is then no longer confined and enclosed. He can see now all round. His width of outlook is enlarged to its full extremity. He sees in every direction. He has a sense of being raised above the world and being proudly conscious that he has raised himself there by his own exertions, he has a peculiar satisfaction and for the time forgets all frets and worries in the serener atmosphere in which he now for a moment dwells.

And it is only for a moment that he can dwell there. For men cannot always live on the heights. They must come down to the plains again and engage in the practical life of the world. But the vision from the heights never leaves them. They want to return there. They want to reach a higher height. Their standard of achievement rises. And so it has come about that mountaineers when they had climbed the highest heights in Europe went off to the Caucasus, to the Andes, and eventually to the Himalaya to climb something higher still. Freshfield conquered the Caucasus, Whymper and Conway the Andes, and the assault upon the Himalaya is now in full swing.

It is therefore only in the natural course of things that men should want to climb the highest summit of the

Himalaya. And though those who set out to climb Mount Everest will probably think little of the eventual results, being perfectly satisfied in their own minds, without any elaborate reasoning, that what they are attempting is something supremely worth while, yet it is easy for lookers on to see that much unexpected good will result from their activities. The climbers will be actuated by sheer love of mountaineering, and that is enough for them. But climbing Mount Everest is no futile and useless performance of no satisfaction to anyone but the climbers. Results will follow from it of the highest value to mankind at large.

For the climbers are unwittingly carrying out an experiment of momentous consequence to mankind. They are testing the capacity of the human race to stand the highest altitudes on this earth which is its home. No scientific man, no physiologist or physician, can now say for certain whether or not a human body can reach a height of 29,000 feet above the sea. We know that in an aeroplane he can be carried up to a much greater height. But we do not know whether he can climb on his own feet such an altitude. That knowledge of men's capacity can only be acquired by practical experiment in the field.

And in the process of acquiring the knowledge a valuable result will ensue. By testing their capacities men actually increase them. By exercising their capacities to the full mountaineers seem to enlarge them. A century ago the ascent of Mount Blanc seemed the limit of human capacity. Nowadays hundreds ascend the mountain every year. And going further afield men ascended the highest peaks in the Caucasus and then in the Andes and have been reaching higher and higher altitudes in the Himalaya. Conway reached 23,000 feet, Kellas 23,180 feet, Longstaff 23,360 feet, Dr. Workman 23,000 feet, Kellas and Meade 23,600 feet and the Duke of the Abruzzi 24,600 feet. It looks therefore as if man by attempting more was actually making himself capable of achieving more. By straining after the highest he is increasing his capacity to attain it.

In this measuring of themselves against the mountains men are indeed very like puppies crawling about and testing their capacities on their surroundings—crawling up on to some obstacle, tumbling back discomfited but returning gallantly to the attack and at last triumphantly surmounting it. Thus do they find out what they can do and how they stand in relation to their surroundings. Also by exercising and stretching their muscles and faculties to the full they actually increase their capacity.

Men are still only in the puppy stage of existence. We are prone to think ourselves very "grown up" but really we are only in our childhood. In the latest discussions as to the period of time which must have elapsed since life first appeared upon this earth a period of the order of a thousand million years was named. But of that immense period man has been in existence for only a quarter or half a million years. So the probability is that he has still long years before him and must be now only in his childhood—in his puppyhood. We certainly find that as he inquisitively looks about his surroundings and measures himself against them he is steadily increasing his mastery over them. In the last five hundred years record after record has been beaten. Men have ventured more and shown more adaptability and a sterner hardihood and endurance than ever before. They have ventured across the oceans, circumnavigated the globe, reached the poles, risen into the air, and it can be only a question of time—a few months or a few years—before they reach the highest summit of the earth.

"What then?" some will ask. "Suppose men do reach the top of Mount Everest, what then?" "Suppose we do establish the fact that man has the capacity to surmount the highest summit of his surroundings, of what good is that knowledge?" This is the kind of question promoters of the enterprise continually have to answer. One reply is obvious. The sight of climbers struggling upwards to the supreme pinnacle will have taught men to lift their eyes unto the hills—to raise them off the ground and direct them, if only for a moment, to something pure and lofty and satisfying to that inner craving for the worthiest which all men have hidden in their souls. And when they see men thrown back at first but venturing again and again to the assault till with faltering footsteps and gasping breaths they at last reach the summit they will thrill with pride. They will no longer be obsessed with the thought of what mites they are in comparison with the mountains—how insignificant they are beside their material surroundings. They will have a proper pride in themselves and a well-grounded faith in the capacity of spirit to dominate material.

And direct practical results flow from this increasing confidence which man is acquiring in face of the mountains. A century ago Napoleon's crossing of the Alps was thought an astounding feat. During the last thirty years troops —and Indian troops—have been moved about the Himalaya in all seasons and crossed passes over 15,000 feet above sea level in the depth of winter. On the Gilgit frontier, in Chitral, and in Tibet, neither cold nor snow nor wind stopped them. In winter or in summer, in spring or in autumn, they have faced the Himalayan passes. And they have been able to negotiate them successfully because of their increased knowledge of men's capacities and of the way to overcome difficulties that constant wrestling with mountains in all parts of the world during the last half-century has given. The activities of the Alpine Club have produced direct practical results in the movement of troops in the Himalaya.

More still will follow. When men have proved that they can surmount the highest peak in the Himalaya they will take heart to climb other peaks and become more and more at home in that wonderful region, extending for nigh two thousand miles from the Roof of the World in the North and West to the borders of Burma and China in the South and East and containing more than seventy peaks over 24,000 feet in height—that is higher than any in the Andes, the second highest range of mountains in the world—and more than eleven hundred peaks over 20,000 feet in height. This great mountain region which in Europe would stretch from Calais to the Caspian is one vast mine of beauty of every varied description. And a mine of beauty has this advantage over a mine of material wealth—that we can never exhaust it. And not only can we never exhaust it, but the more we take out the more we find, and the more we give away the richer we are. We may go on digging into a gold mine, but eventually we shall find there is no gold left. We shall have exhausted our mine. But we may dig into that mine of beauty in the Himalaya and never exhaust it. The more we dig the more we shall find—richer beauty, subtler beauty, more varied beauty—beauty of mountain form and beauty of pure and delicate colour, beauty of forest, beauty of river and beauty of lake and combined beauty of rushing torrent, precipitous cliff, richest vegetation and overtopping snowy summit. And when we have discovered these treasures and made them our own we can actually increase their value to ourselves by giving them away to others. By imparting to others the enjoyment which we have felt we shall have increased our own enjoyment.

We cannot expect those who are first engaged in climbing Mount Everest to have the time or inclination to observe and describe the full beauty there is. They will be set on overcoming the physical difficulties and they will be so exhausted for the moment by the effort they will have made that they will not have the repose of mind which is so necessary for seeing and depicting beauty. But when they have pioneered the way and beaten down a path, others will more leisurely follow after. Many even of these may not be able to express in words or in picture the enjoyment they have felt and be able to communicate it to others. They may not be given to public speech or writing and may have no capacity for painting. The flame of their enjoyment may be kept sacred and hidden within them, and it may be only in the privacy of colloquy with some kindred soul that the white glow of their enjoyment may ever be shown. But, others there may be who have the capacity for making the world at large share with them some little of the joy they have felt—who can make our nerves tingle and our blood course quicker, our eyes uplift themselves and our outlook widen as we go out with them to face and overcome the mountains. Such men as these from their very intimacy with the mountains are able to point out beauties which distant beholders would never suspect. And as Leslie Stephen through his love of mountains has been able to attract thousands to the Alps and given them enjoyment, clean and fresh, which but for him they might never have known, so we hope that in the fulness of time a greater Stephen will tell of the unsurpassable beauty of the Himalaya and by so doing add appreciably to the enjoyment of human life.

Such are some of the advantages which men in general will obtain from the attempt to climb Mount Everest. But it is time now to say something of the mountain itself.

Mount Everest for its size is a singularly shy and retiring mountain. It hides itself away behind other mountains. On the north side, in Tibet, it does indeed stand up proudly and alone, a true monarch among mountains. But it stands in a very sparsely inhabited part of Tibet, and very few people ever go to Tibet. From the Indian side only its tip appears among a mighty array of peaks which being nearer look higher. Consequently for a long time no one suspected Mount Everest of being the supreme mountain not only of the Himalaya but of the world. At the time when Hooker was making his Himalayan journeys—that was in 1849—Kanchenjunga was believed to be the highest.

How it was eventually discovered to be the highest is a story worth recording. In the very year that Hooker was botanising in the Sikkim Himalaya the officers of the

Great Trigonometrical Survey were making observations from the plains of India to the peaks in Nepal which could be seen from there. When they could find a native name for a peak they called it by that name. But in most cases no native name was forthcoming, and in those cases a Roman number was affixed to the peak. Among these unnamed peaks to which observations to determine the altitude and position were taken from stations in the plains was Peak XV. The observations were recorded, but the resulting height was not computed till three years later, and then one day the Bengali Chief Computer rushed into the room of the Surveyor-General, Sir Andrew Waugh, breathlessly exclaiming, " Sir! I have discovered the highest mountain in the world." The mean result of all the observations taken from the six stations from which Peak XV had been observed came to 29,002 feet, and this Peak XV is what is now known as Mount Everest.

The question is often asked, " Why twenty-nine thousand and two ? " " Why be so particular about the two ? " The answer is that that particular figure is the mean of many observations. But it is not infallible. It is indeed in all probability below rather than above the mark, and a later computation of the observed results puts the height at 29,141 feet. In any case, however, there are, as Sir Sidney Burrard has pointed out in his discussion of this point in Burrard and Hayden's *Himalaya and Tibet,* many causes of slight error in observing and computing the altitude of a distant and very lofty peak. The observations are made with a theodolite. The telescope of the theodolite may not be absolutely perfect. The theodolite may not be levelled with perfect accuracy. The graduations on the circle of the theodolite may not be quite accurate. The observer himself may not have observed with sufficient perfection. An error of ten feet may have resulted from these causes. Then there are other and greater sources of possible error. There may be error in the assumed height of the observing station; and the altitudes of peaks are always varying in nature with the increase and decrease of snow in summer and winter and in a season of heavy snowfall or a season of light snowfall. Another source of error arises from the varying effects of gravitational attraction. "The attraction of the great mass of the Himalaya and Tibet," says Burrard, "pulls all liquids towards itself, as the moon attracts the ocean and the surface of the water assumes an irregular form at the foot of the Himalaya. If the ocean were to overflow Northern India its surface would be deformed by Himalayan attraction. The liquid in levels is similarly affected and theodolites cannot consequently be adjusted; their plates when levelled are still tilted upward towards the mountains, and angles of observation are too small by the amount the horizon is inclined to the tangential plane. At Darjeeling the surface of water in repose is inclined about 35″ to this plane, at Kurseong about 51″, at Siliguri about 23″, at Dehra Dun and Mussooree about 37″. For this reason all angles of elevation to Himalayan peaks measured from the plains, as Mount Everest was measured, are too small and consequently all our values of Himalayan heights are too small. Errors of this nature range from 40 to 100 feet."

This then is a considerable source of error, but the most serious source of uncertainty affecting the value of heights is the refraction of the atmosphere. A ray of light from a peak to an observer's eye does not travel along a straight line but assumes a curved path concave to the earth. The ray enters the observer's eye in a direction tangential to the curve at that point, and this is the direction in which the observer sees the peak. It makes the peak appear too high. Corrections have therefore to be applied. But there is no certainty as to what should be the amount of the correction; and it is now believed that the computers of the height of Mount Everest applied too great a correction for refraction and consequently reduced its height too much.

Burrard brings together in the following table the different errors to which the carefully determined height of Mount Everest is liable :—

Source of error.	Magnitude of possible error.
Variation of snow level from the mean . . .	Unknown
Errors of observation	10 feet
Adoption of erroneous height for observing station	10 feet
Deviation of gravity	60 feet, too small
Atmospheric refraction	150 feet, too small

The following table shows how the different values of the height of Mount Everest have been deduced :—

HEIGHT OF MOUNT EVEREST

Observing station.	Year of observation.	Distance in miles.	Height as determined by Waugh.	Determination of height with revised correction for refraction.
			Feet	Feet
Jirol	1849	118	28,991	29,141
Mirzapur . . .	1849	108	29,005	29,135
Joafpati	1849	108	29,001	29,117
Ladnia	1849	108	29,998	29,144
Harpur	1849	111	29,026	29,146
Minai	1850	113	28,990	29,160
Suberkum . . .	1881	87	—	29,141
Suberkum . . .	1883	87	—	29,127
Tiger Hill . . .	1880	107	—	29,140
Sandakphu . . .	1883	89	—	29,142
Phallut	1902	85	—	29,151
Senchal	1902	108	—	29,134
Mean	—	—	29,002	29,141

The height 29,141 is still, Burrard thinks, too small, as it has yet to be corrected for the deviations of gravity. But though it is a more reliable result than 29,002, the latter is still to be retained in maps and publications of the Survey of India.

As to the name, it was called Everest after the distinguished Surveyor-General of India under whose direction the triangulation had been carried out, one result of which was the discovery of the mountain. From the Indian side and Nepal it is not a conspicuous peak on account of its lying so far back. No native name for it could be discovered and Sir Andrew Waugh, the successor of Sir George Everest, called it after his predecessor. From the Tibetan side it is much more conspicuous and, as General Bruce stated in his lecture to the Royal Geographical Society in November 1920, and as Colonel Howard-Bury found in 1921, the Tibetans call it Chomo-lungmo, which Colonel Howard-Bury translated, the "Goddess Mother of the Mountains"—a most appropriate name. But the name Mount Everest is now so firmly established throughout the world that it would be impossible to change it. It is therefore now definitely adopted.

Now, this mountain so coveted by mountaineers is unfortunately situated exactly on the border between two of the most secluded countries in the world—Nepal and Tibet. To reach it the climbers must pass through one or other of these countries and the difficulty of getting the necessary permission is what has so far prevented any attempt being made to attack Mount Everest. But recently access through Tibet has become more possible, and it so happens that it is on the Tibetan side that the summit seems most accessible. From the distant views that could be obtained of it from Sandakphu beyond Darjeeling and from Kampa Dzong in Tibet, a ridge running from the summit in a northerly direction seemed to give good promise of access. Major Ryder and Captain Rawling in 1904, viewing the mountain from a distance of sixty miles almost due north, thought the mountain might be approached from that direction. At the same time the Tibetans were distinctly more favourable to travellers than they had ever been before. The chances therefore of at least exploring Mount Everest were much more promising, and Major Rawling was planning an expedition of exploration when the war broke out and he was killed.

Mr. Douglas Freshfield would certainly have taken the matter up during his Presidency of the Royal Geographical Society, but he had the misfortune to hold that post during the years of the war and no action was possible. But as soon as the war was over interest in Mount Everest revived. In March 1919 Captain J. B. L. Noel read a paper to the Royal Geographical Society describing a reconnaissance he had made in the direction of the mountain in the year 1913. He showed how attention during the last few years had been focused more and more upon the Himalaya and said, "Now that the Poles have been reached, it is generally felt that the next and equally important task is the exploration and mapping of Mount Everest." So he urged that the exploration which had been the ambition of the late General Rawling with whom he was to have joined should be accomplished in his memory. "It cannot be long," he continued, "before the culminating summit of the world is visited and its ridges, valleys and glaciers are mapped and photographed." And at the conclusion of his lecture he said that "some day the political difficulties will be overcome and a fully equipped expedition must explore and map Mount Everest."

It was not clear whether Captain Noel was advocating a definite attempt to climb the mountain and reach the actual summit, and Mr. Douglas Freshfield and Dr. Kellas who followed after him referred only to the approaches to Mount Everest. But Captain J. P. Farrar, the then President of the Alpine Club, seems to have considered it "a proposal to attempt the ascent of Mount Everest," and said that the Alpine Club took the keenest interest in the proposal and was prepared not only to lend such financial aid as was in its power, but also to recommend two or three young mountaineers quite capable of dealing with any purely mountaineering difficulties which were likely to be met with on Mount Everest.

The hour was late, but I was so struck by the ring of assurance and determination in the words of the President of the Alpine Club that I could not help asking the President, Sir Thomas Holdich, to let me say a few words. I then told how General Bruce had made to me, twenty-six years ago, the proposal to climb Mount Everest. I said the Royal Geographical Society was interested in the project and now we had heard the President of the Alpine Club say that he had young mountaineers ready to undertake the work. I added, "It must be done." There might be one or two attempts before we were successful, but the first thing to do was to get over the trouble with our own Government. If they were approached properly by Societies like the Royal Geographical Society and the Alpine Club, and a reasonable scheme were put before them and it were proved to them that we meant business, then, I said, they would be reasonable and do what we wanted. This was a big business and must be done in a big way and I hoped that something really serious would come of that meeting.[1]

Sir Thomas Holdich in closing the meeting advocated approaching Mount Everest through Nepal, and hoped that at some time not very remote we should hear more about the proposed expedition to Mount Everest.

Only a few days after the meeting I met Colonel Howard-Bury at lunch with a Fellow of our Society, Mr. C. P. McCarthy. He was not a mountaineer in the Alpine Club sense of the word, but he had spent much of his time shooting in the

[1] In the enthusiasm of the moment I seem to have displayed a regrettable excess of "nationalism"! According to the record, I expressed the hope that it would be an Englishman who first stood on the summit of Mount Everest. I trust my foreign friends will excuse me! I have this at least to plead in extenuation, that if I have always striven for my own countrymen when they led the way, I have never been backward in helping explorers of other nationalities whom I have met in the Himalaya; and I have received the thanks of both the French and Italian Governments for the help I have given to French and Italian explorers.

Alps and in the Himalaya, and becoming deeply interested in the Mount Everest project, had a talk with Mr. Freshfield about it and made a formal application to the Society for their support in undertaking an expedition. Things now began to move, and the Society applied to the India Office for permission to send an expedition into Tibet for the purpose of exploring Mount Everest. The Government of India in reply said that they were not prepared at the moment to approach the Tibetan Government; but they did not return any absolute refusal.

During my Presidency the Society, in conjunction with the Alpine Club, still further pressed the matter. We asked the Secretary of State for India to receive a deputation from the two bodies, and the request being granted and the deputation being assured of his sympathy we invited Colonel Howard-Bury to proceed to India in June 1920 to explain our wishes personally to the Government of India, and ask them to obtain for us from the Dalai Lama the necessary permission to enter Tibet for the purpose of exploring and climbing Mount Everest. Lord Chelmsford, the Viceroy, received Colonel Howard-Bury most sympathetically and after some preliminary difficulties had been overcome, Mr. Bell, the Political Agent in Sikkim, who happened to be in Lhasa, was instructed to ask the Dalai Lama for permission, and Mr. Bell being on most friendly terms with His Holiness, permission was at once granted.

The one great obstacle in the way of approaching Mount Everest had now at last been removed. What so many keen mountaineers had for years dreamed of was within sight. And as soon as the welcome news arrived—early in January 1921—preparations were commenced to organise an expedition. A joint Committee of three representatives each from the Royal Geographical Society and the Alpine Club was formed under the Chairmanship of the President of the former Society and was named the Mount Everest Committee. The three members of the Society were Sir Francis Younghusband, Mr. E. L. Somers-Cocks (Honorary

Treasurer) and Colonel Jack. The three members of the Alpine Club were Professor Norman Collie, Captain J. P. Farrar and Mr. C. F. Meade. Mr. Eaton and Mr. Hinks were Honorary Secretaries.

Our first business was to select a leader for the Expedition. General Bruce, who had had the idea in his mind for so many years, who knew the Himalaya as no one else did, and who had a special aptitude for handling Himalayan people, was now in England, and it was to him our thoughts first turned. But he had just taken up an appointment with the Glamorganshire Territorial Association and was not then available. In these circumstances we were fortunate in having ready to hand a man with such high qualifications as Colonel Howard-Bury. He had much to do on his property in Ireland, but he willingly accepted our invitation to lead the Expedition, and we could then proceed to the choice of the mountaineers.

From the very first we decided that the main object of the Expedition was to be the ascent of the mountain and that all other activities were to be made subordinate to the supreme object of reaching the summit. It was to be no mere surveying or geologising or botanising expedition which would as a secondary object try to climb the mountain if it saw a chance. To climb the mountain was to be the first object and the mapping and everything else was to come afterwards. The reason for this is obvious. What men really want to know is whether man can ascend the highest mountain.

Knowledge of the topography, fauna and flora of that particular area is of very small consequence in comparison with the knowledge of human capacity to surmount the highest point in men's physical surroundings on this earth. By some perversity of human nature there are men who shy at putting the ascent of Mount Everest in the forefront, because it is adventurous and must therefore, they seem to think, cease to be a scientific object. They profess to be unconcerned with the climbing of the mountain so long as a map is made or plants collected. But the plain man instinctively sees the value of the adventure and knows that the successful ascent of Mount Everest will show what man is capable of and put new hope and heart into the human race.

But while it was decided to make the ascent of Mount Everest the main object of the Expedition, Professor Norman Collie and Mr. Douglas Freshfield from the first insisted that a whole season must be devoted to a thorough reconnaissance of the mountain with a view to finding not only a feasible route to the summit but what was without any doubt the most feasible route. We knew nothing of the immediate approaches to the mountain. But we knew that the only chance of reaching the summit was by finding some way up which would entail little rock-climbing or ice step-cutting. The mountain had therefore to be prospected from every side to find a comparatively easy route and to make sure that no other easier route than the one selected existed. This was considered ample work for the Expedition for one season, while the following season would be devoted to an all-out effort to reach the summit along the route selected in the first year.

On this basis the first year's Expedition had accordingly to be organised. The mountain party was to consist of four members, two of whom were to be men of considerable experience and two younger men who it was hoped would form the nucleus of the climbing party the next year. Mr. Harold Raeburn, a member of the Alpine Club who had had great experience of snow and rock work in the Alps, and who had in 1920 been climbing on the spurs of Kanchenjunga, was invited to lead the mountain party. Dr. Kellas, who had made several climbing expeditions in the Himalaya and had in 1920 ascended to a height of 23,400 feet on Mount Kamet, was also invited to join the climbing party. He had been making experiments in the use of oxygen at high altitudes and was still out in India preparing to continue these experiments on Mount Kamet in 1921.

It was suggested to him that he should make the experiments on Mount Everest instead, and the party would thereby have the benefit of his wide Himalayan experience. This invitation he accepted.

The two younger members selected for the climbing party were Mr. George Leigh Mallory and Captain George Finch, both with a very high reputation for climbing in the Alps. Unfortunately Captain Finch was for the time indisposed and his place at the last moment had to be taken by Mr. Bullock of the Consular Service, who had been at Winchester with Mr. Mallory and who happened to be at home on leave. Through the courtesy of Lord Curzon he was able to get special leave of absence from the Foreign Office.

While we were finding the men we had also to be finding the money. As a quite rough guess we estimated the Expedition for the two years would cost about £10,000, and at least a substantial portion of this had to be raised by private subscription. Appeals were made by their Presidents to the Fellows of the Royal Geographical Society and to members of the Alpine Club, and Captain Farrar was especially energetic in urging the claims of the enterprise. As a result the members of the Alpine Club subscribed over £3,000 and the Fellows of the Royal Geographical Society nearly that amount. Later on with the advice and help of Mr. John Buchan arrangements were made with *The Times* and the *Philadelphia Ledger* for the purchase of the rights of publication of telegrams from the Expedition, and with the *Graphic* for the purchase of photographs. So eventually the financial position of the Expedition was assured.

The equipment and provisioning of the Expedition was undertaken by the Equipment Committee—Captain Farrar and Mr. Meade—and the greatest trouble was taken to ensure that the most suitable and best tents, sleeping bags, clothing, boots, ice-axes, ropes, cooking apparatus, provisions, etc., were purchased and that they were properly packed and listed.

In the same way the scientific equipment was undertaken by Colonel Jack and Mr. Hinks.

Finally the services of Mr. Wollaston, well known for his journeys in New Guinea and East Africa, were secured as Medical Officer and Naturalist to the Expedition.

Throughout these preparations the advice and help of the best men in every line were freely and willingly forthcoming. For such an enterprise all were ready to give a helping hand. Whether they were scientific men, or business men or journalists, they were ready to throw aside their own work and devote hours to ensuring that the Expedition should be a success along the lines on which they severally had most experience.

And most valuable was the encouragement given to the Expedition by the interest which His Majesty showed in conversation with the President, and His Royal Highness the Prince of Wales in receiving Colonel Howard-Bury—an interest which was shown in practical form by generous subscriptions to the funds of the Expedition.

The Expedition was able, therefore, to set out from England under the most favourable auspices, and it was to be joined in India by two officers of the Indian Survey Department, Major Morshead and Major Wheeler, and by an officer of the Indian Geological Survey, Dr. Heron. It was thus admirably equipped for the acquirement of knowledge. But acquirement of knowledge was not the only object which the Expedition had in view. It could not be doubted that the region would possess beauty of exceptional grandeur. So it was hoped that the Expedition would discover, describe and reveal to us, by camera and by pen, beauty no less valuable than the knowledge.

THE NARRATIVE OF THE EXPEDITION

By

LIEUT.-COL. C. K. HOWARD-BURY, D.S.O.

CHAPTER I

FROM DARJEELING THROUGH SIKKIM

Early in May most of the members of the Expedition had assembled at Darjeeling. Mr. Raeburn had been the first to arrive there in order to collect as many coolies of the right type as he could. I had come out a few weeks earlier in order to visit the Indian Authorities at Simla and to make sure that there were no political difficulties in the way. There I found every one very kind and helpful and all were anxious to do their best to assist the Expedition. Owing to the heavy deficit in the Indian Budget, the expenses of every Department had been rigorously cut down, and the Government of India were unable to give us financial assistance. They agreed, however, to take upon themselves the whole of the expenses of the survey, and to lend the Expedition the services of an officer of the Geological Department. The Viceroy, Lord Reading, who, together with Lady Reading, took the greatest interest in the Expedition, kindly gave us a subscription of 750 rupees, and at Darjeeling the Governor of Bengal, Lord Ronaldshay, had not only put up several members of the Expedition at his most comfortable house, but had also given the Expedition several rooms in which to collect their stores for separation and division into loads. Local stores, such as tea, sugar, flour and potatoes had to be bought on the spot. Coolies had to be collected and arrangements made for fitting them out with boots and warm clothing. The coolies were to receive pay at the rate of 12 annas per day while in Sikkim, and when in Tibet were to receive another 6 annas per day, either in cash or the equivalent in rations. The former proved the most acceptable eventually, except during the period when the coolies were up on the glaciers, where there were no villages and consequently nothing could be bought.

A passport had been sent to us by the Government at Lhasa under the seal of the Prime Minister of Tibet, of which the following is a translation:—

To

The Jongpens and Headmen of Pharijong, Ting-ke, Khamba and Kharta.

You are to bear in mind that a party of Sahibs are coming to see the Chha-mo-lung-ma mountain and they will evince great friendship towards the Tibetans. On the request of the Great Minister Bell a passport has been issued requiring you and all officials and subjects of the Tibetan Government to supply transport, e.g. riding ponies, pack animals and coolies as required by the Sahibs, the rates for which should be fixed to mutual satisfaction. Any other assistance that the Sahibs may require either by day or by night, on the march or during halts, should be faithfully given, and their requirements about transport or anything else should be promptly attended to. All the people of the country, wherever the Sahibs may happen to come, should render all necessary assistance in the best possible way, in order to maintain friendly relations between the British and Tibetan Governments.

Despatched during the Iron-Bird Year.
Seal of the Prime Minister.

Our start had been originally arranged for the middle of May, but the "Hatarana," in which were most of our stores, was unable to obtain a berth, as accommodation in the Docks at Calcutta was very insufficient for the large number of steamers that call there; she had therefore to lie out in the Hoogly for a fortnight before she could get room in the Docks. However, by May 11 everything was unloaded at Calcutta. The Darjeeling-Himalayan Railway had generously given the Expedition a free pass over their line for all stores and goods, and as the Customs had granted a free entry into the country, everything was up in Darjeeling by May 14. The time of waiting at Darjeeling had, however, not been wasted. Four cooks had been engaged for the Expedition and some forty coolies. These were Sherpa Bhotias, whose homes were in the North-east corner of Nepal, some of them coming from villages only a few miles to the South of Mount Everest. They were an especially hardy type of coolie, accustomed to living in a cold climate and at great heights. They were Buddhists by religion and therefore had no caste prejudices about food, and could eat anything. They proved at times quarrelsome and rather fond of strong drink; they turned out, however, to be a useful and capable type of man, easily trained in snow and ice work and not afraid of the snow. We later on picked up a few Tibetan coolies in the Chumbi Valley and these proved to be as good as the best of the Sherpas. They were very hardy and got on well with the Tibetans, who were always rather suspicious of our Nepalese coolies. They were also less troublesome to manage and could carry heavy loads at great heights. These coolies had all to be fitted with boots and very difficult this sometimes proved to be, as often their feet were almost as broad as they were long. Blankets, cap comforters, fur gloves and warm clothing were issued to all of them, and for those who had to sleep at the highest camps, eiderdown sleeping-bags were also taken. Arrangements had also to be made for interpreters to accompany the Expedition, as with the exception of Major Morshead, who knew a little Tibetan, no one was able to speak the language. It was a matter of great importance to get hold of the right type of man as interpreter. It was essential to find men of some position and standing who knew not only the Tibetan language, but also all their ways and customs. After many names had been suggested, we were very lucky in getting hold of two men who possessed these qualifications to a great extent. Gyalzen Kazi, who came from Gangtok in Sikkim, where he was a Kazi and landowner, was a young and ambitious man who knew the Tibetan language well and was well read in their sacred writings and scriptures. The other one, Chheten Wangdi, was a Tibetan who had been for a time a captain in the Tibetan army, and who had left them and been attached to the Indian army in Egypt during the war. He was a most energetic, hard-working man, knew all the Tibetan manners and customs, and was up to all their tricks of procrastination and attempts at overcharging. By his knowledge and persuasive powers the Expedition was saved many thousand rupees.

The Expedition when it left Darjeeling included nine Europeans. The Alpine climbers were Mr. Harold Raeburn, Dr. A. M. Kellas, Mr. G. L. Mallory and Mr. C. H. Bullock. Dr. Kellas had unfortunately in the early spring of this year tried his constitution very severely by climbing Narsing,[1] and he had also spent several nights at very low temperatures in camps over 20,000 feet, on the slopes of Kabru,[1] so that when he arrived at Darjeeling a few days before the Expedition was due to start, he was not in as fit a condition as he should have been. The two Surveyors were Major H. T. Morshead, D.S.O., and Major O. E. Wheeler, M.C. These officers had been lent by the Survey of India. Major Morshead had already a considerable experience of travelling in the Eastern borders of Tibet and in the Kham country, where he had carried out some useful survey work, and under him were three native surveyors, one of whom was left in Sikkim to revise the existing maps, which were very inaccurate, while the other two, Gujar Singh and Lalbir Singh, accompanied the Expedition and filled in all the details of the country traversed on their plane tables at a scale of 4 miles to the inch. Major O. E. Wheeler, the other Surveyor, was a member of the Canadian Alpine Club and a very keen climber himself. He was an expert in the Canadian system of Photo Survey—a method especially useful and applicable to a difficult and mountainous country. The Indian Government had also lent the Expedition the services of Dr. A. M. Heron, of the Geological Survey of India, in order to study the geology of the country through which it was about to go, and about which nothing was known, and to investigate the problems which surround the age and the structure of the Himalayan range. Besides these, there was Mr. A. F. Wollaston, a member of the Alpine Club and a very distinguished traveller as well, who had

[1] Narsing and Kabru are two high mountains in the North of Sikkim.

made some most interesting journeys around Ruwenzori in Africa and in the interior of New Guinea. He accompanied the Expedition in the capacity of Doctor, Naturalist and Botanist, and was equipped with a complete collector's outfit.

During our time of enforced waiting at Darjeeling, we came in for the Lebong races—a unique and very amusing entertainment. The course is a small circular one, where the top of the Lebong spur has been levelled, and only genuine Tibetan and Bhotia ponies are allowed to race there. There were always large entries for these races, as they were very popular among the hill-folk, who flocked into Darjeeling from great distances, dressed in their finest clothes and with their women covered with jewellery and wearing clothing of brilliant shades of green and red. There was very heavy betting on each race, and the amount of money that the coolies, sirdars or servants were able to put up was astonishing. In most of the races there was at least a field of ten, which made the start a very amusing affair. The jockeys were all hill-boys, and as they and the ponies were up to every dodge and trick, and were equally anxious to get off first, and as most of the ponies had mouths of iron, it was always a long time before a start could be made, and in nearly every race one or more of the ponies would run out of the course at the point nearest its own home.

On May 13 Major Morshead with his assistant surveyors and fifty coolies left Darjeeling for Khamba Dzong. They went the direct road up the Teesta Valley correcting the Sikkim map as they went along. Their object in going this way was to connect the Indian Survey with the new survey that it was proposed to carry out in Tibet. This would occupy all Major Morshead's time until we should be able to join him at Khamba Dzong in June.

The chief transport of the Expedition consisted of 100 mules belonging to the Supply and Transport Corps and lent to us by the Commander-in-Chief. These arrived at Darjeeling a few days before we were due to start and were camped in the open on the old parade ground at the top of Katapahar. Sub-Conductor Taylor, who had already had experience of mule transport in Tibet in 1904–5, and was to have come in charge of them, was unfortunately laid up at the last moment with a bad attack of influenza. The next man chosen was passed medically unfit, and the third man in temporary charge of the mules was, when he arrived at Darjeeling, already suffering from ague. It was not till May 15 that Sergeant Fowkes arrived, who was to take charge of the mules. He was a very capable and energetic N.C.O., and their subsequent failure was in no way due to him, but solely to the fact that the mules were in no kind of condition to do hard work in the hills, being sleek and fat from the plains where they had had very little work to do. The muleteers, or drabies, were all hill-men and had been picked out specially for us and fitted out with every kind of warm clothing. Though there were a hundred mules, this did not mean that there were a hundred mules to carry our loads—so much extra warm clothing and blankets had been given to the drabies that together with all their line gear it needed twenty-seven mules to carry their kit, which left only seventy-three mules for the Expedition loads, each mule carrying 160 lb., and this was not nearly sufficient for our requirements. A certain amount of our stores had therefore to be left behind at Government House, Darjeeling, for a second journey, and we only took with us sufficient food and supplies for three and a half months, relying on the mules going back and returning with the remainder of the stores in July or August. Owing to the camping grounds being small, and bungalow accommodation limited on the journey across Sikkim, we divided ourselves into two parties with fifty mules and twenty coolies in each party; Wollaston, Wheeler, Mallory and myself being with the first party and Raeburn, Kellas, Bullock and Heron with the second.

The first party left Darjeeling on May 18, and the second party the following day. I remained behind to see the second party off, and then by doing a double march I caught the first party up that evening at Kalimpong, not, however, without noticing on the way that several of our mules were already knocked up. The night before we started rain came down in torrents, and it was still pouring when the mules came round in the morning, and though the rain stopped soon afterwards yet the hillsides were all wreathed in soft grey mists and every moss-hung branch and tree dripped steadily with moisture all day long. The first day's march from Darjeeling was to Peshoke—a seventeen-mile march and down hill all the way after Ghoom. From Darjeeling we gradually ascended some 500 feet to Ghoom and then for 6 miles followed the well-engineered cart road which leads below Senchal to the new military cantonment of Takda which is, I believe, about to be abandoned, as the Gurkhas, for whom it was built, are not at all happy there. During the war it was used as a German internment camp. Along this ridge there are magnificent forests of evergreen oaks, all of which were covered with ferns and orchids and long trailing mosses. This first ridge rising straight out of the plains condenses all the moisture-laden winds that blow up from the Bay of Bengal and causes it almost always to be enveloped in clouds and mists. The path now rapidly descended 4,000 feet, through tea plantations. The whole hillside was covered with tea bushes, neatly planted in lines, and showing a very vivid green at this time of the year. Here and there grew tall tree ferns, 20 feet to 30 feet in height, their stems covered with ferns and Coelogene orchids. The air was now growing hotter and hotter as we descended, but the wonderful and varied vegetation, the beautiful and brilliantly coloured butterflies—for which the Teesta Valley is famous—that flitted across the path in front of us, proved an irresistible attraction, and made us forget the fact that we were dripping with perspiration from every pore. We had already descended nearly 5,000 feet by the time that we reached the P.W.D. bungalow at Peshoke, which was situated in a clearing in the forest. We were, however, still 2,000 feet above the muddy Teesta River which ran down below us in its steamy gorge, and the next morning saw us descending 2,000 feet through a Sal forest by a slippery path of clay leading to the suspension bridge which crosses the mighty river that with its affluents drains the whole of Sikkim. It rushes along with irresistible force in mighty waves and rapids, and though attempts have been made to float timber down it for commercial purposes, yet the current is too swift and the logs were all smashed to pieces. Here at the bridge we were only 700 feet above the sea and the heat was intense. Several mules had been left exhausted at Peshoke and had been unable to proceed the following day and several more only just reached Kalimpong, the second day's march, only 12 miles from Peshoke, but the climb of 3,300 feet up from the bridge over the Teesta in the steamy and enervating heat proved too much for them. The forests here were very beautiful—huge sal trees and giant terminalia abounded with weird and wonderful creepers embracing their stems, or hanging down from their branches. The handsome pothos—the finest of the creepers—grew everywhere. The curious pandanus or screw pine displayed its long and picturesque fronds, while here and there among the dark green of the tropical forest showed up as a brilliant patch of colour the scarlet blooms of the clerodendrons. Above the forests the hillsides had been terraced with immense labour into rice fields, which at this time of year were not yet planted out, but the fields of maize were already ripening. At Kalimpong there was a large and comfortable Dak bungalow, surrounded by a well-kept garden full of roses and scarlet hibiscus with a beautiful and large-flowered mauve solanum growing up the pillars on the verandah. At Kalimpong we were entertained by Dr. Graham and his charming daughters, who showed us true hospitality and kindness. They live in a very pretty house embowered in roses on the crest of the hill and commanding lovely views over the Teesta Valley and up to the snowy peaks of Kanchenjunga. Higher up on the spur are the homes and the industrial schools that many years of hard work have brought into being, thanks to the indefatigable labours of Dr. Graham and the late Mrs. Graham; these now hold between 600 and 700 pupils, both boys and girls, who, when they leave these schools, have all been taught some useful trade and are sent out as useful members of society. They are given as practical an education as could be wished for anywhere. At the Grahams' house I met David Macdonald, the British Trade Agent at Yatung, who was acting temporarily as political agent in Sikkim until Major Bailey arrived from England. He was an old friend of mine, as I had met him before in Tibet. He promised us every assistance in his power and had telegraphed to Yatung and to the Jongpen at Phari to have supplies and anything we wanted in readiness at those places. He told me that an old Tibetan Lama, who knew Mount Everest well, had described it as "Miti guti cha-phu long-nga," "the mountain visible from all directions, and where a bird becomes blind if it flies so high." Throughout our journey across Sikkim the weather was very bad, with heavy falls of rain every day and night. We had had the bad luck to strike the Chota Bursat, or little monsoon, which usually heralds the coming of the proper monsoon a fortnight or three weeks later.

The march to Pedong was an easy one of 14 miles with a gentle climb of 3,000 feet followed by a descent of 2,000 feet past gardens beautiful with their great trees of scarlet hibiscus, daturas and bougainvilleas, which grew with wonderful luxuriance in this climate where frost is almost unknown in winter and where in summer the temperature scarcely ever exceeds 85° Fahrenheit. We passed some of the most wonderful datura hedges that I have ever seen with trees 15 feet to 20 feet in height and laden with hundreds of enormous white trumpet-shaped blooms 8 inches in diameter and fully a foot long. I could only stand and admire. At night these great white flowers glowed as though with phosphorescence in the dark and had a strangely sweet smell. I got thoroughly soaked on the march, for a couple of minutes of these deluges are sufficient to go through any waterproof.

Our mules were now beginning to give us great trouble. Several had to be left behind after each march and fresh animals had to be hired locally to replace those left behind. At Pedong there were more wonderful daturas, and all along the next march we kept passing grand bushes of these flowers. It rained all that night and most of the following day, so that we had a very wet and trying march to Rongli—the distance was only 12 miles, but this included a very steep descent of over 3,000 feet to the bottom of a steamy valley, followed by a climb of 3,000 feet across an intervening ridge and then down another 2,000 feet to the Rongli bungalow. The poor mules were very tired by the end of the march and one had died of colic on the way. Most of the others too were getting very sore backs from the constant rain. On the way Wollaston and I stopped at Rhenock to have a look at the Chandra Nursery kept by Tulsi Dass, where there were many interesting plants, chiefly collected in the Sikkim forests. There was a tree growing everywhere in the forests with a white flower which Sikkim people called Chilauni, and all along the paths the Sikkim durbar had been busy planting mulberry, walnut and toon trees. There was a curious pink ground plant that grew in the forests which I was told belonged to the Amomum species. There were also beautiful orchids in the trees, mauve, white and yellow, belonging to the Dendrobium, Coelogene and Cymbidium families—some with fine sprays of flowers 18 inches long. Here at Rongli the mules were so tired that we had to give them a day's rest before they could go on any further. It was a hot and feverish spot to stop in, and only necessity compelled us to do so, as we were unable to get any extra transport the following morning to supplement the mules that were sick.

All that day we had passed numbers of mules coming down from Tibet laden with bales of wool, and others were returning to Tibet with sheets of copper, manufactured goods, grain and rice which had been bought in exchange. The dark faces of the muleteers with their turquoise earrings formed a pretty picture and they were full of friendly smiles and greetings for us. The mules travelled on their own—if any mule stopped on the path, a stone always aimed with the greatest accuracy reminded him that it was time to go on. Owing to our having to halt a day at Rongli, we had to stop the second party, and were able to do this at Ari, a bungalow 3 miles short of Rongli. I rode up to see how they were getting on, and found they were having the same trouble with their mules that we had been having. On May 23 we left for Sedongchen, or Padamchen as the Tibetans called it. Sedongchen is the old local name, so-called because there once grew there a very large "Sedong" tree. This is a tree that has a white sap which irritates the skin intensely and sets up a rash. Sedongchen was only 9 miles from Rongli, but there was a very steep climb, from 2,700 feet up to 7,000 feet, and our mules only just managed to arrive there. The first part of the way is alongside the rushing stream of the Rongli, through lovely woods and dense tropical vegetation. Caladiums, kolocasias and begonias were growing on every rock, and the giant pothos with its large shining leaves grew up the stems of many of the trees. Climbers of all kinds, such as vines and peppers, hung down from the branches. Here, too, were magnificent forest trees, fully 150 feet high, with clean straight trunks and without a branch for a hundred feet; others nearly equally tall, which the Sikkim people call "Panisage," had huge buttresses and trunks nearly 40 feet in circumference. Every branch here was covered by thick matted growth of orchids. For the first time since leaving Darjeeling the sun shone, and after we left the forests we found the uphill climb very hot. On to-day's march, out of the fifty mules with which we started there were only fourteen carrying our own kit, and of those fourteen we found on arrival at Sedongchen that none would be fit to proceed on the following day. It was therefore with great reluctance that I felt compelled to send back the Government mules, as they could not only not carry their own line gear, but had become an extra and very large source of expense and worry to us. That the mules should have completely broken down like this after a five days' march showed that they must have been in no kind of training and condition and were completely unfitted for heavy work in the mountains. The hill ponies and mules that we had hired to supplement them, although they had been given the heaviest loads, always arrived first, and made nothing of each march. By this failure of the Government transport we were now thrown back on our own resources, and obliged to depend everywhere on what local transport we could obtain, and this often took some time to collect.

At Sedongchen there was a pleasant bungalow, rather Swiss in appearance, with fine views down the Rongli Valley and across all the forest ridges over which we had come, right back to Darjeeling. Opposite us, to the South-east, were densely wooded hills with clouds and mists drifting along the tops, while here and there a waterfall showed up white amidst the dark green vegetation.

Rain came down steadily all night, but the morning proved somewhat finer. Being on the main trade route, we were luckily able to get other transport to replace the Government mules and to arrange for hired mules as far as Yatung. The local animal is a wonderful beast, extremely sure footed, and not minding in the least a climb of 6,000 feet. The path from Sedongchen is really only a stone causeway, very slippery and unpleasant either to walk or ride upon, but probably anything else would be worn away by the torrential rains that fall here. At one place we had to make a wide detour, as the rain of the night before had washed away some hundred yards of the pathway, but luckily this was not in a very steep part, as otherwise we might have been delayed for several days. The constant rain had already brought out the leeches, and on most of the stones or blades of grass beside the path they sat waiting for their meal of blood and clung on to any mule or human being that passed by. The mules suffered severely, and drops of blood on the stones became frequent from the bleeding wounds.

The climb from Sedongchen to Gnatong was very steep with a rise of over 5,000 feet in the first 5 miles, and we soon got out of the zone of the leeches and on to the most wonderful zone of flowering rhododendrons. The rhododendrons in the lower forest chiefly consisted of *R. Argenteum* and *R. Falconeri.* These grew in a great forest of oaks and magnolias, all covered with beautiful ferns among which showed up delightful mauve or white orchids. The lower rhododendrons had already flowered, but as we got higher we found masses of *R. Cinnabarinum,* with flowers showing every shade of orange and red. Then came rhododendrons of every colour—pink, deep crimson, yellow, mauve, white or cream coloured. It was impossible to imagine anything more beautiful, and every yard of the path was a pure delight. Among the smaller flowers were the large pink saxifrage, while the deep reddish-purple primula covered every open space. There was also a very tiny pink primula —the smallest I have ever seen—and another one like a pink primrose, that grew on the banks above the path. We went along quite slowly all the way, botanising and admiring the scenery. The path mostly led along the top of a ridge, and the views and colours of the many-hued rhododendrons in the gullies on either side were very delightful. Gnatong, where we were to spend the night, was a very small and rather dirty village lying in a hollow and surrounded by grassy hills. The fir trees (*Abies Webbiana*) no longer surrounded it, as those anywhere near had been cut down for firewood, or for building houses. From here I was able to telephone to Mr. Isaacs, Mr. Macdonald's head clerk at Yatung, to ask him to make arrangements for ponies and mules for us both at Yatung and at Phari now that our transport had broken down. Wonderful rumours seemed to have preceded our advent. Stories that we were coming with 1,000 mules and 500 men seemed to have been spread about in Tibet.

Gnatong is a most depressing place, and only owes its existence to the fact that it is the first stopping place for the caravans that cross over the Jelep Pass on the British side of the frontier. Rain always falls there, the rainfall in the year being nearly 200 inches, and when rain does not fall the place is enveloped in mist, with the result that the mud was horrible. It poured with rain all the time that we were there and we left again in heavy rain for the Jelep Pass 8 miles distant. We were already over 12,000 feet when we started, and the top of the pass was 14,390 feet, so that it was not a very serious climb. There was no view of any kind to be had as the rain fell steadily all the way and the hillsides were all veiled in mist. We had occasional glimpses of a hillside pink, white or yellow with rhododendrons, which now grew only about 5 feet high. I counted six or seven different varieties of primulas on the way, but near the top there was still plenty of the old winter snow lying about and the Alpine flowers were scarcely out. A big heap of stones marked the summit of the pass and the frontier between Sikkim and Tibet, and a few sticks, to which were attached strings covered with small pieces of rag on which were inscribed prayers, fluttered out in the strong wind that always blows up there. In the cold rain this was not a cheerful spot to linger in, so we hurried on down a steep and stony path and after descending a few hundred feet emerged out of the mist and rain and obtained glimpses of a really blue sky such as we had not seen for weeks. We had arrived at last in Tibet.

CHAPTER II

THE CHUMBI VALLEY AND THE TIBETAN PLATEAU

The range of mountains which here forms the boundary between Sikkim and Tibet runs nearly North and South, and the two main passes across it are the Jelep La and the Nathu La, the latter being a few miles to the North of the Jelep La and about the same height. The Jelep La being the main trade route across which the telegraph line runs, and over which the postal runners travel, is kept open all the year round, though often after a heavy blizzard it is closed for ten days or a fortnight. On the Sikkim side the snow-fall is always the heaviest; this range of mountains stops most of the moist currents that drive up from the Bay of Bengal, with the result that the rainfall in the Chumbi Valley on the Tibetan side is only about a quarter of what it is at Gnatong on the Sikkim side.

The descent into the Chumbi Valley was very steep and stony, as there was a drop of over 5,000 feet from the top of the pass. The beauty of the valley and its wild flowers made up, however, for the badness of the path. The rhododendrons on the descent were extremely fine, and the whole character of the vegetation was altered and became more European. The great pink rhododendron *Aucklandi* showed up splendidly in the dark forests of silver fir (*A. Webbiana*) which here grows into a fine tree. There was also the yellow rhododendron Campylocarpum and a white rhododendron, probably Decorum; the beautiful *R. Cinnabarinum* with its orange bells of waxy flowers relieved the darkness of the firs. There was a small Tibetan rest-house called Langra where our coolies wanted to stop, but we pushed on past this and descended steeply through more wonderful forests. As we got lower we found birch, sycamore, willow and elder still clothed in the light green of early spring. A fine white clematis, a pink and white spiræa, a yellow berberis, white roses and the dark purple iris grew in profusion on either side of the path. Underneath these were the small flowers of the wild strawberry, which the Macdonald family collected later on in the year and made into jam in great quantities.

Near the entrance to this side valley we came to Old Yatung with its Chinese custom-house and wall built right across the valley to keep the British from going any further. All this was now deserted and in ruins. Soon afterwards we arrived in the main Chumbi Valley where were broad fields filled with potatoes and ripening barley. The houses here were mostly built of stone and wood and in two stories. In character they much resembled Tirolese houses except for the elaborate carving over the doors and windows and the many colours in which they were painted. We passed through the prosperous villages of Richengong, Phema and Chumbi before arriving at New Yatung, or Shassi as the Tibetans still prefer to call it. Here was a comfortable bungalow overlooking the bazaar on the other side of the river. Knowing that we had had a long and tiring march and that our coolies would only arrive late that night, Mrs. Macdonald had with much thoughtfulness sent over her servants who had tea and dinner prepared for us on a generous scale. No attention could have been more acceptable. It rained steadily all that night—a somewhat unusual occurrence in this valley—but the next morning it cleared up and the day was delightful.

The Chumbi Valley is one of the richest valleys in Tibet. Yatung lies at a height of 9,400 feet. Apples and pears do well here, and barley, wheat and potatoes are grown in great quantities. At this time of the year the air is scented by the wild roses which grow in large bushes covered with hundreds of cream-coloured and sweetly scented flowers.

The villages all look extremely prosperous and an air of peace and contentment seems to pervade the valley. We had to hire a new lot of animals to take us on to Phari—28 miles further up the Chumbi Valley. These all arrived in good time, and by eight o'clock on May 27 our loads were all on their way. Before leaving, I sent off a telegram to Sir Francis Younghusband to announce the arrival of the Expedition in Tibet, a telegram which arrived opportunely at the Anniversary Dinner of the Royal Geographical Society, just at the commencement of dinner.

There is a small garrison at Yatung, consisting of twenty-five men of the 73rd Carnatics. There was also a hospital and a supply depot from which we were able to purchase sugar, flour, ata (coarse native flour) and potatoes, while later on we were able to send back to it for further supplies. We formed quite an imposing procession as we started off: Wollaston and myself on our ponies, Gyalzen Kazi and Chheten Wangdi, our interpreters, on their ponies which they had brought along with them. There was Mr. Isaacs, the head clerk, with a red-coated chaprassi and a syce also mounted, who accompanied us on a visit to two monasteries further up the valley. The path followed close to the banks of the Ammo-chu, which was now a clear stream and contained many a likely pool for fish. The valley was full of delightful flowers; curious ground orchids, with several beautiful varieties of the ladies' slipper grew there; the wild roses, especially the large red one, were very sweet-scented and filled the air with fragrance. Berberis, clematis and some charming dwarf rhododendrons abounded. After going about 3 miles the valley narrowed, and we passed the spot where the Chinese had built another wall across the valley to keep us out. Just above this wall there was a deserted Chinese village, for now all the Chinese have been driven out of the country and are not allowed to go back and live there. High above us on the hillside was the Punagang Monastery belonging to the old sect of the Bhompo's, who turn their prayer wheels the opposite to every one else and always keep to the right of Chortens and Mani walls. This monastery was too far off the path for us to visit it. We soon afterwards passed the large and flourishing village of Galinka surrounded by fields of barley. Here we turned aside to visit the Galinka Monastery, which stood in the midst of the village. This was quite a new building, with a great gilt image of Buddha inside it. The monks were still busy painting pictures of scenes from the life of Buddha on the walls. They apparently did quite a good trade in selling clay images of Buddha in his different forms and postures. These were stamped by a very well cut brass die, which the monks told me had been made at Shigatse. In a side room was a huge prayer wheel some 12 feet high and 5 feet to 6 feet in diameter. It was covered over with painted leather inscribed with the usual Om Mani Padme Hum (Hail, jewel of the lotus flower). They told us the inside was also filled with prayers, and that it contained one and a half million of these, so that each time the wheel was turned a million and a half prayers were said for the person who turned it. After each complete revolution it rings a bell. We were allowed to turn it several times, so that I hope the many million prayers sent up may benefit us. After leaving the monastery, the path rose steeply and the river came down in a series of waterfalls. Above us were masses of pink and mauve rhododendrons, flowering cherries, viburnum, berberis, roses and other delightful shrubs. Soon afterwards, at the entrance to the Lingmatang plain, we crossed the river and rode up a rocky spur formed of great boulders that had some time or another fallen down and blocked up the valley, forming a lake some 2 miles long, but this lake no longer existed, and there was only a flat grassy plain grazed over by yaks and ponies. On the top of the spur was the Donka Monastery in a grand situation, commanding beautiful views up and down the valley. I had hoped to see my friend the Geshe Lama or Geshe Rimpoche, as he is sometimes known, with whom I had lunched last year at the hot springs at Kambu, but unfortunately he was away at Lhasa. He is a man of very great learning and held in high veneration throughout these valleys.

On entering the big stone courtyard of the monastery a crowd of children and Lamas at once flocked round us. We were shown over the main temple, but it was badly lit with a few butter lamps and we could see little of its contents; amongst these were several statues of Buddha under his different forms. There were also kept there 108 volumes of the Tangyur, one of the Buddhist sacred writings. These books were very curious. Each volume consisted of a number of loose oblong parchment sheets 2 to 3 feet long and from 8 inches to a foot wide. These were kept together by two elaborately carved boards between which they were pressed. The writing was all done by hand by the Lamas, who copied out and illuminated books with the greatest care and skill in the same manner that the monks in the Middle Ages illuminated their missals. The book-shelves of the library consisted of a number of pigeon-holes in the walls in which these volumes were kept. Here, too, they were busy making clay images to bury under the Chorten that they were building above the monastery. Next door was another and newer temple, built to house the Oracle, and called the Sanctuary of the Oracle. He, too, was unfortunately away, as he was taking the hot waters at Kambu, but we were shown his throne and the robes that he puts on when he prophesies. There was a curiously shaped head-dress of silver, adorned all round with silver skulls, and a very quaintly shaped bow and arrow which the Oracle held in one hand while a huge trident was grasped in the other. I am told that he is consulted far and wide and has a great reputation for truth. We were then taken upstairs to a sunny verandah, just outside the Geshe Rimpoche's private room and commanding fine views up and down the valley. Here we were given Tibetan tea, made with salt and butter, and served up in agate cups with beautifully chased silver covers. After drinking this tea we were shown over the Geshe's private apartments and chapel, the prevailing colour scheme of the room being yellow. The little shrines with their silver bowls in front—the incense burner and the flame that is never allowed to go out—were all very interesting to us. We then took a photograph of the Lamas in front of their temple, after which the head Lama accompanied us some way down the path to say good-bye, hoping we would come and see them again on our return.

I have alluded several times to the hot springs at Kambu. These springs are two days' journey from Yatung up the Kambu Valley, but can also be reached quite easily from Phari. There is a curious account of these springs written by an old Lama and translated by Major Campbell. The writer describes the Upper Kambu Valley as quite a pleasant spot where cooling streams and medicinal plants are found in abundance. Medicinal waters of five kinds flow from the rocks, forming twelve pools, the waters of which are efficacious in curing the 440 diseases to which the human race is subject. The springs are then made to describe their own qualities in the first person :—

1. The Lhamo Spring (The Spring of the Goddess): My virtue is derived from the essence of stone—I am guarded by the Goddess Tsering, and my virtue therefore consists in purging the sins and obscurities of the human body. Those who bathe first in my waters will be purged of all sin and the power of all diseases will be abated.

2. The Chagu Spring (The Spring of the Vulture): My virtue is derived from black sulphur. As regards my properties, a vulture with a broken wing once fell into my waters and was healed. I benefit diseases of women, also sores, gout and fractures. I possess particular virtue for all diseases below the waist. I do not benefit neuralgia, nervous diseases, or loss of appetite.

3 and 4. The Pon Springs (The Springs of the Official): We two brothers derive our properties from both yellow and black sulphur. One of us provokes catarrh, while the other allays it. A learned man, who wished us well, once said that we were beneficial in cases of hemorrhoids, kidney diseases and rheumatism. We are not aware of possessing these qualities, and rather tend to cause harm in such cases.

5. The Traggye Spring (The Spring born of the Rock): My virtue is derived from a combination of sulphur and the essence of stone. I was formerly efficacious in cases of diseases of the arteries and nerve trouble, but later on the Brothers of the Pon Spring rushed down on poor me like tyrants so that no one now regards me. The caretaker of the Springs

and visitors treats me like a beggar and pays no attention to me. Even now if some person with the permission of the Brothers of the Pon Spring would carry out some repairs, so as to separate my waters from theirs, I would guarantee to benefit those suffering from arterial diseases, nerve trouble, impurities of the blood and bile.

6. THE SERKA SPRING (The Spring of the Crevice): My virtues are derived from sulphur and carbon. I am not beneficial to those suffering from ailments arising from nerve trouble, bile and acidity. I am beneficial to those suffering from chapped hands and feet due to hard work among earth and stones and also in cases of diseases of the kidneys and bladder. I am somewhat hurtful to those suffering from headache arising from nervous catarrh, or impurities of the blood.

7. THE TANG SPRING (The Spring of the Plain): My virtues are derived from carbon and a little sulphur. I am beneficial in cases of hemorrhoids, kidney disease, rheumatism and other diseases below the waist, also in cases of venereal disease. There is a danger of the waist becoming bent like a bow through too much bathing in my waters.

8. THE TRAGGYAB SPRING (The Spring behind the Rock): I am beneficial in cases of disease of the arteries and anaemia—I am not aware that I am harmful in other cases.

9. THE TONGBU SPRING (The Spring of the Hole): My virtues are derived from a large proportion of crystalline stone and a little sulphur. I guarantee to be beneficial in cases of white phlegm, brown phlegm and other forms of phlegmatic disease. Also in diseases arising out of these, and in cases of impurities of the blood and colic pains. Please bear this in mind.

10. THE NUB (The Western Spring): My virtues are derived from a little carbon. I am beneficial in cases of liver disease, impurities of the blood, flatulence, kidney disease, dyspepsia, brown phlegm, tumours, gout, rheumatism, gleet, and complications arising from these. I do not boast in the way that the other Springs do.

11. THE DZEPO SPRING (The Leper's Spring): I am cousin to the Western Spring. He guarantees to cure diseases arising from two or three causes, also kidney disease, flat foot, rheumatism and gout. I am beneficial in cases of hemorrhoids, gout, rheumatism and diseases of the feet. I possess particular virtue in cases of leprosy, sores and wounds.

12. THE LAMA SPRING (The Spring of the Lama): My virtues are derived from a large proportion of lime and a little sulphur. I am beneficial in cases of lung disease, tumours, dyspepsia, both chronic and recent, poverty of the blood and venereal diseases.

WRITTEN BY TSEWANG IN THE HOPE THAT THE PEOPLE OF BHUTAN, SIKKIM, AND THE SURROUNDING COUNTRY WILL BEAR THIS IN MIND.

COPIED BY TENRAB, CLEARLY AND EXACTLY, FROM THE ORIGINAL IN THE MALE IRON DOG YEAR IN THE FIRST HALF OF THE EARTH MONTH.

After leaving the monastery we had a pleasant gallop across the Lingmatang Plain, after which the valley narrowed again and the path followed close beside the rushing stream. It was a delightful ride through forests of birch, larch, juniper, spruce, silver fir and mountain ash. Never anywhere have I seen birch trees grow to such a size. They were grand rugged old trees that matched the rugged scenery of the gorge. Blue poppies, fritillaries, ground orchids and sweet-scented primulas grew along the path, and mixed up everywhere in the forest were great bushes of *R. Cinnabarinum*, which varied in shade from yellow and orange to deep red. Wagtails and white-crested redstarts dodged about from rock to rock in the rushing stream, and the clear note of the shrike could usually be heard above the noise of the waters. The weather had luckily kept fine all day, so that we were able to dawdle along and enjoy the scenery and flowers.

After going about 12 miles we came to the bungalow of Gautsa, situated at a height of about 12,000 feet, and at the bottom of the gorge; here we spent the night. During the night there was heavy rain, and when we woke in the morning, fresh snow was low down on all the hills and within 1,500 feet of the bungalow. However, the day again proved brilliantly fine. For breakfast we had been given some large wild-goose eggs belonging to the bar-headed goose. Mine I had boiled, and found excellent, though one was sufficient for a meal. Two that the others had were rather *passé*, and were not equally appreciated. The day's path was at first very stony and climbed steadily uphill beside the torrent of the Ammochu. Pale blue iris, yellow primulas, a pink viburnum and a large yellow-belled lonicera grew beside the path, but the rhododendrons were still by far the most wonderful of the flowering shrubs. We passed many big blue meconopsis, and some of these flowers measured fully 3 inches across. Dwarf rhododendrons, only a foot high—some pure white and others pink, continued up until about 13,500 feet, and then the hillsides became purple from another little rhododendron, which looked in the distance like heather and gave the rounded hills quite a Scotch appearance. As we rose higher the flowers decreased in number. Larks and wheatears ran along the ground in front of us, and small tailless marmot rats dodged in and out of their holes as we approached. The distance from Goutsa to Phari was about 16 miles, of which the last 8 miles were over flat country with a springy turf, on which it was a pleasure to be able to canter again after having passed over so many miles of stony roads. Chomolhari, the Mountain of the Goddess, stood up as a wonderful sight with its sharp peak outlined against the clear blue sky. On its summit the wind was evidently very strong, as we could see the fresh snow being whirled off in clouds.

Phari is an extremely dirty village dominated by a stone fort and lying under the shadow of the great mountain Chomolhari, 23,930 feet high. It is 14,300 feet above sea level, and the climate there is always cold, as it is never without a strong wind. In the afternoon the Jongpen, or Governor of the district, came to call on me. He was a young man with an intelligent and pleasant face, and came from the country between Khamba Dzong and Shekar Dzong, so that he was able to give us much useful information about the road; he promised that he would write to his brother, who was acting as agent for him at his home, telling him to entertain us and give us all facilities in the matters of transport and supplies. He told us that he had received written instructions from the Lhasa Government to arrange for supplies and transport for us, and he promised that he would do his best. I gave him photographs that I had taken last year of his fort, and also of Chomolhari; these pleased him very much, and in return he presented us with a dried sheep which looked mummified and smelt very strongly, but which proved very acceptable to our coolies. It was necessary to stop here for several days as the second party had to catch up, and they too needed a day's rest. Also the transport that was to carry us along to Khamba Dzong would not be ready for several days, so the following morning I went to call on the Jongpen in his fort, where I found him living in some very dark rooms. I presented him with one of the new lever electric torches, which he much appreciated, though at first he and his servants were rather frightened by it. He gave us tea and sweetmeats, and soon afterwards the head-men of all the villages came in, and were given orders about our transport. Their quaint attitudes of respect and their darkly bronzed faces, that just showed up in the light, reminded me forcibly of an old Dutch picture. Some men, too, had been sent from Khamba Dzong for orders and to know when we should be likely to arrive there. In the course of the afternoon Dr. Heron and I rode over to a monastery about 3 miles away where I had been last year, and where I had taken some photographs. Some prints of these I brought back to the monastery, and the monks were very pleased with them. They were in the middle of a service when we arrived, as it was some kind of festival, and the dark temple was illuminated by hundreds of little butter lamps. The monks were all chanting their scriptures, and this they continued to do all the afternoon.

On returning to Phari, we found that a message had come from the Jongpen to ask us to dine with him the following evening. The change in the climate and the bad cooking had affected the stomachs of all the members of the Expedition, and none of us was feeling very well. Dr. Kellas was the worst, and as soon as he arrived at Phari he retired to bed. The following morning was misty and the ground was all white with hoar-frost, though it was the last day in May; but as I was anxious to get some photographs of Chomolhari we rode, with the Chaukidar as a guide, through the mist across the plain to some hills just to the South of the great mountain; after a few miles we found ourselves above the clouds with the sun shining in a brilliant blue sky. The whole of the Phari Plain was covered by a sea of clouds. On the far side rose the Pawhunri group of mountains, while further to the South, Kanchenjunga towered above all the other peaks, such as Siniolchum,

Kabru and Jonsong, all of which stood out very clearly in this brilliant atmosphere. I rode up a delightful little mountain valley full of dwarf rhododendrons and Alpine primulas until I reached a height of 16,000 feet. We then left the ponies and climbed on to the top of the hill, which was about 17,500 feet; from this point we had glorious views of Chomolhari immediately across the valley, while on the other side we looked over to the snowy peaks and ranges in Bhutan far to the South of us. We found the wind very keen at this height, and after taking several photographs we rode back again to Phari.

Here I found the place full of troubles. Our Coolie Sirdar was, as we were beginning to find out, not only useless, but very mischievous, and he was evidently at the bottom of an attempted mutiny among our coolies, who refused to go on. The Sirdar strongly objected to our interpreters, who were preventing him from fleecing us in the matter of stores and supplies. However, after much talking they were all satisfied. Then it was the turn of the cooks, all of whom the Sirdar had chosen. I should not have minded one or two of these going, as they were very bad cooks and usually drunk, and the fact that all of us had been ill was solely due to their bad cooking; but I could not let them all go, so it was necessary to find out which were the most useless, and this we were able to do in the course of the next few days. Dr. Kellas was getting no better; he refused to take any food, and was very depressed about himself. At Phari I was able to change a certain number of our rupees into Tibetan currency. The then rate of exchange was 33 rupees to 1 sersang—a gold coin—and 4½ silver trangkas to 1 rupee. The trangkas were a thin and very badly stamped coin about the size of a two-shilling piece. We found them, however, to be the most useful form of currency as the gold coin, though much easier to carry, could only be exchanged at a few places, and it was seldom that we met people who were rich enough to be able to change them.

That night four of us went over to have dinner with

the Jongpen. First we were given tea and sweetmeats, followed by strong ginger wine, which was most comforting to our stomachs in their delicate condition. Then came dishes of mutton in varying forms with vegetables and macaroni. They were all served up in Chinese fashion in little dishes and some were quite appetising. We were very late in starting the next morning as all the loads had to be sorted and laid out for the very miscellaneous transport that had been given us. This consisted of ponies, mules, donkeys, bullocks and yaks. For riding-animals we were given mules, which trotted well and covered the ground quite quickly, though some of the Alpine climbers found them hard to manage and were apt to part company with their steeds. Our transport was by now becoming rather complicated as forty-four animals were going right through to Khamba Dzong and forty-four were being changed at every stage. Dr. Kellas was not well enough to ride and was carried in an arm-chair all day. Soon after starting I passed two of our cooks on the road hopelessly drunk, and left them there. Our way led over the Tang La, a very gentle and scarcely perceptible pass, 15,200 feet, but important as being the main Himalayan watershed. All day there was a very strong South wind blowing, but it was luckily at our backs, and we did not feel it too much. We then quickly trotted the 10 miles across the absolutely level Tang-pün-sum Plain. Here I saw several herds of kiang, the wild ass of Tibet, and got within 50 yards of one lot, but unfortunately the coolie who was carrying my camera was not up with me at the time. We also passed a certain number of Tibetan gazelle, but they were all very wary. The Monsoon clouds came up to the South of us in great rolling billows, but not a drop of moisture came over the Tang La. Chomolhari was a magnificent sight all day with its 7,000 feet of precipices descending sheer into the plain. Tuna (14,800 feet), about 20 miles from Phari, was our first halt. We were still on the main road to Lhasa and found a comfortable rest-house into which the eight of us all managed to stow ourselves. Dr. Kellas, though rather better the next day, was still too weak to ride, and was carried for the next march on a litter. We were now in the true Tibetan climate, with brilliant sunshine, blue skies, still mornings and strong winds all the afternoon.

The next march from Tuna to Dochen was still on the Lhasa Road. I did not follow the path, but rode with a local man from the village over the great Tang-pün-sum Plain in search of goa—Tibetan gazelle. We saw many of them on the plains, but they were the wiliest and most difficult animals to approach, and in this flat and bare country it was not possible ever to get within 300 yards of them. As a rule they ran off when we were still half a mile away. They are restless little creatures, always on the move, and never at any time an easy mark to hit. I thoroughly enjoyed this ride over the plains and our glorious views of Chomolhari and the great snow-covered and glaciated chain to the North of it along the foot of which we were travelling. A curious pink trumpet-shaped flower grew in great quantities on the plain; the leaves were buried under the sand and only the flower showed its head above the ground. There were also white pin-cushions of a kind of tiny saxifrage. This plain, over which we were riding, was evidently once upon a time a lake bed, as the pebbles were rounded and there were distinct evidences of former shores along the sides of the hills. Many kiang were grazing on it and many thousands of sheep were being pastured there. As we approached the lake called Bamtso, the country became very marshy, and our ponies got bogged several times. The bungalow at Dochen was situated near the shores of the Bamtso. Never have I seen a lake with so many colours in it. It was very shallow, and the shades varied from deep blue and purple to light green, while in places it was almost red from a weed that grew in it. Behind it was a background of snow and glacier-covered mountains, which in the still mornings was reflected faithfully in its waters and formed a charming picture. Swimming on this lake were many bar-headed geese and Brahminy ducks, and along the shores were many terns and yellow wagtails.

That evening an amusing thing happened in the kitchen. One of our cooks was heating up a tin of tinned fish and had put it in some hot water without previously opening it. When he thought it was sufficiently hot, he started to open it, with the result that it exploded violently, covering him and every one else in the kitchen with small pieces of fish. I was able then to explain to the Tibetans who were carrying our loads that our stores were very dangerous, and that if any were at any time stolen, they would be liable to explode and hurt them. It was, of course, the rarefied air that had caused this, for Dochen is at a height of 14,700 feet above sea level.

Every day on from now the wind used to blow with great violence all the afternoon, but would die down after sunset. It must have been of a local nature caused by the rapid changes from high temperature to low, because the clouds above at the same time were hardly moving. I sent back Dorje, one of our cooks, from this place, as it was the fourth time that he had been drunk, and this I hoped would be a lesson to the others. We now left the Lhasa Road and turned off Westwards, having henceforward to rely on our tents.

From Dochen to Khe was a short march of 11 miles over the Dug Pass, 16,400 feet. I did not follow the road taken by the transport animals, but took a local guide and rode over the hill-tops in search of ovis ammon. I did not see any, however, though we sighted two or three goa, but they were very wild and would not allow me to approach within 500 yards of them. There were numbers of blue hares, however, and some ram chakor, the Himalayan snow cock. But beyond this the hillsides were very bare of game. There were pin-cushions of a beautiful little blue sedum growing at a height of over 17,000 feet, also there was a big red stonecrop. Khe is now only a small and dirty village with practically no water except a half-dried muddy pond, but

Loading up at Dochen.

at one time it must have been a place of some importance, as ruins and buildings of considerable size extend over an area of more than a mile. The Kala-tso evidently at one time came right up to this ruined town of Khetam, and the fact that it is deserted now is probably due to the shrinkage of the lake. This was only one of the many signs of desiccation that we saw in our travels in Tibet. There were some curious ruins which looked like old crenellated walls, but these walls were only places on which barley dough used to be exposed to feed the crows as a sign of prosperity. It was a curious custom and could only have prevailed in a very fertile valley, which this place is no longer. The age of the city I could not find out, but the few survivors told me that the holy shrine at Tashilumpo, which now is at Shigatse, ought to have been built here. According to a local legend, there was a certain stone in Khetam shaped like a ewe's-womb, and one day a donkey driver finding that his loads were unequal in weight, picked up this stone and put it on the light load to balance the other, quite unaware of the importance of the stone. This stone was then carried from Gyantse to Shigatse, where a high and important Lama saw it, and recognising that this was a very holy stone, had it kept there. The powerful monastery of Tashilumpo was built over this stone. We passed two small nunneries called Doto and Shidag in snug little valleys to the North of the plain, and on asking why there should be so many nunneries in these parts when in the greater part of Tibet men predominated, I was told that this was due to the fact that it was close to the Nepalese frontier where there had always been much fighting, so that most of the men had been killed and only women had survived. After a short and easy march we came to a small pocket in the hills called Kheru. Here were encamped some people belonging to a nomad tribe who always lived in tents. They were very friendly, put tents at our disposal, and did their best to make us comfortable. They told us that they came here every year in the twelfth month, about January, and left again in the fifth month of the Tibetan year (June) for a place near Tuna, where they disposed of their wool, butter and cheese at the Phari market. There were altogether about twenty families here owning some 200 yaks and 3,000 sheep. Dr. Kellas was slightly better, but Raeburn was not feeling at all well, and Wheeler was suffering from indigestion, so that we were rather a sick party. Kheru lies at a height of 15,700 feet, but it had been very hot all day in the brilliant sunshine, and on the way we had passed lizards and a number of common peacock butterflies. Next morning our march was to Tatsang (Falcon's Nest), a distance of 15 or 16 miles, and over two passes 16,450 and 17,100 feet. The going was easy all the way, as the gradients both up and down the passes were very gentle. Between the two passes was a broad valley, filled with huge flocks of sheep and herds of yaks, and after crossing the second pass, we descended into a great barren and stony plain, more than 10 miles across which was Tatsang and over which the wind blew very keenly. To the South of us appeared the snowy crests of Pawhunri, Kanchenjhow and Chomiomo and the Lhonak peaks. Again I did not keep with the transport, but followed the crests of the hills, where I had lovely views; on the way I saw plenty of gazelle, and was lucky enough to shoot one of them, as they are very good eating. Our camp at Tatsang was pitched just below the nunnery there, which is on the top of a rock and where there are about thirty nuns. Our camp was on a pleasant grassy spot where some excellent springs bubble up out of the ground. These within a few yards formed quite a big stream full of small snow trout. They do not really belong to the trout family, although they have somewhat similar spots, and are very good to eat. Bullock, with his butterfly net, and the coolies with their hands, managed to catch quite a number of fish, and we had them for dinner that night. The ground round our tents was full of holes out of which the marmot rats kept appearing. They were very tame, and did not seem to be in the least afraid of us. Dr. Kellas had had a very trying day. He had been rather better, and had started riding a yak, but he found this too exhausting and coolies had to be sent back from Tatsang to bring him on in a litter, so that he did not arrive at Tatsang till late in the evening. Tatsang is 16,000 feet, so the night was cold, the thermometer inside the tent registering 7° of frost, though it was June 4; outside there must have been quite 15° as the running streams were all frozen over, but once the sun had risen everything warmed up and we had a beautiful warm day. Dr. Kellas started off in his litter at 7 a.m. in quite good spirits. I did not start till an hour later, as I had wanted to see everything off, and then went up to visit the nunnery, over which the lady abbess showed me. There were thirty nuns living there, all with shorn heads and wearing a curious wool head-dress. The place where they worshipped was full of prayer wheels, both large and small. They sat down behind these, and each nun turned one or two of them if they could manage it. The room was very dark, with a low ceiling, and at the end were several statues of Buddha covered over with gauze veils. In another room there was a large prayer wheel which they said contained half a million prayers.

After leaving the nunnery we jogged along a dry and barren valley which gradually rose in about 12 miles to a pass 17,200 feet. On the way we passed Dr. Kellas in his litter, who then seemed to me to be still quite cheerful. I then rode on and at the top of the pass saw three ovis ammon, and after a chase of about a mile I shot one, which afforded plenty of food for the coolies for some days. It was a full grown ram about five years old and we had great trouble in getting the carcass on to a mule, as it was enormous and very heavy. After this I rode on down the valley for another 10 miles to Khamba Dzong. There were actually a few bushes in this valley, which was carpeted with the pretty pink trumpet-shaped flower mentioned above, also with light and dark blue iris. Suddenly the valley narrowed into a fine limestone gorge, and all at once the fort of Khamba

Dzong appeared towering above us on the cliffs. It was really a very impressive sight and some of the architecture of the round towers was very fine. I found that Morshead had been waiting here for about nine days, but had employed his time in fixing the old triangulation points. Soon after I arrived the Jongpen came down to pay us a visit. He was quite a young fellow, only about twenty-four, but very pleasant and polite.

While we were talking, a man came running up to us very excitedly to say that Dr. Kellas had suddenly died on the way. We could hardly believe this, as he was apparently gradually getting better; but Wollaston at once rode off to see if it was true, and unfortunately found that there was no doubt about it. It was a case of sudden failure of the heart, due to his weak condition, while being carried over the high pass. His death meant a very great loss to the Expedition in every way, as he alone was qualified to carry out the experiments in oxygen and blood pressure which would have been so valuable to the Expedition, and on which subject he was so great an expert. His very keenness had been the cause of his illness, for he had tried his constitution too severely in the early months of that year by expeditions into the heart of the Himalayas to see if he could get fresh photographs from other angles of Mount Everest. The following day we buried him on the slopes of the hill to the South of Khamba Dzong, in a site unsurpassed for beauty that looks across the broad plains of Tibet to the mighty chain of the Himalayas out of which rise up the three great peaks of Pawhunri, Kanchenjhow and Chomiomo, which he alone had climbed. From the same spot, far away to the West—more than a hundred miles away—could be seen the snowy crest of Mount Everest towering far above all the other mountains. He lies, therefore, within sight of his greatest feats in climbing and within view of the mountain that he had longed for so many years to approach—a fitting resting-place for a great mountaineer.

KAMPA DZONG.

CHAPTER III

FROM KHAMBA DZONG THROUGH UNKNOWN COUNTRY TO TINGRI

Our camp at Khamba Dzong* was pitched in a walled enclosure at the foot of the fort, built on a great crag that rose 500 feet sheer above us. They called this enclosure a Bagichah, or garden, because it once boasted of three willow trees. Only one of these three is alive to-day, the other two being merely dead stumps of wood. The Jongpen here, who was under the direct orders of Shigatse, was very friendly, and after our arrival presented us with five live sheep, a hundred eggs, and a small carpet which he had had made in his own factory in the fort. Next afternoon Morshead, Wollaston and myself went up to pay the Jongpen a visit in his fort. It was a steep climb from our camp, past long Mendongs or Mani walls covered with inscribed prayers. The Jongpen was at the entrance waiting to receive us. He then showed us over his stables, where he had several nice Tibetan ponies, which strongly objected to Europeans and lashed out fiercely as we approached them. After looking at them we went up many flights of most dangerously steep stairs, almost in pitch darkness the whole time, until we came to a small courtyard. Then after climbing up more steps, we were ushered into a small latticed room where we were given the usual Tibetan tea and sweetmeats. I presented the Jongpen with one of the new lever electric torches, with which he was much pleased, saying it would be of much use to him in going up and down his dark staircases. After tea he took us up on to the roof of the fort, which was quite flat, and from which we had a most magnificent view. We stood on the top of a great precipice

* Dzong means fort.

and looked straight down at our camp, which lay many hundred feet below but almost within a stone's throw. From here too we could look across the wide plains and valleys of the Yaru and its tributaries to the main chain of the Himalayas which formed the Southern boundary to the picture. From this side they do not appear nearly as imposing as they do when seen from the South. Seen as they are from a height of over 15,000 feet, the distance to the sky line is not nearly so great, and as a rule we found the Northern slopes to be much less steep than those on the Southern side. The snow line, too, was also several thousand feet higher. Every day great masses of moist cumulus clouds came rolling up and round the peaks to the South of us, indicating heavy falls of rain and snow on the South, but very little of this came over the watershed—only an occasional slight hailstorm or a few drops of rain. From this point we could see as far West as Mount Everest, still over a hundred miles away. After spending some time up there and admiring and discussing the view, we descended once more into the fort, where the Jongpen showed us some of the carpets that his womenfolk were busy making and promised to have some ready for us by the time that we came back. We also much admired the curious old locks by which the doors and boxes were fastened ; before leaving, he made me a present of one of these locks.

June 7 saw us still at Khamba Dzong, as the transport would not be ready till the following day. Raeburn, who for some time had been suffering from the same complaint as Dr. Kellas, was unfortunately getting no better and was getting weaker every day. We were therefore reluctantly compelled to send him back again into Sikkim to Lachen, where he could be taken charge of by the lady missionaries and properly looked after. Wollaston and Gyalzen Kazi were to accompany him down to Lachen, and if possible to rejoin us by the time that we got to Tingri. This break-up of our climbing party was most annoying and seriously weakened our party, obliging us to alter our plans for reconnoitring in a thorough manner the various approaches to Mount Everest. The following day, after a good deal of delay and argument about the loads, we got everything loaded up and started off for Lingga, a march of about 16 miles to the West. For the first few miles we rode across a great plain on which were several small herds of goa, but these were very wary and kept well out of shot. The path then took us alongside a small isolated rocky hill in which we kept putting up numerous hares who often got up right under our ponies' feet. We crossed the Yaru River, now only a small stream, at the picturesque village of Mende with its fine willow trees, and then after passing over a spur, formed of slaty rock, we descended into another great plain which extended all the way to Tingri. Five miles across this plain was the village of Lingga, surrounded by marshes and ponds, with barley fields and rich grass growing between the patches of water. There were several other villages in sight, so that the plain was evidently fertile and could support a considerable population. This was the first place where we became bothered by sand flies, which in the morning were very troublesome; but when the wind got up, as it always did in the afternoons, it blew them away, and for once was welcome. The villagers were very hospitable; they produced tea and beer brewed from barley for us as soon as we arrived there. The latter is quite a pleasant drink on a hot day, but it did not agree with my inside at all. The people here had never seen a European before, and though at first inclined to be rather shy, they soon became very friendly and curious. Some pieces of silver paper from chocolates quite won the hearts of the children who flocked around and did not in the least mind being photographed. To the South extended the chain of snows of the main range of the Himalayas, and on the way we had several clear and distinct views of Mount Everest. Morshead, who had left the day before, was camped at a small monastery a few miles to the North of us in order to follow the crest of the ridge of hills and to survey both sides, but was to join us again at Tinki. The weather now was really delightful, though to the South of us we still saw heavy clouds which brought showers of snow as far as the mountains, but they did not reach us.

From here to Tinki was about 13 miles over a perfectly level plain. The midges or sand flies were very troublesome the whole way and came in hundreds round one's head, got inside one's topee, and were thoroughly objectionable. The plain appeared very fertile, as there seemed to be plenty of water and great herds of yaks and flocks of sheep were grazing upon it. In the marshes and ponds were many bar-headed geese, Brahminy ducks, mallard and teal. After the rains, it is evident that a great part of this plain is under water. About a couple of miles from Tinki we crossed some curious sand dunes, about 20 feet high, which are evidently on the move, and soon afterwards the Jongpen of Tinki came riding out to meet us with a few mounted followers, he himself riding a fine white pony. He was very Chinese in appearance, wearing finely embroidered silks with a Chinese hat and a long pigtail, and his manners were excellent. He escorted us to the place where our camp was to be, and had had three or four tents already pitched for us. Tea and country beer were at once served, and we rested in the shade of his Chinese tents until our transport arrived.

We were encamped in a very picturesque spot beside a large pond that was full of bar-headed geese, Brahminy ducks and terns. On the opposite side of this pond rose the walls and towers of the fort of Tinki. As soon as we had settled down, the Jongpen came again to pay us a formal visit, presented us with four sheep and a couple of hundred eggs and promised to do everything he could to help us and to forward us on our way. Half a mile above us was a large village and a big monastery belonging to the Yellow Sect of Buddhists who also owned a fine grove of willows. The bottom of the valley was all covered with barley fields, now a tender green and coming up well. As the fresh transport

TINKI DZONG.

had not arrived, we had to spend the following day there. This gave an opportunity for Abdul Jalil, our photographic assistant, to rejoin us. We had sent him back to Phari in order to change some more rupees into Tibetan currency, as we found that Indian notes or rupees were not accepted any further to the West. Abdul Jalil had been very nervous about travelling with so much money and had borrowed a revolver and a rifle from members of the Expedition besides two large Tibetan swords and a dagger which he obtained from the Jongpen. In the morning, with Bullock, I went to return the call of the Jongpen. His fort at the time was under repair, so he was living in a small house outside the main building. He was very affable and gave us tea: we were then able to make all the arrangements for transport except the actual fixing of the price. For this he said he would have to consult his head-men. Just as we were about to leave he insisted on our eating the large meal which he had had prepared for us. He gave us small dishes of excellent macaroni and mince, seasoned up with chillies and very well cooked—much better than anything our cooks could produce. This we had to eat with chopsticks—a somewhat difficult proceeding, as we were not yet used to them. Later on, however, after much practice, we found no difficulty in consuming the numerous bowls of this excellent dish that the Tibetans always set before one. The Jongpen told us that he had been twenty-nine years in Government service, and he was expecting to have a better post than this shortly. His health was poor and he said he had been suffering much from indigestion, so I gave him some pills and tabloids, for which he was very grateful. On the return journey, he told me that he had greatly benefited by my treatment. The bar-headed geese and the wild duck here were extraordinarily tame, allowing us to approach within five yards of them and showing no signs of fear. They would come and waddle round our tents, picking up any scraps of food. The Jongpen had begged us not to shoot or kill any of them, as he said a Lama had been sent specially from Lhasa some years ago in order to tame the creatures, and certainly the result was extraordinary; it was most interesting to watch these birds, ordinarily so wild, from so close a distance. In the evening the Jongpen came over to see us again, and after a good hour's bargaining over the price of the transport, we finally reached a reasonable and amicable agreement. Every evening, to the South of us, there were constant flashes of lightning all along the horizon. In the morning I woke up to the unusual sound of drops of rain, but this only lasted for five minutes and then cleared up, though the sky remained clouded all the morning. There was the usual fighting and confusion about the loads, each person trying to get the lightest loads for his own animal. The result was that there was much talking and fighting, and nothing was actually done until some head-man would come and take control and decide the dispute. The method of adjudication was as follows:—From each of the families who were regarded as responsible for the supply of a transport animal was taken one of the embroidered garters by which the man's felt boots are kept in their place. These garters were shuffled, as one might shuffle a pack of cards, after which a single garter was laid upon each load. The family to which the garter belonged thereupon became responsible for that load and had to pack it upon the animal's back. Although we had only ninety animals, there were forty-five different families supplying them.

The march from Tinki to Chushar Nango was about 14 miles and was up the valley behind Tinki to the Tinki Pass. On the way we passed well-irrigated fields of barley and then climbed up a spur covered with a small yellow cistus. After this a long gentle pull brought us to the top of the pass, 17,100 feet. There was a very fine view from here to the East looking over Tinki and Khamba Dzong and along the Northern slopes of the Himalayas. I climbed up a hill about 600 feet above the pass, whence I had a more extensive view still. I could see far away to the East to Chomolhari, while in the foreground was the large and picturesque lake called Tsomotretung backed by the rugged chain of peaks that separated us from the valley of the Brahmaputra. To the West we looked down into the valley of the Yaru, which flowed gently through a broad and flat valley. To the South-west was a range of sharp granite peaks rising up to 22,000 feet, which ran North and South and forced the Yaru to flow round them before it could find its way into Nepal. The descent from the pass was much steeper. We passed many of our old friends the pink trumpet-shaped flowers, also a curious white and pink flower, rather like a daphne in shape, and smelling very sweetly, which grew in masses along the path. It was evidently poisonous as no animal would touch it. I picked some flowers of it and put them in my buttonhole, but was warned by the Tibetans not to do so, as they said it was poisonous and would give me a headache. Lower down the valley was full of small dwarf gorse bushes—1 foot to 18 inches high—which carpeted the ground. Everywhere were flocks of sheep and cattle grazing in the valley. Our camp was pitched on a grassy flat just below the village of Chushar Nango with its fine old ruined tower of stone with machicolated galleries all round it. To the South of us was the Nila Pass, which afforded an easy way into Nepal. The climate here was fairly warm, but the wind blew very strongly all that evening. Next day we saw the mountains all covered with fresh snow down to 16,000 feet, but we only experienced a slight drizzle as most of the snowflakes evaporated before they reached the ground, though clouds remained overhead all the morning. Morshead and his surveyors had been kept very busy up till now surveying and plotting in the intervening country from the tops of the hills, but owing to the clouds they were unable to do anything. We were all very late in starting, as our transport animals had been changed and the yaks that were supplied to us were very wild. In the first few minutes after starting we saw the plain strewn with our kits and stores, and yaks careering off in every direction with their tails in the air.

The march to Gyangkar Nangpa to-day was only a short one and led across a wide plain through which flowed the muddy and sluggish waters of the Yaru. The existing maps of this country were quite misleading and we could no longer depend on them. The rivers flowed in opposite directions to those shown on the map and mountains were shown where there were none. After about 2 or 3 miles, we had to ford the river, which was about 80 yards wide and not quite 3 feet deep. We then rode on across the plain, which was in some parts sandy and in others muddy or gravelly; evidently during the rainy season a shallow lake. In places the dwarf gorse grew on it. The sandy tracks were covered with curious hillocks 5 to 6 feet in height formed by the drifting sand and the gorse bushes. These in order to keep alive were compelled to push their branches through the sand which in its turn became piled up around them. Towards the West end of the plain were marshes and shallow lakes around which we had to make big detours.

Gyangkar Nangpa, which was our destination, was the country residence of the Phari Jongpen. His brother, who was acting as agent for him, rode out to meet us and escorted us to his house, a fine solid stone building dominating all the small houses. The tops of the walls were covered with gorse and juniper, rather suggestive of Christmas decorations. Tents were pitched for us in a grass paddock close to a grove of willows. We were then conducted upstairs into a pleasant room where were some fine gilt Chinese cabinets and some good Chinese rugs. Here the Jongpen had a meal prepared for us. We were first given tea, milk and beer, after which some fifteen dumplings apiece, each as big as a small apple, were put down in front of us together with three other bowls. In one of these was a black Chinese sauce, in another a chillie paste, and a third contained a barley soup. We were then given chopsticks with which we were expected to convey the dumplings into the barley soup, break them up there, season them with the various sauces, and then convey them to our mouths—a not too easy feat. This meal was so

Gyangka Range from near Chushar.

satisfying that we felt that we did not want to eat anything for a long time afterwards. We were told that in the rainy season the river here was unfordable, as it rose several feet and flooded over the plains, and it was then necessary to keep to the North or to the South of it. In the evening the agent came to make an official call and presented us with a sheep and a number of eggs. We invited him to dinner and gave him his first taste of such European cooking as could be provided by our native cooks.

There was a slight frost during the night, but the day turned out very fine. Our host accompanied us to the village of Rongkong, one of the villages belonging to his brother, and here he said good-bye to us. The day's march was uninteresting. We followed along the left bank of the Yaru past well-irrigated barley fields, for there was any amount of water here, until the valley narrowed and the sides came down steeper, when it became covered with gorse bushes. This valley we descended for about 10 miles until it debouched into another, a broader sandy valley where the Yaru changed its course to the South. We forded it at a point where it was about 90 yards wide and 3½ feet deep, and we then sat down and waited for our transport to come up. Beyond us lay a wide sandy valley through which a stream flowed sometimes on the surface, but more often underground, when it formed dangerous quicksands. When the transport came up, our drivers were very anxious to cross immediately, as there was a strong wind blowing and a violent sandstorm. They said that it would be much safer to cross now that all the fresh sand had blown over the wet sand. In the morning, they said, after a still night, it was very dangerous, so following their advice we started off, every one dressed up as though for a gas attack, with goggles over the eyes and comforters or handkerchiefs tied over the mouth and nose to keep the sand out. At first we wound our way through big sand dunes, off which the sand was blowing like smoke. Under one of these sand dunes we found our coolies halted and lost. Some of the donkeys, too, had been unloaded here, as they could not find their way across in the sandstorm. After leaving the dunes, there were wide stretches of wet sand to cross, over which the dried sand from the dunes was being blown like long wisps of smoke so that the whole ground appeared to be moving. In places where the wet sand shook and quivered we galloped along. Eventually we and our transport arrived on the far side of the plain in safety. It was now too late, however, to go on any further, so we camped on the dunes near the quicksands in the teeth of the gale. The sand was being whirled up on to us and into our tents until everything and every one was full of sand. Water was handy, but yak dung, our only fuel, was scarce and scanty.

Just before dark a very beautiful and lofty peak appeared to the Southwards. Our drivers called it Chomo Uri (The Goddess of the Turquoise Peak) and we had many discussions as to what mountain this was. In the morning, after taking its bearings carefully, we decided that this could be no other than Mount Everest. We found out afterwards that the name, Chomo Uri, was purely a local name for the mountain. Throughout Tibet it was known as Chomo-lungma—Goddess Mother of the Country—and this is its proper Tibetan name.

Next morning, after an uncomfortable and windy night, we rode for several miles across a plain covered with sand dunes 20 feet or more in height. On reaching the entrance to the valley of Bhong-chu, I determined to separate myself from the main party in order to explore a peak which attracted my attention on the North side of the valley and seemed to promise good views of Mount Everest and its surroundings. After a climb of some 3,000 feet, I found myself on a spur from which I had a very wonderful view. The view extended to the East from beyond Chomolhari—over 120 miles away —and embraced practically all the high snow peaks from Chomolhari to Gosainthan, a distance of some 250 miles. In the centre Mount Everest stood up all by itself, a wonderful peak towering above its neighbours and entirely without a rival. I spent four or five hours at the top of this hill, basking in the sun, as it was delightfully hot. I saw several swallow-tailed butterflies, also a number of bees, wasps and horse flies. Major Morshead and his surveyors soon afterwards joined us, intending to take advantage of the fine view. In the afternoon I left the peak and descended into the valley in search of our new camp, for we had now left the Yaru and had turned up into the valley of the Bhong-chu, a river that flowed from the West, with a very considerable volume of water. As there was rinderpest in the valley, our transport consisted now of donkeys only, many of them being very diminutive in size, but quite accustomed to carrying heavy loads. Our camp was pitched at a place called Trangso Chumbab, where there was an old Chinese rest-house. The Bhong-chu here was nearly 200 yards in width, but there was quite a good ford across it to Tsogo. Here we found many flourishing villages and much cultivation. We seemed to be entering a much more populated part of the country; from the top of the hill I counted in one valley no less than fifteen villages and quite a number of willow groves. From here a longish march of 18 miles up the valley of the Bhong-chu brought us to Kyishong—a pretty little village on the banks of the river. There were a few willow trees here and a lot of sea buckthorn. I did not keep to the road, but started early across a big plain on which I was lucky enough to shoot a goa with quite good horns. The day was very hot and sultry, and after crossing the plain I went up a side valley which turned out to be extremely pretty. It was very narrow and a mass of wild rose bushes. These roses were all of a creamy yellow, and every bush was covered with hundreds of sweet-smelling flowers. There was also a curious black clematis and several species of broom and rock cistus. Here and there were grassy patches with bubbling springs of crystal clearness. Rock pigeons, Brahminy ducks, blackbirds and numerous other varieties of small birds came down to drink here and did not mind us at all. About two o'clock the weather suddenly changed and violent thunderstorms started all round us, first on the opposite side of the valley and then on every side. Heavy hail came down at the same time and the ground soon became white. On descending into the valley, I put up what was to me a new kind of partridge, also numerous mountain hares. On emerging into the main valley, I noticed a group of five large Chortens. I was told that the centre Chorten had been built over a very bad demon, and that it kept him down. The other four Chortens at the corners prevented his ever getting away.

The next day's march to Shekar Dzong was a short one of only 12 miles. We followed the main valley for about 6 miles through some interesting conglomerate gorges alternating with open spaces covered with sea buckthorn. We then turned off Northwards up a side valley which led us to the town and fort of Shekar. This place was very finely situated on a big rocky and sharp-pointed mountain like an enlarged St. Michael's Mount. The actual town stands at the foot of the hill, but a large monastery, holding over 400 monks and consisting of innumerable buildings, is literally perched half-way up the cliff. The buildings are connected by walls and towers with the fort, which rises above them all. The fort again is connected by turreted walls with a curious Gothic-like structure on the summit of the hill where incense is offered up daily. On our arrival the whole town turned out and surrounded us with much curiosity, for we were the first Europeans that they had ever seen. A small tent had been pitched for us, but there was such a crowd round it that I retreated to a willow grove close by, which was protected by a wall. As the Jongpen had not come to see us, Chheten Wangdi went over to find him; presently he came along with a basket of eggs and with many apologies for not coming before, but he said that he had had no warning of our arrival. This was but partly true, for though our passport did not particularly mention this place, it authorised all officials to help us to their utmost, and the Jongpen certainly knew and had heard that we

SHEKAR DZONG.

were coming. I asked him to give orders that no intoxicating spirits should be served out to our followers, remembering the trouble we had had in one or two places before owing to their all getting drunk. Our tents were all pitched inside an enclosure and in the shade of the willow grove, and above us towered the picturesque buildings of the fort and the monastery. This was by far the largest and most interesting place that we had yet come across. For our mess tent we were given a fine Chinese tent such as they always seem to keep for the entertainment of guests of honour. As in most places, there were two Jongpens residing here, one lay and the other ecclesiastical, and finding that Tingri was under their jurisdiction, we asked them to issue orders to their representatives at Tingri to help us in every way with supplies and transport.

June 17 we spent resting at Shekar. In the morning Morshead and I went to call on the Jongpen; he lives in a poor house at the foot of the hill, his official residence being three-quarters of the way up, but he wisely prefers to live at the bottom, not being very fond of exercise. He was busy adding on to his house, and we were shown into the old part in which he was living. He gave us the usual Tibetan tea and sweetmeats and then insisted on our having macaroni and meat seasoned with chillies, which was excellent, followed by junket served in china bowls. He had some very fine teacups of agate and hornblende schist with finely chased silver covers, which I admired very much. That afternoon several of us went up to visit the big monastery of Shekar Chö-te. This consisted of a great number of buildings terraced one above the other on a very steep rocky slope. A path along the face of the rock brought us to several archways under which we passed. We then had to go up and down some picturesque but very steep and narrow streets until we came to a large courtyard. On one side of this was the main temple. In this temple were several gilt statues of Buddha decorated all over with turquoises and other precious stones, and behind them a huge figure of Buddha quite 50 feet high. Every year, they told us, they had to re-gild his face. Around were eight curious figures about 10 feet high and dressed in quaint flounces which they said were the guardians of the shrine. We then went up steep and slippery ladders, in almost pitch darkness, and came out on a platform opposite the face of the great Buddha. Here were some beautifully chased silver teapots and other interesting pieces of silver, richly decorated in relief. Inside the shrine, which was very dark, the smell of rancid butter was almost overpowering as all the lamps burnt butter. The official head of the monastery showed us round. He was apparently appointed from Lhasa and was responsible for all the revenues and financial dealings of the monastery. We were given very buttery tea in the roof courtyard, which was a pleasant spot, and here I photographed a group of several monks. They had never seen a camera or photographs before, but they had heard that such a thing was possible and were very much interested in it. Before leaving we went in to see the Head Lama who had lived over sixty-six years in this monastery. He was looked upon as being extremely holy and as the re-incarnation of a former abbot, and they therefore practically worshipped him. There was only one tooth left in his mouth, but for all that he had a very pleasant smile. All around his room were silver-gilt Chortens inlaid with turquoises and precious stones and incense was being burnt everywhere. After much persuasion the other monks induced him to come outside and have his photograph taken, telling him that he was an old man, and that his time on earth was now short, and they would like to have a picture of him to remember him by. He was accordingly brought out, dressed up in robes of beautiful golden brocades, with priceless silk Chinese hangings arranged behind him while he sat on a raised dais with his dorje and his bell in front of him, placed upon a finely carved Chinese table. The fame of this photograph spread throughout the country and in places hundreds of miles away I was asked for photographs of the Old Abbot of Shekar Chö-te, nor could I give

The Abbot of Shekar Chöte.

a more welcome present at any house than a photograph of the Old Abbot. Being looked upon as a saint, he was worshipped, and they would put these little photographs in shrines and burn incense in front of them.

About midnight that night I was suddenly awakened by yells and loud shouting and hammering close to my tent and next to that in which Bullock and Mallory were sleeping. The latter turned out and found that a Tibetan had seized an ice axe and a mallet and was busy hammering on our store boxes. He gave chase, but failed to catch the intruder. Some of our coolies, however, found out where he had gone to, and Chheten Wangdi had him handed over to the Jongpen. On investigation in the morning the man proved to be a madman whom his parents always kept locked up during nights when the moon was full, but he had managed to escape, so we handed him back to his family.

Our transport was very slow in arriving, and there were so many delays that it was midday before the procession finally moved off. The loads, too, were very badly put on and kept falling off, also the transport was quite the worst that we had yet had. For about 5 miles the path went up and down hill and through much sand until we came to the bridge over the Bhong-chu. This bridge consisted of four or five stout pillars of loose stones which acted as piers, on which were laid a few pieces of wood, on which flat stones were placed. It was a rough form of bridge, but served at ordinary times for its purpose. During the course of this summer, however, after heavy rain, these piers so dammed up the water as to cause it to rise some 4 or 5 feet on the upper side of them with the result that the immense weight of water swept the whole bridge away. Bullock and Mallory with half a dozen coolies had left early in the morning, intending to bivouac out for a couple of nights and climb one of the hills to the South of the Bhong chu in order to get a view of Mount Everest. After we had gone about 5 miles we met them close to the bridge, as they had lost their way and had been walking for about 15 miles:

not having found the bridge, they had forded the river and had got wet up to their necks in crossing it. At dusk we reached the village of Tsakor, where we found a tent pitched for us, and here we spent the night. Our transport did not turn up till nearly nine o'clock, and so we all slept in the mess tent. From here to Tingri was still another 20 miles—the path following the right bank of the Bhong-chu the whole way. In places the river was as much as 200 yards wide and flowed very sluggishly. We were told that the waters were very low, but that next month, when the rains had broken, the river often filled the whole of the bottom of the valley. On the way we passed some very handsome black-necked cranes as large as the Saurus crane. These had black heads and bills, with red eyes, light grey bodies and black tails with fine feathers. On this march the midges were dreadfully annoying the whole way, and we were surrounded with clouds of them the whole time. Their bite was very tiresome and extremely irritating. On the way we passed a Mongolian who had taken eleven months in coming from Lhasa and who was on his way to Nepal. His method of progression was by throwing himself at full length down on the ground. He then got up and at the spot where his hands touched the ground repeated the motion again. As we approached Tingri, the valley widened out and bent round to the South. Tingri itself was situated on the side of a small hill in the middle of a great plain, from which, looking to the South, was visible the wonderful chain of snowy peaks, many of them over 25,000 feet in height, which extends Westwards from Mount Everest. We crossed the Ra-chu—a tributary of the Bhong-chu, partly by bridges and partly by fords; it was split up into a number of small and very muddy channels that took their rise from the Kyetrak Glacier. Tingri was to be our first base for reconnoitring the Northern and North-western approaches to Mount Everest. It was June 19 when we arrived there, so that it had taken us just a month's travelling from Darjeeling to perform this part of our journey.

CHAPTER IV

TINGRI AND THE COUNTRY TO THE SOUTH

Tingri is a place of some importance, with a considerable trade at certain seasons of the year. It is the last place of any size on this side of the Nepalese frontier and boasts of a military governor. The garrison, however, when we visited it, consisted only of a sergeant and four or five soldiers. There were about three hundred houses in Tingri, all clustered together on the slopes of a small isolated hill standing in the middle of the great plain. On the top of the hill was the old Chinese fort, now all falling into ruin, but still littered with papers and books, written in Chinese characters, left behind by the Chinese on their hasty departure. Inside were quaint mural frescoes of curious old men riding stags or winged dragons painted in many colours. All the way up the valley of the Bhong-chu we had seen ruins of walls and evidences of much fighting. These all dated back, we were told, to the time of the Nepalese invasions of Tibet in the eighteenth century when the Gurkhas penetrated so far into Tibet that they actually got to Shigatse, and the Tibetans had to call upon the Chinese Empire for help. The Chinese came into the country with a large army, defeated the Gurkhas, drove them out of Tibet and crossed the Himalayas with a considerable army into Nepal, an extraordinary military feat considering the enormous difficulty of moving an army in these unhospitable regions over the high mountain passes through which it is approached. The Chinese, after this, never left Tibet until they were driven out by the Tibetans only a few years ago. In the hills round Tingri we came across many evidences of the fighting which then took place. This probably accounted for the large number of ruined and deserted villages that we saw in the valleys around. At the foot of the hill was a large Chinese rest-house which was only used to house Tibetan officials when they came there on duty. The Tibetans themselves did not like to live in or use the place, as many Chinese had died there and they thought that their ghosts haunted the spot. This rest-house was, however, swept out and prepared for our reception, as we had told the Tibetans that we should probably stay there for some time and should want a house to protect us from the wind and to provide a dark room for developing our photographs. The rest-house consisted of three courtyards; in the outer one we put the coolies, in the middle one the surveyors, and the inner one we kept for ourselves. In appearance the building was quite picturesque with its mural paintings of flying dogs and fierce dragons; but in spite of its picturesqueness outside and its handsome appearance, the rooms inside were small, and when the rain came it poured through the roof and our beds had to be shifted many times during the night to avoid the drips of water. It however provided an excellent dark room for us after we had well plastered the walls, the floor and the ceiling with mud and got rid of the dust of ages. To do any photographic work in Tibet a house is a necessity, as with the violent wind that blows every day all one's belongings get covered with dust which would ruin any negative. At first we found water a great difficulty as the local water was full of mud, but we eventually discovered a beautifully clear spring, about half a mile away, which bubbled up in a deep bluey green basin, and this water we used always, both for drinking and for photographic work. Tingri had many advantages as a base. Stores, supplies and transport were always available there, as it was the headquarters of the district. It also provided an easy means of approach to Mount Everest from the North-west and to the high group of mountains that lay to the West of Mount Everest. After sorting out all our stores and equipment and seeing in what state they were after the journey, our next business was the making of a dark room, as we had taken many photographs on the journey that required developing. The weather at this time was very fine, but the Tibetans kept on telling us that the rainy season ought to be starting, so we determined as soon as possible to send out parties in different directions to make the most of the favourable opportunity. The first morning after our arrival we were up on the top of the hill by six o'clock in the hope of getting a good view to the South, but the clouds were already over most of the mountains. Everest we could see quite clearly, and Cho-Uyo, the great 26,800 feet peak that lies to the West of Mount Everest. The Depon here, who was acting as the Governor of the place, was a nice young fellow and very cheery, and later on I got to know him very well and went over to his house and was entertained by him and his wife. He told me that the Tibetans still paid tribute to Nepal for all that part of the country, and that the amount they had to pay was the equivalent of 5,000 rupees per annum. The Nepalese kept a head-man at Tingri and another at Nyenyam to deal with all criminal cases and offences committed by Nepalese subjects when in Tibet. I found later on that the Tibetans were very frightened of the Nepalese, or of having any dealings with a Gurkha. I took photographs of the Depon's wife and all their children, and of his mother-in-law, which delighted them immensely; the wife at first was very shy of coming forward, but after many tears and protestations her husband finally induced her to be photographed. The great semi-circular head-dresses that the women wear are usually covered with turquoises, and coral, and often with strings of seed pearls across them. Round their necks hang long chains of either turquoise or coral beads, sometimes mixed with lumps of amber. Suspended round the neck by a shorter chain is generally a very elaborately decorated charm box, those belonging to the richer or upper classes being of gold inlaid with turquoises, the poorer people having them made of silver with poorer turquoises. The officials, as a rule, have a long ear-ring, 4 or 5 inches long, of turquoises and pearls, suspended from the left ear, while in the right ear they wear a single turquoise of very good quality. Nearly every one carries a rosary, with which their hands are playing about the whole day. We were told that the laws governing marriage in those parts were strictly regulated. Owing to the excessive number of males, a form of polyandry prevails. If there were four brothers in a family, and the eldest one married a wife, his wife would also be the property of the three younger brothers; but if the second or third brother married, their wives would be common only to themselves and their youngest brother. In Tibet, when, owing to the severe climate, digging is impossible for about six months in the year, if a man dies his body is handed over to professional corpse butchers, of whom there are one or two in every village. These butchers cut the body up into small pieces, which are taken out on to a hill-top and scattered about for the birds of the air or the wolves to devour. If by any chance there is a delay in consuming these remains, this is looked upon as a sign that the man has led an evil life during his lifetime.

On June 22 Wollaston rejoined us again. He had escorted Raeburn to Lachen, and had there arranged for an assistant surgeon to come up and take him back as far as Gangtok. Wollaston had then come on as fast as possible to rejoin us. His kit did not arrive till the following day, as he had ridden in direct from Shekar Dzong. The following day Bullock and Mallory left us, making direct for Mount Everest, and intending to reconnoitre the North and North-western slopes. Looked at from here it is certainly a very wonderful mountain, as it seems to stand up all by itself, but from this side it looks far too steep to be climbed. On June 25 Wheeler and Heron went off to Kyetrak, from which point Wheeler was to begin his photographic survey. I had intended to start the following day and join them, but the acid hypo that I had been using for fixing had given off so many sulphur fumes that I had been quite "gassed" for several days and had lost my voice in consequence. Unfortunately my orderly and Wheeler's bearer, who were both Mahommedans, were taken ill with enteric. Wheeler's bearer was in a very bad way, and a few days after my departure he died, but my orderly, after a bad attack, recovered, and when I returned three weeks later he was able to be up and to walk about a little. As Wollaston was likely to be detained here for some time owing to these cases of sickness, and as Morshead wanted to get in some surveying all round Tingri, I thought it would be a good opportunity to visit the different parties that we had sent out, and also to get, if possible, some information about Kharta, which I intended should be our second base. The coolies that we had still with us at Tingri were kept busy by Wollaston, and daily they would bring in rats, birds, lizards, beetles, or fish which they had collected for him. The local people would not make any attempt to collect these animals, as they said it was against their religion. On June 26 I started out to the South and camped the first night at Sharto, a small village about 9 miles across the plain to the South of Tingri. On the way we passed numbers of bees that seemed to be coming up out of the ground and swarming. These were all of a very light brown colour. Sharto is only a small village, but there are no other houses between it and Kyetrak, so that it was necessary to stop there. As the wind always blows with great strength here, the tents were pitched within some sheltering walls. In every place that we went to now we managed to get some kind of green food which was turned into spinach; a small kind of weed that grows in the barley fields was generally thus used. At other times we tried turnip leaves, or again, when we were higher and above the limits of cultivation, the young shoots of the nettle which grows up to 17,000 feet, and is really very good. I had taken with me this time a Tibetan whom we had picked up on the way. He was called Poo, and he turned out to be an excellent cook who could make any of the Tibetan dishes. As he was a sensible fellow, and very seldom drunk, I made a good deal of use of him. He accompanied me in all my wanderings, and I could not have found a more useful servant when travelling, as he never seemed to mind the cold or the height and could always produce a fire of some kind, even though he had forgotten to bring any matches. That evening at Sharto there was a curious false sunset in the East with rays of light in the deep purple of the sky. All the hills stood out with wonderful sharpness, and the colours were very beautiful. Towards nightfall we saw a number of kiang, which came quite close up to the camp and started feeding on the barley fields in spite of the pillars of stones and the strings which are put round the fields to keep both them and the hares away from the crops. The next morning I started off early as I intended to climb a hill 17,700 feet, on the way to Kyetrak. This hill, however, proved further off than I anticipated, and we had some difficulty in crossing a glacier stream, so that I did not get up to the top till 9 a.m., by which time the clouds had hidden a great part of the mountains to the South of us. The view, nevertheless, was extraordinarily fine. The top of Everest just showed above a great icy range to the East of us, and South-east was that great group of mountains of which Cho-Uyo, 26,800 feet, is the highest. Immense granite precipices descended sheer for several thousand feet until they reached great winding glaciers, while from over the Khombu Pass long wisps of cloud came sailing round these peaks and eventually hid them from our view. To the North the view extended right up to the watershed of the Brahmaputra, 80 to 100 miles distant. The different colours of the hills, the light and shade from the clouds, all formed a charming picture. Once over 17,000 feet, I met my old friend the dwarf blue poppy (*Meconopsis*) and many pretty white, blue and yellow saxifrages that grew on the rocks. Descending from this hill into the Kyetrak Valley, we passed a number of goa which were quite tame, but unfortunately they were all females. We had two more big glacial torrents to cross which later in the afternoon would probably have been impassable as by that time they would have risen another 2 feet, due to the melting of the snow and the ice by the hot sun in the morning; indeed, we only just managed to get across when we did. The main Kyetrak stream comes from the great glacier that descends from Cho-Uyo and the Khombu Pass. Opposite the village of Kyetrak it is luckily divided into a number of small streams, so that it is usually possible to get across it, though in the afternoons it is always somewhat difficult.

This village lies at a height of 16,000 feet, at the foot of the Khombu or Nangba Pass and the Pusi Pass. The former is a high glacier-covered pass, about 19,000 feet, that leads into the Khombu Valley in Nepal. The other, the Pusi Pass, is a much lower and easier pass that leads into the Rongshar Valley. Between these two passes lies a very beautiful glacier-covered peak called Chorabsang. Here at Kyetrak I met Heron and Wheeler encamped in the shelter of some walls close to the village, which consisted of a few dirty stone houses and a big Chorten. The people told me that they lived here all the year round, and that they owned the grazing for many miles to the North and possessed herds of yaks several thousand in number. Traffic could be kept up over these passes, they said, at all times of the year, though only with great difficulty, and with much danger, whole convoys being sometimes wiped out by blizzards when trying to cross the Khombu Pass, as the fine powdery snow is blown down into their faces from every direction and they finally get suffocated by it. That night there was a sharp frost, and the following morning Heron and I started to go up towards the Khombu Pass, following at first the East side of the Kyetrak Glacier. For about 6 or 7 miles we rode beside the great moraine that extended along the East side of this glacier; every now and then we climbed up on to a mound on the edge of the glacier in order to take photographs of it. The ice was all torn and riven into wonderful shapes and opposite us was the finely crevassed peak of Chorabsang. I pushed on, leaving Heron to come on at a slower pace, as I was anxious to get to the top of the pass before the clouds should have come up and hidden all the views. Every day it cost us a race to get up to a point of vantage before the clouds should have come up and hidden everything. Leaving the pony behind, with one coolie, I pressed forward for some 4 miles up a very stony and slippery moraine on the glacier. Here were many curious ice formations—ice tables with a big flat rock superimposed, curious upright pillars of ice, and the main glacier itself was worn by stone and water into the weirdest shapes and forms. In places, too, we came across that curious formation which in South America is called Nieve Penitentes. As we passed onwards, new glaciers opened up in every valley. The views up some of these side valleys, which often widened out into great amphitheatres, were very grand, especially that of the huge glacier that swept down from below the rock walls of Cho-Uyo.

On arriving at the end of the moraine, the boots that my coolie was wearing came to pieces and he said he could go no further across the snow, so shouldering the big camera, I started off alone. At first the ice was firm, but soon I came to soft snow and much water underneath it: they made the going very unpleasant and I kept floundering about up to my knees in snow and water. At length I came to a large crevasse along the edge of which I followed for over half a mile as most of the snow bridges across it were unsafe. At last I found my way across and by climbing on to some rocks was able to look over the top of the pass and down into Nepal. The height of the pass seemed to be about 19,000 feet, and as the day was very hot, I lay down and went sound asleep, only waking up when it began to snow. I then started, none too soon, on my homeward journey: all the way back snow fell heavily. I was very thankful to meet my coolie again and to hand over the camera to him: carrying a camera for five or six hours in soft snow at a height of over 18,000 feet is a heavy tax upon the endurance of anyone unaccustomed to carrying weights. Wheeler meanwhile had moved up his camp from Kyetrak to a spot on the moraine East of the glacier and intended to spend a week or fortnight in that valley.

The next morning Heron and I started to go over the Pusi Pass (Marmot Pass), so called because of the number of marmots that frequent the Southern slopes. After fording the Kyetrak River, we climbed up the moraine to the West of the Kyetrak Glacier and then turned up some easy grass hills until we came to the top of the pass, 17,700 feet. Here at the very top were growing some delightful little dwarf forget-me-nots—not an inch high—also many white and yellow saxifrages. Most of the views were unfortunately hidden by clouds, though one fine triple-headed peak showed up well to the South. We passed several flocks of female burhel (*Ovis nahura*), which were quite tame, and allowed us to ride up to within 50 yards of them. The hillsides were bare at first and grassy and the air felt distinctly cold and damp. We now commenced our long descent, and at 16,000 feet began to meet with juniper bushes and many dwarf rhododendrons. As we got lower, many more varieties of bushes appeared. There were two or three kinds of berberis, loniceras, white and pink spiræas, and quantities of white roses; besides these were masses of primulas and anemones, and pink, white or mauve geraniums. We now followed the right bank of the Shung-chu, a great glacial torrent, which joined by several others became an unfordable stream. The path was well engineered, sometimes close to the river, and sometimes built out on rocks high above the stream. All of a sudden the valley narrowed into a great gorge. We had left all the granites and slates behind and had suddenly come into the zone of the gneiss, which extended many miles to the South. A little way further down, at a place where two other valleys meet, we caught sight of some green barley fields lying round the small village of Tasang where we encamped on a terrace for the night. We were now at a height of only 13,300 feet, and were able to get fresh eggs and vegetables again. It was a great pleasure once more to have wood fires in place of the yak dung with its acrid smoke, which caused all one's food to taste unpleasantly. Here we used as fuel the aromatic wood of the juniper.

This valley is looked upon as a holy one, owing to the number of juniper bushes that grow in it, and several hermits and nuns had taken up their abode in it and shut themselves up in caves in order to meditate. The nearest village used to supply them with food, and morning and evening could be seen ascending the blue smoke of the juniper, which they burnt as incense before the entrances of their dwelling places. There was a hermit who lived close to the village and whose cave we could see high up in the rocks above. The villagers told us that after meditating for a period of ten years, he would be able to live on only ten grains of barley a day, and they were looking forward to that day. There was another anchorite female who was supposed to have lived here for 138 years and who was greatly revered. She had forbidden any of the animals in the valley to be killed, and that was the reason why the flocks of burhel we had passed were so extremely tame. The next day, giving our transport a rest, Heron and I walked for 7 or 8 miles down the valley. On the opposite side of the valley the only trees were birches and willow, and it was curious that, at these comparatively low heights, there were no large rhododendrons or fir trees. On the other side of the valley, the vegetation consisted wholly of juniper, berberis or wild roses. We descended to 12,000 feet, most of the time going through narrow gorges. At one place we came across a number of gooseberry bushes covered with young gooseberries, of which we gathered a sufficient supply to last us for several days. The rose bushes were charming all the way. At first they were all of the white creamy coloured variety, but lower down we came on the big red one with flowers often more than 3 inches in diameter. Wherever there were springs of water there grew masses of anemones and yellow primulas. We now returned to our camp at Tasang, and rain then started and continued the remainder of the day. The people told us that this valley was passable for animals for three days' journey, after which the river entered into some terrible gorges down which it was only just possible for a coolie to get along, and these latter gorges formed the boundary between Tibet and Nepal. On July 1 we started to return to Kyetrak; the morning was misty when we started, and though the higher peaks were all hidden in the clouds, the sun shone brightly and the day was quite hot. Our kit did not arrive till between five and six o'clock, and the yaks had a great deal of trouble in getting across the Kyetrak River, as it had risen considerably. Wheeler was still at his high camp further up the valley, waiting for a really clear day. The clouds, too, were his great enemies, as they came up very early every morning from over the Khombu Pass.

From here Heron and I had decided to go on and see how Mallory and Bullock had been faring in the next valley, so the next morning, after breakfasting at 5 a.m., we started off. It was one of the coldest mornings we had had, with a very hard frost, and being on the shady side of the valley we did not get the sun till several hours after we had started. After going down the valley for about 6 miles, we turned off to the East and crossed several easy passes, the higher of them, the Lamna La, being 16,900 feet. The country was very barren of flowers and vegetation, but there was a certain amount of grazing for yaks and sheep. The march to Zambu was a fairly long one of 20 miles, but the yaks came along well. This was a more prosperous-looking village than most of them, and the houses were all white-washed. We were still too high for barley fields as we were just 16,000 feet, but the wealth of the village lay in its herds of yaks and sheep; the villagers told us they owned 3,000 yaks. Shepherds in this country are but poorly paid, getting only thirty trangkas (10*s.*) per annum. But house servants are still worse off, getting only eight trangkas (2*s.* 8*d.*) per annum. However, they seem to thrive under those wages and there is no discontent or trades unionism among them. Our camp was pitched in a sunny spot not far from the village, looking straight over towards Mount Everest, whose top appeared over the opposite hills. From this side its precipices looked most formidable and there was also a magnificent ridge which we had not seen before. There was a slight frost again that night.

Breakfasting, as usual, at 5 a.m., I started up the hill South of the camp and was lucky enough to get a clear view of Everest and the Rongbuk Valley that led up to it. This valley ran right up to the foot of Mount Everest and seemed an easy enough approach, but the mountain itself looked absolutely unscalable from this side, showing nothing but a series of very steep precipices. The day turned out to be a very hot one. I descended into the valley below, and started to ride up towards Mount Everest. Presently I came to an unfordable stream, and after making several attempts to get across this, found myself compelled to return several miles down the valley to the monastery of Chöbu, where there was a slender footbridge. The pony that I was riding was swum across, a rope being attached to its head. He was then pulled over to the far side, a proceeding he did not at all enjoy. The yaks, too, were unladen, and the loads carried by hand over the bridge. After this the yaks were driven into the river and made to swim across, but they only went as far as an island in the middle of the river. From this place they would not budge in spite of stones, curses and threats, until at length a man with a sling, fetched from the monastery, hurled stones at them with great violence: this procedure apparently so stung them up that they thought it advisable to cross the remainder of the stream. At the entrance to the valley, we passed some very tame burhel within a few yards of the path, and then went along at the foot of some fine cliffs with limestone on the top and layers of hornblende and granite below. At first there was quite a rich vegetation growing here, considering we were just on 16,000 feet. There were juniper bushes, clematis, willows, a genista, rock roses, and even some yellow primulas, but as we got further into the valley it became more stony, and on either side of the path were small piles of stones heaped up by pilgrims. The valley was considered very sacred and was apparently a great place of pilgrimage. We found the base camp of the Alpine climbers pitched close to the Rongbuk Monastery, where there lived a very high re-incarnated Lama who was in meditation and not allowed to see anyone. This valley was called the Rongbuk, or inner valley—a name well suited to it; the legend was that from this valley there used to be a pass over into the Khombu Valley, but the high Lama who lived here forbade the use of it, as it disturbed the meditations of the recluses and hermits, of which there were several hundred here. At first these good people did not at all approve of our coming into this valley, as they thought we should be likely to disturb and distract their meditations.

The Rongbuk Monastery lies at a height of 16,500 feet, and is an unpleasantly cold spot. This monastery contains twenty permanent Lamas who always live there, together with the re-incarnated Lama. Besides these, there are three hundred other associated Lamas who come in periodically, remaining there for periods of varying length. These Associate Lamas are mostly well-to-do, and having sufficient money to support themselves are not a drain upon the villagers. They will often invest several thousand trangkas with some village, and in return for this money the village will supply them with food, barley, milk, eggs and fuel. Higher up the valley there was a smaller monastery, and dotted along the hillside were numerous cells and caves where monks or nuns had retired to meditate. Every animal that we saw in this valley was extraordinarily tame. In the mornings we watched the burhel coming to some hermits' cells not a hundred yards away from the camp, to be fed, and from there they went on to other cells. They seemed to have no fear whatever of human beings. On the way up the valley we passed within 40 to 50 yards of a fine flock of rams, but they barely moved away, and on the way back we passed some females that were so inquisitive that they actually came up to within 10 yards of us in order to have a look at us. The rock pigeons came and fed out of one's hand, and the ravens and all the other birds here were equally tame; it was most interesting to be able to watch all their habits and to see them at such close quarters. On July 4, Heron and I walked up the valley to see Mallory and Bullock, who had got an Alpine camp some 7 miles further up the valley at a height of 18,000 feet, where they were training their coolies in snow and ice work and trying to find out whether there was any possible way of attacking Mount Everest from this side. It was a beautiful morning when we started, and on the way we passed one or two small monasteries and numerous cells where hermits and recluses were living in retirement and meditation. After crossing several small lake beds and old moraines—for the big Rongbuk Glacier seemed to have been retiring in the last few years—we came to the big moraine-covered Rongbuk Glacier. This glacier appeared to be about 8 or 9 miles long, starting immediately below an immense circle of cliffs which formed the North face of Mount Everest. We found afterwards that there were several other side glaciers that joined in it, which were even larger and longer than the centre glacier. After some steep scrambles up the moraine-covered glacier and on to a high terrace on the West side of it, we found Mallory and Bullock with their coolies encamped in a pleasantly sheltered spot with plenty of water close at hand and commanding the most magnificent views of Mount Everest, which here seemed to be only about 6 miles away and towered up above the glacier, showing immense cliffs 10,000 feet high. Mallory and Bullock were hard at work training the coolies in snow and ice work and exploring all the different glaciers from that side. They were, however, much handicapped by there only being two of them, which made the work more strenuous. After spending the day with them, Heron and I returned to our camp in the evening. The evening light on Mount Everest was wonderfully beautiful. The weather seems nearly always to clear up about sunset, and its summit then usually towers far above the clouds in a clear sky. At dusk several of the Lamas came for medicines of different kinds, which we gave them, and much to our surprise in the morning they presented us with a number of fresh eggs in gratitude. Having seen Mallory and Bullock well established in this valley, our next most important duty seemed to be to select a site for our next base camp. Some place on the East side of Mount Everest would have to be chosen, and it seemed that somewhere in the Kharta Valley would be the most likely spot. Heron and I therefore determined that we would make a quick reconnaissance of that district before returning to Tingri. On the following day we moved down from the Rongbuk Monastery.

CHAPTER V

THE SEARCH FOR KHARTA

After leaving Mallory and Bullock to continue the search for a possible route up Mount Everest from the Rongbuk side, Heron and I, on July 5, started off down the Rongbuk Valley in order to visit Kharta. We had been told that it was only two days' easy march from the monastery to get there. It was a cold morning when we started off; there had been a sharp frost during the night and the sun did not reach us till late in the morning. Mount Everest stood out at the head of the valley wonderfully clear and clothed with a fresh mantle of white. Instead of crossing over the river by the bridge, at Chöbu, we kept straight on down the valley till we came to Chödzong, where were the first barley fields and cultivation. There was plenty of water here for irrigation purposes, and some fine grassy fields on which many ponies were grazing. We had to change our transport in this village and get fresh animals, so that it was not till three o'clock in the afternoon that we got started again. In Tibet they have a system of stages, and animals from one village are taken, as a rule, for one stage only. As each stage usually ends at the next village, and as villages are frequent, this is a most awkward and inconvenient arrangement—as it necessitates three or four changes a day. In order to avoid these constant changes, we used to persuade the villagers by promises of extra baksheesh, especially where we had a large number of animals, to undertake two or three stages. After leaving Chödzong we climbed up over a steep pass 1,200 feet above the valley and found a still deeper descent to the village of Halung, which lay at our feet. Here we waited for our transport, but as this did not arrive till dark, we decided to camp there, though we had only done 18 miles from Rongbuk; the yak travels very slowly. We were now again at 14,800 feet and found a much warmer climate, with green barley fields and here and there patches of yellow mustard. A large rhubarb with a curious crinkled leaf grew here and there in the fields. We tried to eat this rhubarb; it had an unpleasant taste, but this disappeared when it was cooked and it proved a welcome addition to our diet. The Tibetans do not use it for food, as sugar—without which it would be uneatable—is scarce and expensive in the country. The plant serves, however, as an acid for dyes.

Halung is a very prosperous-looking village with well-built houses. The villagers soon had three tents pitched for us on a grassy field between the village and the river; cushions, cooking pots and fuel were also brought out for us. Here we camped for the night in reasonable comfort. On the following morning the loads were all carried by hand across a fragile bridge over the glacier stream, while the yaks and the ponies were driven across it. We then rode for a mile down the green and well-watered valley, and afterwards turned up into another valley where every flat space was green with barley-fields intermixed with brilliant patches of yellow from the fields of mustard. A small glacier stream fed this valley and supplied plenty of water for irrigation. After passing several small villages we rode across a spur also covered with barley-fields to Rebu, where we had to change our transport. This was quite a picturesque village situated on a rocky knoll, part of the village being on one side and part on the other of the river. Along the various irrigation canals were wild flowers of all kinds. Monkshood grew there, also black and yellow clematis, rhubarb, ranunculus and primulas of different kinds. By ten o'clock our transport was changed and we were given ponies instead of yaks: they travel much quicker and we had apparently a long way to go yet before we could reach the next village. We were expecting all the time to get to Kharta that evening, but where distances are concerned all Tibetans are liars, and after doing 26 miles we stopped, Kharta being apparently as far off as ever. After leaving Rebu the path led for some miles up an uninteresting valley, in which limestone cliffs on one side and sandstone cliffs on the other came down almost to the stream, the waters of which, in contrast to the muddy glacier streams that we had been meeting the whole time, were as clear as crystal. There were many small birds along the banks, all of them wonderfully tame; these, when we were resting for lunch, hopped all round us and under our legs, carrying off crumbs or any morsels of food. We now climbed up on to a pass called the Doya La, 17,000 feet, from the top of which were fine views of great rocky peaks on either side, those on the South being covered in parts with hanging glaciers. About a quarter of a mile from the top of the pass we struck some granite soil on which grew an extraordinary variety of Alpine flowers; the blue poppy abounded, pink, yellow and white saxifrages covered all the rocks, and besides these were many other plants which I had not seen before and which were quite new to me. The range which we now crossed acts as a barrier against the approach of the Monsoon clouds and prevents them from passing over into Tibet. Over on the North side the country is mostly dry and very little grows there, whereas on the South there is a rich and varied vegetation and the air feels soft and moist. The road from the pass led by an easy descent into a fine valley with a green lake lying at its head under the dark cliffs of some bold rocky peaks. We followed this valley for many miles, a strong head wind blowing against us the whole of the time, and found ourselves before long once more among the junipers and willows. We also saw pink and white rhododendrons, and in places a small yellow one with waxy blossoms. The yellow rock cistus, spiræas, roses, yellow primulas, blue monkshood, campanulas, blue anemones, and hundreds of other wild flowers formed a rich flora which showed that a considerable precipitation from the Monsoon fell in this valley.

At last we came to a village, but every one fled at our approach, and we could get no information about the route. A little further on we came across more villages, in one of which, with much difficulty and after a long chase, we captured a man and made him guide us to the village of Chulungphu, where we decided to stop the night. After a little time we induced some of the villagers to come out from their hiding-places, and to produce tents and fuel for us. The camp was pitched in a field of sweet-scented primulas near the village. The architecture of these houses was quite different from what we had met before—they all appear to be strongly fortified, as they have practically no windows and there are only small loopholes facing outwards. They are all built of a brown stone—a kind of gneiss, and have sods on the parapet over which are laid branches of juniper. The next morning we woke to the sound of pattering rain and found all the hills wreathed in grey mist. This was their first rain this year, so the inhabitants told us. It was pleasant to one's skin after the dry climate and biting winds that we had been experiencing on the other side of the passes to feel oneself wrapped in a softer and milder air. We rode down this valley for about 6 miles until it debouched into the main Arun Valley. The people, however, do not know it by this name here, but call it still the Bhong-chu until it reaches Nepal. We passed villages all the way, villages brown in colour and built of a brown gneiss, around which grew fields of barley and mustard. After the barren valleys which we had left, these appeared very fertile; rose and currant bushes surrounded every field, while the hillsides were covered with juniper and willows. Along the path grew spiræas and clematis, while beside every watercourse were yellow marsh marigolds and primulas. A feature of the Arun Valley, which was fairly wide here, was the old terraces on its slopes, now all covered with barley, pea and mustard fields, the latter being a blaze of yellow. There were many villages here and some pleasant country houses surrounded by groves of willows and poplars. Down here the people were not quite so frightened of us as they were in the valley from which we had just come, where they had run away from us whenever we approached. The Bong-chu here is a large river with a very great flow of water, and quite unfordable. The nearest place where it could be crossed is at a rope bridge some 18 miles higher up, and during the rainy season this bridge is impassable, and communication with the other side completely cut off. To the South and close by, at a height of 12,000 feet, the Bhong-chu enters a terrific gorge on either side of which tower up great cliffs with snowy peaks high above them. On some of the slopes which are not quite so steep there are thick forests of fir trees and rhododendrons where, I was told, the muskdeer lived. After descending the valley for 3 miles, we turned up a side valley pointing Westwards. Down this flowed a very large and unfordable glacial stream. This evidently came down from the neighbourhood of Mount Everest, but local information as to its source was very vague, and it was evident that we should have to prospect for ourselves. Some 3 miles up this valley we came to a place called by the natives Kharta Shika, where the Governor of the Kharta District resides. Kharta was not apparently a village at all, but a district including a number of small villages. We halted a short distance below Kharta Shika and presently the Governor came out to meet us with a present of sweetmeats and the usual scarf. He apologised for not meeting us before, as he said that he had no information as to the date of our arrival. He begged that we would come over to his garden where he had ordered a fine Chinese tent to be pitched for us. We crossed the river by a wooden bridge, and after going through the village came to the Governor's house. Crossing through the courtyard we entered his garden, which lay in a nice sheltered spot surrounded by willow trees with a stream of clear water running through it. Big wild roses grew there and a few

European flowers that he had planted, while under a very ancient poplar there was a large painted prayer wheel, some 8 feet high, which was turned by a stream of water. Here in his garden he provided us with a meal of excellent macaroni and a very hot chilli salad. It was very pleasant to rest the eyes on the luscious green of the well irrigated garden, and to be for once sheltered from the wind. During the night we were awakened by a regular shower bath. The Chinese tent, beautiful as it was in outward appearance, was sadly lacking in waterproof qualities. As it rained steadily most of the night, we had to take cover under our mackintoshes on which were pools of water in the morning. There seemed to be no doubt that the proper Monsoon had at last broken, and the Jongpen himself told us that this was the first really heavy rain that they had had. All the people considered that we had brought this rain with us and were very grateful in consequence; later on, when we left, they begged us not to stop the rain, as they wanted it badly for their crops.

As it cleared up a little about nine o'clock in the morning, though the hills were still all in cloud, we rode out with Chheten Wangdi, the Jongpen and Hopaphema, who was the largest landowner about here, to look out for a site for our next base camp. We wanted, if possible, to get a house that could be used as a store-room and also for photographic purposes. We rode down into the main valley, and after looking over several houses, we eventually selected one on an old river terrace with fine views all around and standing quite by itself well away from any village. The water supply was good and handy, and there was a pleasant garden of poplars and willows, in which we could pitch our tents. After a certain amount of bargaining, the owners were willing to let us have the house and the garden for the large rent of one trangka ($3\frac{1}{2}d.$) a day. It was apparently the first time anyone in that valley had ever wanted to rent a house, and there were no house agents there to run one up into exorbitant prices. We then rode on to Hopaphema's house, which was a fine solidly built dwelling surrounded by large juniper trees, willows and poplars. Later on we got to know this man very well, and used to call him always the "Sergeant," as he was supposed to do any recruiting for the Tibetan army that was needed in that valley. He had a very kindly disposition, was always very hospitable, and had a great sense of humour. He had a tent pitched for our reception under a very old poplar with a grass plot in front surrounded by bushes of wild red roses. Here we were given tea, milk and beer, and then the usual macaroni and mince was produced. On leaving, he insisted on my taking away a large quantity of turnip leaves, as he knew I was very fond of green food, and they made an excellent "spinach." The Tibetans that we met have invariably proved very kindly and hospitable.

On returning to Kharta, where I had left Heron, I found that it had been raining all the time, though in the main valley we had had it quite fine. In the evening I took a walk up to an old fort not far from our camp. This fort in old days had commanded the only path from here that led into Nepal, but now it had all fallen into ruin. Close by it, however, was a delightful dell full of hoary willow trees, underneath which the ground was carpeted with yellow primulas growing among the bushes of scarlet roses. Near by were two old poplar trees, whose trunks measured between 20 and 30 feet in circumference and were evidently of a very great age. The primulas everywhere were really astonishing. They outlined every watercourse with yellow and often grew between 2 and 3 feet high with enormous heads of sweet cowslip-scented yellow flowers. It rained again during the whole of the night, and the fine spray that came through the Chinese tent made sleep rather difficult. The next morning we started to go back to Tingri, and for the first day's march were given coolies for our transport. In this district coolies are used a great deal as all the trade with Nepal has to be carried on by them, the paths over the passes being quite impassable for pack transport; the Jongpen told us that we would find them quite as fast as ponies.

To-day's march was to Lumeh—a distance of about 17 miles—and the coolies arrived very soon after we did, having come along extraordinarily well. Our route for the first 3 miles was down the Kharta Valley until it joined the valley of the Bhong-chu; we then followed the right bank of this for some 10 miles. On the way we stopped at the house of Hopaphema, who insisted on giving us a meal of milk, macaroni and mince, although it was only just over an hour since we had had breakfast. On our departure he gave us a basket of eggs and some more turnip leaves to take along with us, and altogether showed himself a most friendly and hospitable host. At first we rode through fields of barley, peas and mustard for several miles, the valley then became much more barren and the path occasionally was taken high up on the face of a cliff, where the river swept round close beneath the mountain side. At other times we crossed broad stony terraces. We came eventually to the village of Dak, where the monks from the monastery had pitched tents for us and had another meal provided for us. Coolies had to be changed here, our old coolies arriving while we were having our meal; after the loads had been transferred, our new transport proceeded along to Lumeh, where we intended to spend the night. The path after Dak was in places dangerous owing to falling stones, and our guide every now and then urged us to hurry, as owing to the heavy rain of the preceding night many stones had been loosened. The main Bhong-chu suddenly turned off to the East from here, unexpectedly forcing a passage through a very curious and deep gorge, where it burst its way through the highest mountains. We did not, however, follow the valley of the Bhong-chu, but kept on up what appeared to be the main valley; this was really only the valley of the Lower Rongbuk that in its lower portion is called the Dzakar-chu. This river we crossed by a wooden bridge, built on the cantilever principle, and which a couple of months later was washed away. After riding for a couple of miles over a nice grassy turf we came to Lumeh. Here was a very fine country house around which were grouped a few smaller houses. This was the residence of Ngawangyonten, who was managing the district for the big monastery at Shekar Dzong, whose property it was. He had tents already pitched for us, and fuel, milk and eggs already prepared. Around this house were five of the largest poplar trees that I have ever seen. The largest was almost 40 feet in circumference at the base, and the others were all between 20 and 25 feet in circumference. The villagers told us that they thought these trees had been planted about 500 years ago. Magpies and hoopoes were very common in this valley—the former were quite tame and allowed us to approach very close. The barley-fields seemed to hold many hares. Some fine crops of wheat as well as barley were grown here, although the height was 12,800 feet. Every night now we had heavy rain which brought fresh snow down to 16,000 feet. As the clouds remained low all day we seldom got any distant views.

The march to Pulme, our next point up the valley of the Dzakar-chu, was 22 miles, a very dull and uninteresting ride. The going was bad—we often had to follow the bed of the river, which was now in flood and extended to the cliffs on both sides—at other times we kept high up on the steep sides of a gorge, sometimes of gneiss, sometimes of limestone rock. In places where the valley widened out, the river bed was full of bushes of tamarisk and sea buckthorn, but otherwise the vegetation was scanty. After going 15 miles we were to change coolies; but the Lumeh coolies, who were extremely poor and very different from those that we had taken from Kharta, took eleven hours to cover the 15 miles, and did not arrive till six in the evening. Much to Heron's disgust, I proposed to push on to Pulme, late as it was; but the road was good, and we trotted the 7 miles in an hour and a half, though the coolies and the donkeys did not arrive till well after dark. Fortunately we found tents as usual pitched for our reception. We had originally intended to ford the Dzakar-chu that evening and camp on the far side, but it was too dangerous to do it in the dark, though the villagers told us that by morning the stream would be a couple of feet higher. The river is a great obstacle at this time of the year, as there is no bridge over it here, the next bridge being at Chöbu, 20 miles higher up the valley.

The following day I started on my return journey to Tingri, leaving at 5.30 in the morning with Chheten Wangdi. I succeeded in fording the Dzakar-chu, which was deep and very swift. My pony was swept off his legs once and I got very wet, the icy cold water coming right over the saddle.

Heron and the coolies were to follow on slowly and were to take two days in reaching Tingri, but I was anxious to get back, having been away already longer than I intended. Four miles away, at Tashi Dzom, I changed ponies and procured a guide who was to take me on to Tingri, leaving Chheten Wangdi behind with Heron. This guide proved quite an amusing fellow, and suddenly surprised me by counting in English one, two, three, four, and then saying "Right turn" and "Left turn," and other military words of command. On inquiring where he had learned this English, I found that at one time he had served as a soldier at Lhasa, where the military words of command are in English, and these were the only English words that he knew. After leaving Tashi Dzom we turned up into a broad side valley with villages every half-mile and surrounded by barley, mustard and pea fields. What was, however, especially noticeable about all these valleys that we had been passing through for the last two days, was the extraordinary number of ruined villages that there were everywhere. This was not due to lack of water, for there was plenty of water in all the streams; these valleys, however, must have at one time been very thickly inhabited, and it is probable that the dearth of population to-day is due to the wars with the Gurkhas in the eighteenth century. We had a very wet ride—one storm after another overtook us, and a cold rain fell heavily all the way to Tingri. We gradually ascended out of the cultivation and crossing a low pass, about 16,000 feet, looked down again on the great Tingri Plain. There was still, however, a long way to go, and it was not till after five o'clock in the evening that I reached Tingri, drenched to the skin. It had been a ride of between 36 and 40 miles.

At Tingri I found Wollaston and Morshead. The former had been very busy all the time I had been away in collecting insects, butterflies, rats, mice, birds and flowers, and had amassed quite a number of specimens. Morshead had been out a good deal with his surveyors to the North and to the West, but had been driven in by the bad weather of the last few days. This had apparently been general and we might say that the rainy season this year had begun on July 7, which the Tibetans considered very late for those parts. The following afternoon Heron arrived, and my kit also, which I was very glad to get, as I had only had a spare tent to roll around me the previous night.

The next day or two was spent mostly in reading letters and newspapers. Our postal arrangements were at first rather complicated, there being no regular postal service to the provinces in Tibet. We had, therefore, to make an arrangement with each Jongpen to forward on our mail. Phari was the last post office, and the postmaster there had to arrange with the Phari Jongpen for a messenger every week to go with our posts to Khamba Dzong; we had left money with him for the purpose of paying the postman. At Khamba Dzong we had arranged with the Jongpen there that he should forward our letters to Tinki, and at Tinki we had made further arrangements for them to be sent on to Shekar Dzong and from Shekar Dzong they were to be sent to Tingri. We had left money for this purpose with the various Jongpens, and each Jongpen as he received the mail bag was to affix his seal on it and send it on as quickly as he could to the next Jongpen. This system worked very well for the first two months, but after we had moved to Kharta, partly owing to floods, and partly perhaps to the laziness of the Shekar Jongpen, our mails were all held up and we eventually had to send coolies back from our camp to Phari to bring them along. The best plan another time would be to take with the Expedition a certain number of coolies to be used purely for going backwards and forwards with the mails. On July 13 Morshead and Wollaston left to go to Nyenyam in response to a cordial invitation from the Jongpen, asking that some of the Expedition should visit the place. We were glad to accept, and this should be a very interesting part of the country botanically.

CHAPTER VI

THE MOVE TO KHARTA

I had arrived back at Tingri on July 11, and remained there in the Chinese rest-house until July 24, when I started to move the base camp and all the stores round to Kharta. During the time I was not left always alone, for Heron came in occasionally for a night between his various geological expeditions to the North. Wheeler also came down for a change and a rest, and to develop the photographs that he had taken. He had been having a very trying and provoking time in the high camps, as the weather had been bad, with frequent snowfalls. Nearly every day he climbed up to a spur 20,000 feet or more in height, yet in spite of waiting all day there in the icy cold winds or driving snow, it was but seldom that he was able to get a photograph, and then the clouds would only lift for a few minutes.

There was always plenty to do at Tingri, so the time passed quickly. Much photographic work had to be done and much developing and printing of the many photographs that were being sent in by the various members of the party. Supplies had also to be sent out and arrangements made for the comforts of the climbing party in the Rongbuk Valley. There were also several expeditions to be made round Tingri, and these were full of interest. Anemometers were very popular in this district; they were fixed by the Tibetans above small prayer wheels, and owing to the constant winds, it was seldom that the prayer wheels were not revolving. Many yaks' horns, carved all over with prayers, were lying about on the different Chortens or Mani walls. The barley, which was only just coming up when we arrived, was now 18 inches high and coming into ear, and though we were over 14,000 feet, the crops looked very healthy and even. Every evening during this period we had heavy storms of rain with much lightning and thunder, and fresh snow used to fall during the night as low as 15,000 feet, but most of it melted again during the day. During this period the plains round Tingri were rapidly becoming marshes and the rivers quite unfordable. The storms always gathered to the North of us, along the Sipri limestone ridge, and the high mountain chain that formed the watershed between the Brahmaputra and the Bhong-chu. These storms generally worked down towards the South. Occasionally fine days came to us when there was a strong South wind to blow the rain back, and it was seldom that the Monsoon clouds brought rain directly to us from the South. The Sipri range was a very conspicuous limestone range to the North of us, the limestone being worn into the most curious shapes. It was looked upon by the Tibetans as being a holy mountain, and on its slopes were many small monasteries. Hermits also took up their abode in the limestone caves below the summit. Pilgrims used to come from great distances to make the circuit of the mountain. This took generally five days, and much merit was acquired by doing so.

On July 17 I made an excursion out to the Hot Springs at Tsamda, about 7 miles away to the North-west across the plain. The valley of the Bhong-chu narrows there for a few miles before opening out again into the wide Sutso Plain. There were two or three hot springs here, but only one large one, and this was enclosed by walls within which were little stone huts in which people could change their clothes. The water was just the right temperature for a nice hot bath. When I went there, there was one man bathing and also washing his clothes in it. The Tibetans said, however, that this was not the proper season for bathing. The autumn was the correct time for them to have their annual bath before the winter sets in. The water was saline and had, I think, a little iron in it, but was not very unpleasant to the taste. The rocks from which it gushes out are very extraordinary, the strata forming a very steep arch, on the top of which there is a crack, from the very end of which, and at its lowest point, the springs came bubbling out. Near by in the valley there were also a good many saline deposits. In one of the smaller springs there were a number of little pink worm-like animals that were swimming about and clinging with their mouths to the sides of the rock. Riding back to Tingri by a different way across the plain, I saw a number of kiang and a few goa, but they were very wild and would not allow us to approach to within 500 yards. I also passed three of the handsome black-necked cranes. The way across the plain was rather boggy, and we had some difficulty in finding it. When I got back I found that Heron had come in for a couple of nights, and the following day Wheeler too joined us, having walked in from Nezogu, the bridge over the Kyetrak River. He was anxious to develop some photographs, and as the weather was very bad, he could do no good by remaining in his high camp.

On July 20 we had very brilliant flashes of lightning, followed by a heavy storm of rain during the night. This was too much for the flat earth roof of the rest-house, and the water poured into all our rooms, causing us to move our beds many times during the night in search of a dry spot. I started off early in the morning as I had intended to climb the hills to the East of Tingri, but the rain that had fallen at Tingri had meant a heavy fall of snow on the mountains and the snow had fallen as low down as 15,000 feet. We passed several goa on the way, but they were too shy to allow us to get a shot, also some kiang, which were very tame, and showed up well in the snow. As we got higher, the snow became about 4 inches deep, but was melting rapidly. The glare and the heat were intense. I saw a good many flocks of burhel, but no very large heads. The views as I followed the crests of the hills were extremely fine; on the North I looked down into the valley of the Bhong-chu, which was in flood and had filled the whole of

Military Governor, his Wife and Mother.

the bottom of the valley with water, and on the other side I looked over the Tingri Plain to the great range of snow peaks which finally ended in the mighty mass of Gosainthan. The weather had been very hot and oppressive all day, and as usual in the evening we had another very severe thunderstorm with heavy rain all through the night. The following day was more like an English November day—cold and grey with drizzling rain—and with the snow on the hills down to 15,000 feet. I bought a Tibetan pony during the morning for the large sum of £7. It was a bay, an excellent ambler, and very surefooted. The Tibetan name by which he was known was Dug-dra-kyang-po, which means "The bay pony like a dragon."

I went over to have lunch with the Depon's representative. His family were all dressed up very smartly for the occasion, the women folk wearing their best head-dresses of turquoises, coral and pearls. He gave us rice and raisins as a *hors d'œuvre*, and an *entrée* of junket, followed by some pickled turnips, which I thought very nasty, after which we had the usual macaroni and mince. He had been very friendly and kindly to us the whole time that we were at Tingri, and had always supplied us with everything we asked for. On July 22 we saw a very fine solar halo with well-marked rings of yellow, brown, green and white, but the rain continued steadily nearly all the time. The day before we were to leave Tingri I sent away my orderly, together with two coolies who had been sick, and whom the doctor had recommended that we should send back to Darjeeling. They were given sufficient food to take them back to Darjeeling and an extra fifteen days' pay, the orderly also being given a horse to ride. Towards evening the weather improved and we had some lovely views of Mount Everest and that great group of snow peaks of which Cho-Uyo is the highest. They all looked very white under their new coating of snow, which lies thickly down to 16,000 feet.

On July 24 we eventually got off from Tingri; the last few days had been spent in packing up and re-arranging all the stores. There was the usual talking, shouting and arguing, but all the loads were eventually packed on to the animals, or loaded on to the backs of the coolies by nine o'clock. We then took a last farewell of the Depon's representative, who was very sorry to see us go, and who had done so much to make our stay pleasant there.

The first march was to Nezogu, where there was a bridge over the Kyetrak; this was about 19 miles, partly across the Tingri Plain and then over a tiresome moraine. While crossing the moraine, I shot a goa which had quite a good head. Wheeler had accompanied me, as he had left his camp at the bridge, and on arrival there we found his tents all pitched and his cook waiting ready to receive us. Our own kit did not arrive till it was getting dark, when the weather looked very ominous. Rain fell steadily most of the night, and just before dawn this turned to snow, so that when we woke up there were a couple of inches of fresh snow on the ground. As it was still snowing steadily, we were in no great hurry to start, and did not get off until nine o'clock. The weather than gradually improved and the fresh snow soon melted, though the ground was left in a very boggy condition. The march to Chöbu was about 15 miles over the easy Lamna Pass. Knowing the way, I climbed on to a ridge to the South, where I had a fine view again of Mount Everest and the Rongbuk Valley. We pitched our camp on the far side of the Rongbuk River, our loads being carried across the frail bridge by the villagers, and our ponies being swum across. Here Mallory and Bullock joined us. They had been experiencing latterly very bad weather in the Upper Rongbuk Valley, and constant heavy falls of snow had seriously hindered their reconnaissance work. Their coolies, too, were getting rather tired and stale from remaining at such heights for a considerable time, and were badly in want of a rest. I had therefore arranged for them to meet me here and to accompany me round to Kharta, from which place they could then explore the Eastern approaches of Mount Everest.

During the night I suffered much from inflammation of the eyes, due to the snow that had fallen the day before. They were so painful as to make sleep quite impossible. I was not, however, the only one to suffer, as Chheten Wangdi, the interpreter, Acchu, the cook, and several of the coolies that were with me were all suffering from the same complaint in the morning. Though the sun had not been shining and the day had been misty, the glare from the new snow had been very much more powerful than anything we had expected and taught us a lesson that whenever there was the slightest fall of snow, we should always wear our snow goggles. From Chöbu we marched to Rebu—a distance of about 15 miles. Knowing the way, I took Mallory and Bullock by the upper road over a pass to Halung; from the top of this pass we branched off on to a spur where there was a very fine view of Mount Everest and the mountains to the North and North-east of it. There had been so much fresh snow everywhere that it was often very difficult to recognize the peaks, but Mount Everest from this side looked as impossible as ever with the great black bands of perpendicular cliffs that seemed to encircle it.

The day was actually fine and the march was a pleasant one through a fertile valley full of fields of barley, mustard and peas. The wild flowers all round Rebu were still very beautiful. Our camp was pitched on a grassy spot on the bank of a rushing stream and close to the village of Rebu.

The following morning the weather was again fine, and as the yaks were all ready for us, we were started by 7.30 a.m. This start was quite amusing; we ourselves had first to cross a flooded stream over which there was a very wobbly stone bridge. With much excitement and noise the yaks were then driven across the stream, but the current was too strong for the bullocks, which had to be unloaded and their loads carried over. While this was being done, the bridge collapsed, and a good lady and a bullock that were trying to get over by the bridge all fell into the water together. There was then a terrible excitement and mix-up, every one shouting and screaming, but they both scrambled safely to the shore, and beyond a wetting, no one was any the worse. We then took the road that I had travelled three weeks before over the Doya La. Knowing that there was a good view to be got from the top of the pass, I hurried ahead and climbed a rocky hill, 17,700 feet, close to the pass, where I saw a wonderful scene. Range upon range of snowy mountains extended right away to Kanchenjunga, and the course of the Arun could be traced wandering down through Nepal, while to the South towered up the great walls of Makalu. Mount Everest itself I could not see, as there were a good many clouds about, but to the South-west were some fine snow and rock peaks of which I took several photographs. I then basked in the sun for a couple of hours and enjoyed the view. The wild flowers on the top of the pass were delightful; I found three different kinds of gentians and the blue poppies were as numerous as ever. The primulas, however, had many of them already gone to seed, but the saxifrages still covered the rocks, and it was a delight to wander along and note the different varieties. Riding on to Chulungphu, we found tents pitched for us and fuel and milk all ready. In place of the primulas the ground was now carpeted with gentians. From here to Kharta the march was only a short one, but we thoroughly enjoyed riding along between the bushes of wild rose or juniper. The former were no longer in blossom, but there were many other new varieties of flowers appearing. I rode on ahead to the spot that I had chosen, three weeks previously, for our new base camp, and I found that Hopaphema had already pitched some tents for us. He had also prepared a meal for us and made every arrangement for our comfort. Our camp was pitched under the willows and poplar trees in the garden, and it was pleasant to hear the rustle of the leaves in the wind once more. We were now at a height of only 12,300 feet, and the change in altitude was a very great relief to the climbing party and the coolies who had come down from the high camps. There were also plenty of green vegetables to be got here, and the coolies appreciated the change enormously. Just below us flowed the Arun, now a majestic river over a hundred yards wide. A mile lower down in its course it entered into the great gorges in which within a space of 20 miles it dropped from 12,000 feet to 7,500 feet, a drop of over 200 feet in the mile. From our camp we used to watch the Monsoon clouds come up every day through the gorge in thin wisps, but every day they melted away always at the same spot; and though rain fell heavily a mile below us, yet with us the sun shone brightly, and it was rare for any rain to reach us. Twenty miles away to the North again were heavy clouds and storms, and rain fell there daily, so that we seemed to be living in a dry zone between the two storm systems. The forests of fir and birch trees came up to the limit of the rainfall and then ceased suddenly where the rain stopped a mile below us. At this point the Kharta River formed a sharp dividing line between the wet and dry zones.

The next day was spent in settling down, arranging all our stores and making a new dark room in the house we had rented. The climate here was delicious and a great change from Tingri. The temperature in my tent used to go up to 75° Fahr. during the day.

The day after we arrived the Jongpen came down to pay an official call and brought a welcome present of a hundred eggs and five animals laden with fuel. He apologised for not coming the day before, but said he had been very busy trying a murder case where eighteen people had been poisoned by a family that had a feud with them, the poison used being aconite, with which they were evidently quite familiar. He told us that our coolies could collect fuel anywhere on the right bank of the Kharta River, but begged that we would not collect it anywhere near where we were living, as the villagers would object.

On July 30 I started off to explore a neighbouring pass

and valley which looked interesting. Mallory and Bullock were having a few days' rest before starting off again, and so they remained in camp. Riding a few miles up the Kharta Valley, I crossed the river by a bridge at the first village, and then had a very steep and stony climb of nearly 3,000 feet to the Samchung Pass, 15,000 feet. As we approached the pass, and entered a moister climate, the vegetation increased rapidly. On these slopes there were rhododendrons 5 feet high, mountain ash, birch, willows, spiræas and juniper. At the top of the pass there was not much of a view, but prowling round I came across some very fine saussuræas with their great white woolly heads and a wonderful meconopsis of a deep claret colour that I had never seen before. There were fifteen to twenty flowers on each stem, and it grew from 2 to 3 feet high. Eight varieties of gentians also grew in the same valley, and a quantity of other attractive Alpine plants. From the pass we descended about 500 feet into a delightful high level glen full of small lakes, evidently once upon a time formed by glaciers which must have filled the whole of the valley. I counted fourteen lakes in this valley, two or three of them being nearly half a mile long, and all of them of different colours varying from a turquoise blue to green and black. For some miles we rode and walked up the valley. The road consisted of big loose stones, often with water flowing underneath them, and usually with big holes in between, so that our ponies were lucky in not breaking their legs. There was then a steep climb which brought us on to a second pass, the Chog La, 16,100 feet, close to which were three small glaciers. Across the top of the pass there was a wall built many years ago as a second line of defence against the Gurkhas, the first line being on the top of the Popti Pass. Unfortunately the clouds now came up, and it began to rain, so that we had no view into the Kama Valley, though later on I was to make the acquaintance of this most charming valley. For an hour and a half I sheltered behind the wall, but as the clouds did not lift I returned towards Kharta.

THE DZONGPEN OF KHARTA AND HIS WIFE.

As we descended into the valley again the glimpses of the lakes seen between the mists reminded me much of the upper lakes at Killarney. There were the same ferns, willows, birch and rhododendrons, and much the same moist atmosphere.

Next day, with Bullock, I went to pay an official visit to the Jongpen at Kharta Shiga. He had made great preparations to receive us, and had put up a large tent in which Chinese carpets and tables were set out with pots of flowers arranged all round. Soon after our arrival we were given a most copious meal: bowl after bowl of well cooked macaroni and mince with pickled radishes and chillies were set before us. After we had finished this meal, I induced the Jongpen and his young wife to be photographed. She had a most elaborate head-dress of coral and pearls, with masses of false hair on either side of her head. It was not becoming. Barely had we finished taking the photograph when another meal was put in front of us: this time it consisted of Tibetan dumplings and mince patties, of which I gave the Jongpen's little dog the greater part surreptitiously; I then hurried off before I should be compelled to eat a third meal.

On August 2 Mallory and Bullock started off with thirty-two coolies to explore the Eastern approaches to Mount Everest. It had been very hard to get any information about Mount Everest. The people knew the mountain by name, but told us that the only way to get near it was by crossing over the ridge to the South of the Kharta Valley, when we should find a big valley that would lead right up to Chomo-lungma. Where the Kharta River came from they could not tell me, and whether it took its source from the snows of Mount Everest they did not know. Tibetans' ignorance of any valleys outside their own was really extraordinary. I could seldom get any definite information about places outside their valley, and on asking two or three people, they would invariably give contradictory answers. It was the same as regards distance. They would tell you a place was one, two or three days' march away, but for shorter distances they had no time-table, and the nearest approach to this was a measurement by cups of tea. I remember one day asking a village yokel how far off the next village was, and he surprised me by answering, "Three cups of tea." Several times afterwards I got the answer to a question about distance given me in cups of tea, and I eventually worked out that three cups of tea was the equivalent of about 5 miles, and was after that able to use this as a basis for measurements of distances.

Two or three hours after Mallory and Bullock had gone, Wollaston and Morshead arrived from their trip to Nyenyam. They had had bad weather the whole time. Here, too, the weather remained overcast and threatening, with a strong South wind, the mountains remaining covered in clouds above 16,000 feet. To the South of us rain fell steadily all day, but the rain did not come up as far as our camp. One afternoon Morshead, Wollaston and I went over to have tea with our hospitable Zemindar Hopaphema about a mile away from us. On this occasion he gave us pods of fresh peas and the red hips and haws of the wild rose as a kind of *hors d'œuvre*, followed by a junket served with pea flour. Then came bowls of hot milk with macaroni and minced meat, seasoned with chillies, together with potatoes and a kind of fungus that grew in the woods. After this meal, from which we suffered no ill effects, for our stomachs were getting accustomed to queer foods, he produced an old painted musical instrument with two sounding boards, on which he played and sang at the same time some old Tibetan love songs. Some of these had quite a catching and plaintive melody. He showed us also some Tibetan dances. Our interpreter, unfortunately, refused to give us a literal translation of some of the love songs, though he seemed very amused at them.

Another afternoon I rode with Wollaston some 5 miles up the Kharta Valley to the Gandenchöfel Monastery. This was situated in a delightfully sheltered spot surrounded by poplars and ancient gnarled juniper trees of great size.

On arrival we were shown into a picturesque courtyard, the walls of which were covered with paintings depicting scenes from the life of Buddha. Cushions and tables had been arranged for our reception and placed on a verandah where, on arrival, we were given cups of tea and hot milk. The Head Lama presently came out and after taking some tea with us, proceeded to show us round his temple. This was a curious building, square in shape, and surmounted by a cupola. It was very solidly built of stone and was, they told us, about 500 years old. It was founded by a saint called Jetsun-Nga-Wang-Chhöfel, who after a great flood which swept down the valley, destroying all the houses in it, had taken a large frog (which animal is believed to represent the Water God) and buried it under the centre pillar of the temple. With great reverence they showed us the spot under which this unfortunate frog had been immured in the centre of the shrine. This immolation of the frog had apparently not been completely efficacious in preventing the floods as two other floods had subsequently occurred, and two small Chortens had been erected to make quite certain that the frog could not get out again and cause more floods. The interior of the temple was very dark in spite of numerous butter lamps. As our eyes gradually became accustomed to the dim light, we made out three figures of Buddha—a large one in the centre and smaller ones on either side. On the pillars were figures of the saint who had founded the monastery. In this temple were also represented some Indian saints, but these were shown as dark figures, very black and very ugly. Tibetans always despise the Indian and they therefore represent him as quite black and with the ugliest features imaginable. Around the shrine were twelve great plaster figures—about 12 feet to 15 feet in height—the guardians of the shrine, figures monstrously ugly, and evidently made so in order to frighten away the evil-doer. Outside the sanctuary there was a curious passage in the thickness of the walls leading all round the building, in which were stencilled and painted curious representations of Buddha. In one of the side rooms there was a huge prayer wheel, which rang a bell every time it was turned; it contained, the priests told us, many million prayers. After visiting the shrine, I took a photograph of the monks with their long trumpets, their bejewelled clarionets and their drums. After our tour of inspection we were given further refreshment in the way of macaroni and meat in a small secluded garden where the monks used to walk reading the Scriptures and meditating.

On another day Wollaston and I made an excursion down to the gorges of the Arun. We first rode up the Kharta Valley, crossing the river by the first bridge, and then following the right bank of the river as far as we could go. After riding only a short way, we entered into a country and a scenery where we might have been a hundred miles away from Tibet. The change was extraordinarily sudden—a dense forest covered the hillsides, mostly of fir (*Abies Webbiana*) and birch, many of them fine old trees. The undergrowth consisted of rhododendrons, 8 feet to 10 feet in height and extremely difficult to get through. Besides these there were many larch and willow trees growing on the hillside, together with many new and delightful flowers. We went on until we were brought up by a series of perpendicular cliffs that descended 700 feet sheer down to the river below us. It was a grand sight from here to see the mighty Bhong-chu or Arun River, narrowed now to one-third of its former width, forcing its way in a series of rapids through these stupendous gorges covered with woods wherever the precipices allowed a tree to grow and with trees dipping their branches far below us in the flooded waters of the river. On the opposite side of the gorge we saw a small track wandering along the cliffs; the inhabitants told us it was impossible to get across the river lower down at this time of the year until you reach Lungdö, where there was a bridge some 20 miles lower down. Kharta now remained the base headquarters of the Expedition until it was time to return to India in October, and all the expeditions that

Lamas of Kharta Monastery.

we made up the Kharta Valley, or into the Kama Valley, were made from Kharta. The Jongpen there and Hopaphema did everything they could to assist us by giving us coolies and arranging for supplies to be sent up to the various camps.

CHAPTER VII

THE KAMA VALLEY

We had not been able to gather much information locally about Mount Everest. A few of the shepherds said that they had heard that there was a great mountain in the next valley to the South, but they could not tell us whether the Kharta River came from this great mountain. The easiest way to get to this valley, they told us, was by crossing the Shao La, or the Langma La, both of which passes were to the South of the Kharta Valley, and, they said, led into this new valley. They called this valley the Kama Valley, and little did we realise at the time that in it we were going to find one of the most beautiful valleys in the world. Mallory and Bullock had already left Kharta on August 2 to explore this route, which we thought would lead us to the Eastern face of Mount Everest. As Wollaston and Morshead had now arrived at Kharta, there was nothing to prevent my following the others and learning something about the geography of the country. Eleven mule-loads of rations, consisting of flour, potatoes, sugar and rations for the surveyors, had just arrived; there was therefore now no cause for me to worry about shortage of supplies. These had been sent off from Yatung on June 15, but had only arrived at Kharta on August 2. Learning that I was about to start off, Hopaphema, the old Zemindar, hurriedly came round with a large basket full of spinach, potatoes, and turnips, which he insisted on my taking with me.

On August 5, taking with me Chheten Wangdi and a dozen coolies, I started off in the tracks of Mallory and Bullock. For the first few miles we travelled up the Kharta Valley, through rich fields of barley, by far the best that I

MAKALU
from 21,500 foot peak on ridge south of Kama-chu.

had seen so far in Tibet. The crops were very even and everywhere quite 3 feet in height. The valley was thickly inhabited, containing villages nearly every mile, and many monasteries, some of which were surrounded by fine old gnarled juniper trees. Our local coolies made very poor progress, taking six hours to cover the first 6 miles, as they stopped at every village for a drink. After passing the last village, there was a steep climb of 1,000 feet. Here our coolies were very anxious to stop and spend the night, but I pushed on ahead, and they came on behind very slowly and reluctantly. Seeing that it was impossible to get over the Langma La, I stopped at the limit of firewood and camped at a height of 16,100 feet. Poo, who was acting as my cook, had forgotten to bring any matches with him, and I watched him with much interest lighting a fire of damp rhododendron bushes with the flint and tinder that he always carried. The day had been clear and very warm; and on the way up we had had some fine views of the great snowy peaks on the Eastern side of the Arun River. The villagers had told us that this pass was impossible for ponies, and I accordingly left mine behind at Kharta, though we found out that ponies could quite well have crossed the pass. Opposite our camp was a peak of black rock with a glacier just below it. During the night there was a little rain and the morning was unfortunately cloudy. As our coolies had informed us that there were three passes to be crossed in the next march, I had them all started off by 5.30 a.m., after which I left with my coolies, Ang Tenze and Nyima Tendu, who always accompanied me carrying a rifle, a shot-gun and three cameras of different sizes. Above the camp there was a steep climb of 1,000 feet on to a broad, rocky shelf in which was a pretty turquoise-blue lake. This was followed by another steep climb of 500 feet on to another great shelf, after which a further climb of 500 feet brought us to the top of the Langma La, 18,000 feet. The three steps up to this pass were evidently the three passes that the coolies had told us about, as from the top we looked down into the next valley. All the coolies who were carrying loads complained of headaches, due no doubt to the steep climb and the high elevation of the pass. To the East there was a curious view looking over the Arun towards some high snow peaks. Clouds were lying in patches everywhere on the hillsides, as the air was saturated with moisture. To the West our gaze encountered a most wonderful amphitheatre of peaks and glaciers. Three great glaciers almost met in the deep green valley that lay at our feet. One of these glaciers evidently came down from Mount Everest, the second from the beautiful cliffs of Chomolönzo, the Northern peak of Makalu, of which we unfortunately could only get occasional and partial glimpses, an ice or rock cliff peeping out of the clouds every now and then at incredible heights above us. The third glacier came from Kama Changri, a fine peak to the North of the Kama Valley which later on we climbed. The clouds kept mostly at a height of about 22,000 feet, and prevented us from seeing the tops of the mountains. After waiting for an hour at the top of the pass in hopes of the clouds lifting, I started the descent, catching on the way a very pretty Marmot rat, with huge eyes and ears for his size, and a pretty bluish grey fur. Meeting shortly afterwards some of Mallory and Bullock's coolies, I gave this animal to them to take back to Wollaston. We now descended through grassy uplands for nearly 3,000 feet, past another beautiful blue lake called Shurim Tso, and came to a curious long and narrow terrace about 1,000 feet above the bottom of the valley. Here there was a tent belonging to some yak herds; and as wood and water were plentiful I determined to stop and spend the night with them. They called the place Tangsham. It was certainly a most glorious place for a camp, for it overlooked three great valleys and glaciers. Opposite us, on the other side of the valley, were the immense cliffs of Chomolönzo, which towered up to nearly 26,000 feet, while Mount Everest and its great ridges filled up the head of the valley. I spent the whole afternoon lying among the rhododendrons at 15,000 feet, and admiring the beautiful glimpses of these mighty peaks revealed by occasional breaks among the fleecy clouds. The shepherds were able to give me much information about the district, which proved very useful to us afterwards. They come up here every year for a few months in the summer and in the winter cross over to the valley of the Bong-chu.

After a slight frost during the night, we had one of the few really perfect days that fell to our lot in the Kama Valley. As soon as I had finished breakfast I climbed up 1,000 feet behind the camp; opposite me were the wonderful white cliffs of Chomolönzo and Makalu, which dropped almost sheer for 11,000 feet into the valley below. Close at hand were precipices of black rock on which, in the dark hollows, nestled a few dirty glaciers. Mount Everest being some way further off, did not appear nearly as imposing. Our object now was to get as close to it as possible; we therefore descended into the valley, a steep drop of nearly 1,000 feet, through luxuriant vegetation. A very beautiful blue primula was just beginning to come out. This Wollaston had already discovered a fortnight before near Lapchi-Kang. We then crossed the Rabkar Chu, a stream which came out of the Rabkar Glacier, by a very rickety bridge over which the water was washing. Beyond this was a very fertile plain covered with rhododendrons, juniper, willow and mountain ash. On it were a couple of small huts which were occupied by some yak herds. From here we had to follow along the edge of the Kang-do-shung Glacier which, coming down from Chomolönzo, plunges across the valley until it strikes against the rocks of the opposite side. Between the glacier and these cliffs was an old water-course up which we travelled, but stones kept frequently falling from the cliffs above and the passage was somewhat dangerous. This had evidently been the old channel of the stream that has its source in the glaciers of Mount Everest, but owing to the advance of the Kang-do-shung Glacier, is now compelled to find its way through this glacier and hurls itself into a great ice cavern in it. Opposite this ice cavern we had a steep climb for 500 feet, and found ourselves among pleasant grassy meadows, after a few miles of which we came to a place called Pethang Ringmo, where we found some yak herds living. We found that Mallory and Bullock had chosen this place to be their base camp. It was a most delightfully sunny spot at 16,400 feet, right under the gigantic and marvellously beautiful cliffs of Chomolönzo, now all powdered over with the fresh snow of the night before and only separated from us by the Kangshung Glacier, here about a mile wide. Great avalanches thunder down its sides all the day long with a terrifying sound. Everest from here is seen to fill up the head of the valley with a most formidable circle of cliffs overhung by hanging glaciers, but it is not nearly such a beautiful or striking mountain as Makalu or Chomolönzo. The shepherds would insist that Makalu was the higher of the two mountains, and would not believe us when we said that Mount Everest was the higher. Next morning was foggy, but there was a glimpse of blue sky behind the mists, so after breakfast I hurried up the valley, intending to climb a ridge exactly opposite to Mount Everest which I had marked down the night before. After walking for an hour up the valley in a thick fog, by luck I struck the right ridge, which proved a very steep climb. Glimpses of blue sky and white peaks, however, gave us hopes of better views higher up. It took me two and a half hours to climb 3,000 feet, which at last brought me above the mists. The top of the ridge was 19,500 feet high, and from it we had most superb views. Mount Everest was only 3 or 4 miles away from us. From it to the South-east swept a huge amphitheatre of mighty peaks culminating in a new and unsurveyed peak, 28,100 feet in height, to which we gave the name of Lhotse, which in Tibetan means the South Peak. From this side the mountain appeared quite unclimbable, as the cliffs were all topped with hanging glaciers, from which great masses of ice came thundering down into the valley below all the day long. Between Mount Everest and Makalu, on the watershed between Tibet and Nepal, there stands up a very curious

CLIFFS OF CHOMOLÖNZO
from camp at Pethang Ringmo.

conical peak, to which we gave the name of Pethangtse. On either side of it are two very steep, but not very high, passes into Nepal; both of them are, however, probably unclimbable. To the South-east towered up the immense cliffs of Makalu, far the more beautiful mountain of the two. The whole morning I spent on this ridge, taking photographs whenever opportunity offered. The clouds kept coming up and melting away again and were most annoying, but they occasionally afforded us the most beautiful glimpses and peeps of the snow and rock peaks by which we were surrounded. At a height of over 19,000 feet, I had a great chase after a new kind of rat; but it finally eluded me, and I was not able to add it to our already large collection. Even at these heights I found both yellow and white saxifrages and a blue gentian. From the top of this ridge I had been able to see Kanchenjunga and Jannu, though nearly 100 miles away, but their summits stood up out of the great sea of clouds which covered Nepal.

On returning to camp in the afternoon, I found that Mallory and Bullock were there. They had climbed a snow peak on the North side of the Kama Valley, about 21,500 feet, and from this view point had been unable to discover a possible route up Mount Everest on the Eastern face; they thought, however, that there might be an alternative approach from the next valley to the North. They therefore intended returning to the Kharta Valley to follow that river to its source.

Next morning was cloudy, and neither Everest nor Makalu were to be seen; but towards the East the view was clear, though the mountains appeared to be much too close. We started all together down the valley. On the way I climbed 1,000 feet up among the rocks opposite to the big glacier that descends from Chomolönzo. I failed, however, to get the good view of Makalu which I had been hoping for, owing to the clouds, and returned to my old camping ground at Tangsham, Mallory and Bullock branching off from here towards the Langma La. The shepherds had told us that there was another pass into the Kharta Valley called the Shao La, rather more to the South. I therefore intended to make use of this pass on the return journey to Kharta. As usual, in the evening, the clouds came up and enveloped us in a thick mist. Every night this happened in the Kama Valley, and was evidently due to the excessive moisture of the air. When we started the following morning, there was still a thick Scotch mist which made the vegetation very wet. We descended the Kama Valley, most of the time keeping high up above the river. On the opposite side of the valley were immense black cliffs descending sheer for many thousand feet. On the way we passed through acres of blue iris, mostly over now, and then through a very luxuriant vegetation which grew more and more varied as we descended lower. There was a lovely emerald-green lake beside the path, and like white sentinels on the hillsides grew the great rhubarb of Sikkim, the *Rheum nobile.* This was a most conspicuous plant with columns of the palest green leaves sheathing the flower spikes which grew fully 5 feet in height. There were several other varieties of rhubarb here, but none were as handsome as this. At one place we descended as low as 13,000 feet and came once more amongst dense forests of juniper, silver firs (*Abies Webbiana*), mountain ash, willow, birch and tall rhododendrons. From every tree hung long grey lichens attesting the moisture of the climate. Wherever there was an open space in the forest, it was carpeted with flowers. Two delightful varieties of primula were new to me, and were just coming out, one of them being almost black in colour. The big deep red meconopsis grew here, too, in great luxuriance. Gentians of all kinds abounded and many other varieties of flowers and ferns, due to the fact that Makalu seems to attract all the storms, causing the moist Monsoon currents to be drawn into this valley. As the day went on, the weather improved; the sun came out, and the clouds melted away, disclosing the magnificent peaks of Makalu. A big glacier descended from the East face from a side valley into the

THE KAMA VALLEY.

floor of the valley below us at a height of about 12,000 feet. It was very curious to see fir trees, birch and juniper, and a very luxuriant vegetation growing on either side of the ice and on the moraines beside it.

Below this glacier the valley became quite flat with grassy meadows and patches of forest dotted about the pastures—a very unusual type of valley for the Himalayas. Almost opposite to this glacier we turned into a side valley; the path and the stream that came down this valley were often indistinguishable. All round the valley were great black cliffs; in one place where they were less precipitous the path found its way upwards. Our camp was pitched that night on a shelf above the cliffs where for a short time we had some very wonderful views. This place was called in Tibetan "The Field of Marigolds," though at the time we were there they were all over. We were at a height of 15,300 feet, and Makalu's two peaks were almost exactly opposite to us. The cloud effects were very striking; the storms seemed to gather round Makalu, and first one peak and then the other would appear out of the great white cumulus clouds whose shapes changed every minute. As usual, the mists came up in the evening, and we were enveloped in a very wet Scotch mist with a temperature of 46° Fahr. Next morning, instead of getting the lovely view that we had expected, a thick Scotch mist prevented our seeing more than 20 yards away. We crawled up to the top of the Shao La, 16,500 feet, in driving rain, but after crossing over it we emerged into finer weather. On the descent we passed several fine lakes, on the cliffs above which were numerous ram chakor (Himalayan snowcock). I pursued a covey of these, and after a chase managed to shoot one. They are very fine birds, weighing between 5 and 6 lb.; they are extremely noisy and fond of their own voices. The parent birds are always very loth to leave their young, and early in the summer it is possible to approach very close to them; but later on in the year, when the young have become nearly full grown, they are very wily, and having excellent eyesight, do not allow anyone to approach within a couple of hundred yards. That afternoon I arrived back at Kharta, where the weather had been quite fine, and where there had been but little rain during my absence.

During that night a thief broke into our store-room, forcing and breaking the lock outside. The only thing he took, as far as we could find out, was one of Wheeler's yak-dans (a leather mule trunk). The thief had probably mistaken this one for one of mine, which contained a considerable amount of money, and knowing that I was away, he thought that my kit must be packed away in the store-room. We informed the Jongpen and the head-men of the villages around of the theft, and had a couple of suspicious characters watched; but we never found any trace of the stolen articles, which luckily were of very small value. For the next fortnight I remained at Kharta.

On August 19 Heron suddenly arrived back after a very interesting trip, during which he had explored all the mountains North of Tingri and Shekar Dzong up to the Brahmaputra watershed. He had had very bad weather all the time. Every night there had been heavy thunderstorms and practically all the bad weather had come from the North. The whole country was under water, and it was very difficult to get about. Some of the rivers that we had crossed earlier in the season were now a mile or more wide.

On the following day Bullock and Mallory returned to Kharta after having explored the Upper Kharta Valley. They thought that they had found a possible way up Mount Everest from this valley, but at present the weather was too bad for them to carry on with their reconnaissance, and they had come down for a fortnight's rest, hoping that the Monsoon would be over by the beginning of September and that they would then be able to make a proper attack on the mountain. As Mallory and Bullock were likely to be at Kharta for some time, Wollaston and I seized this opportunity to visit the lower valley of the Kama-chu.

Therefore, on August 23, with eleven of our own coolies and several Tibetan coolies, we climbed the Samchung Pass (15,000 feet), and then descended into the valley of the fourteen lakes, and after crossing the Chog La camped on the far side of the pass near a dark green and sacred lake called Ruddamlamtso. On the way we saw a new species of black rat in the moraine of a glacier; but Wollaston's servant, who had the collecting gun with him, was unfortunately far behind; he was always rather fond of drink and loth to leave the villages. The weather was cloudy, and there were no views from the top of either pass. The march was a strenuous one, taking the coolies thirteen hours to cover the whole distance, and they did not arrive till after dark. The Ruddamlamtso, the lake by which we were camped, had wonderfully clear water; I could see every stone at a depth of 20 feet, and it was evidently very deep. It is looked upon as a sacred lake, and to it people make yearly pilgrimages, walking round it burning incense and throwing spices into its waters.

The following morning the clouds were low down everywhere on the hillsides and we had no views. There was a steep descent for 4 miles to Sakeding—12,100 feet, through the most interesting zones of vegetation. We followed the edge of the rushing stream, always white from the rapidity of its descent. On one side of the valley grew rhododendrons of many varieties and mountain ash, and on the other were hoary old junipers with twisted stems. Grey lichens hung down from every branch, and were often 5 or 6 feet in length. We came across some of the finest and largest red currants that we had yet seen. Of these we collected a great quantity, and they formed a very excellent stew. Birches, wild roses and berberis were the commonest shrubs, while nearly every rock was covered with an extremely pretty rose-coloured creeper, which in places caused the hillsides to look quite pink. Earlier in the year the iris must have been a very beautiful sight, as we passed through acres of their leaves. A big yellow rock-rose with flowers 2 inches across was also to be met with here, and many of the lower leaves of the rhododendrons were turning yellow to scarlet, making a great show of colour on the dark green of the hillside. Deep purple-coloured primulas and monkshood, as well as a curious hairy mauve-red monkshood with a very graceful growth, were also to be seen. The pretty white-crested red-start flitted about from rock to rock, and numerous tits of various kinds flew about in flocks from tree to tree as we descended.

Sakeding (Pleasant terrace) had been at one time a village of considerable size, but a pestilence sent by the local demon had wiped out all its inhabitants. This demon was still reputed to be very active, and no one had dared to re-build the old houses of which the ruins, overgrown with weeds and bushes, could be seen here and there. It was a very pleasant site for a village, situated as it was on a terrace that projected out into the valley 1,000 feet above the stream below. During the summer months there is quite a trade passing through this place, the Tibetans bringing salt from the North, and the Nepalese coming up from Nepal with rice, dyes and vegetables, which they exchange. The rate of barter at this time was two measures of rice or three measures of madder dye for one measure of salt, and no money changes hands. Everything that was brought here was brought on the backs of coolies, and these Nepalese coolies were sturdy, cheery fellows, and thought nothing of carrying 80 lb. of salt on their backs up and down the execrable paths of the district.

From Sakeding we descended steeply through a forest of the finest juniper trees that I had yet seen. These grew 80 to 90 feet high, and many of their trunks were 18 feet to 20 feet in circumference. As a rule they had clean stems, without a branch for 50 feet or 60 feet. The branches were all hung with grey lichens. We now descended beside the muddy and tempestuous waters of the Kama-chu. The juniper forest gradually gave way to silver firs—wonderful trees of enormous size and great age. We passed through many open glades, park-like in appearance, with grand clumps of fir trees or sycamore dotted here and there. The hillsides were absolutely running over with water, and often for several hundred yards we walked along logs put down to try and avoid the mud and the running water. As many of these rounded logs were very slippery, both we and our coolies had to proceed with caution, and even so we experienced many a fall. At Chu-tronu—10,200 feet—there was a well-made wooden bridge, 60 feet long, which spanned the river where it flowed in a narrow channel between two great rocks. We crossed this bridge, and finding a broad open space there, I selected a spot suitable for our camp and ordered the coolies to cut down some of the grass where we intended to pitch the tents. I could not at first make out why they kept jumping about when thus engaged, but on going to investigate, I found that the place was alive with leeches; however, as there was no other better place in which to camp, we had to make the best of it. The men collected some dry bamboos out of an old shepherd's hut which was close by; these they burnt on the sites where we were to pitch our tents, hoping by this means to drive away the leeches. This method, however, was not very successful, for all that evening we were busy picking leeches off our clothes, legs, hands or heads. They climbed up the sides of the tents and dropped down into our food, our cups and on to our plates. Wollaston invented the best way of killing them, which was by cutting them in two with a pair of scissors. Our interpreter remonstrated with him, as he said this method increased the number of leeches, thinking that both ends of them would grow. After a somewhat restless and disturbed night, due to these leeches, we started off next morning to go down to the junction of the Kama River with the Arun. The distance as the crow flies was only about 6 miles, but we did not realise the kind of path that we should have to traverse. In that short distance we must have risen and fallen quite 5,000 feet. The path was never level and always very rough and stony.

At first it led through beautiful glades running with moisture and over logs buried, most of them, inches deep in the water; they were, however, better to walk on than the soft mud there was on either side. The silver firs were now at their best—trees over 100 feet in height, and with stems 20 feet to 25 feet in circumference. Here grew great hydrangeas 20 feet or more in height covered with flowers. Our only halts on the way down, and they were pretty frequent, were to pick off the leeches from our clothes. We took them off by tens at a time; they were very hungry, and varied in size from great striped horse-leeches to tiny ones as thin as a pin and able to penetrate anywhere. The track now left the upper terraces and descended very steeply towards the river, at times climbing sharply upwards again to avoid precipitous rocks and cliffs. During the descent, we gradually passed from the zone of the silver firs into that of the spruce, meeting the lovely *Picea Brunoniana*, which grew to an even greater size than the silver firs. Many of the trees were over 150 feet in height and without a branch for 70 feet or 80 feet; their stems too, were often 25 feet to 30 feet in circumference. This valley is so inaccessible that I am glad to think that these glorious forests can never be exploited commercially. After passing a great overhanging rock called Korabak, which is evidently much used as a halting-place, we descended steeply to the river, which now forms a series of cascades, leaping from rock to rock, a very remarkable spectacle. During the last 6 miles of its course, this river—the product of four large glacier streams—descends at the rate of 450 feet every mile. In places there were waterfalls of 20 feet and more, where the river hurled itself into seething cauldrons; in one place I saw it confined to a breadth of barely 5 feet. The junction of this river with the Arun is only 7,500 feet above the sea; just above the junction is a bridge which leads to the village of Kimonanga, a picturesque village situated on a terrace some 700 feet above the river and surrounded by some fine trees. In this valley we came across a few blue pines (*Pinus excelsa*) and also a large-leafed alder; near its junction with the Arun were many trees and orchids of a semi-tropical character. On the opposite side of the valley is a forest of evergreen oak trees, but as I was unable to cross the river I could not say to what species they belonged. On the way we passed many yellow raspberries on which we slaked our thirst. Our guide also dug up some of the roots of the wild arum to show us; it is a great flattish tuberous root, rather oval in shape. This the inhabitants dig up and, after allowing it to ferment by burying it in a hole for several days, pound it up, and then eat it; it was much esteemed by the villagers. It is necessary to ferment it first, as otherwise the root is extremely poisonous. We tasted a slice of bread made out of this root, and I have seldom tasted anything nastier. It is supposed, if not properly fermented, to cause all the hair to fall out of the head; but I should be inclined to imagine that it would do this even if it were properly fermented. Near the junction of the Kama and Arun Rivers, we climbed up on to a terrace 1,200 feet above, on which was situated the village of Lungdö. The great Arun gorges here become a considerable valley; for 20 miles above this point up to Kharta the Arun runs through a narrow and practically impassable gorge, but here the valley widens out for a few miles and contains several villages; a short distance below it enters again into another great gorge. The river now was in full flood and covered the whole of the bottom of the valley, being in places many hundred yards in width. At one spot, where it contracted, there was a well-made bridge leading to the village of Matsang. I was astonished to meet with maize growing at this height—8,700 feet. The villagers also grew cucumbers, pumpkins and several kinds of millet, including an extremely pretty red one. The head-man of Lungdö gave me some millet beer, which was very refreshing after the long march. Wollaston did not care for it, but between us we managed to eat three large and juicy cucumbers. The head-man was very friendly; and a local official was staying here who had just come from Kharta, who recognised us, and presented us with some excellent honey cakes. We neither of us looked forward to the uphill return journey, but after five and a half hours' hard walking I reached camp just before dark. Wollaston did not arrive till later, and I had to send a coolie with a lamp to bring him in. We were both of us much exhausted, as the day had been a long and trying one. That night we had a grand camp fire of rhododendron and fir logs. Hundreds of moths insisted on flying into the fire instead of entering the tent where Wollaston was ready with his cyanide bottle to catch them.

The following morning the weather was dull and cloudy, and did not look very promising. We determined, however, to visit the Popti La, the pass between Tibet and Nepal, over which all the local traffic passes. Leaving the camp, we entered a small side valley to the South, the path climbing steeply upwards under big rhododendrons (*R. Falconeri* and *R. Argenteum*) with leaves 18 inches long. Noticing many of their leaves strewn on the path, I inquired the reason for this. Our guide informed us that the carriers fastened these leaves together with thin strips of bamboo and thus provided an excellent waterproof cover for themselves and for their loads. After climbing about a mile, we saw some bamboo huts in the forest and a number of cows were grazing round them. These belonged to some Nepalese herds who come over here in the summer, bringing their cattle to graze. The path now followed the side of a rushing torrent, peaty brown in colour, which came hurrying down under the shade of birch, sycamore, silver firs, juniper and rhododendrons. As we ascended higher, the open spaces became more frequent, though the grass and weeds grew fully 3 feet in height, attesting the constant rainfall of this district. On leaving the path to collect a few seeds from some plants growing a short distance away from it, I found myself in a few moments covered with leeches which apparently thrive here at an altitude of over 12,000 feet; this must be almost a record height for these pests. The path climbed up steeply, the rhododendrons growing gradually smaller in size as we ascended. After going for four hours, we reached the top of the pass—14,000 feet. Here on the top was a stone half hidden in a pile of rocks with a notice, written in Chinese characters, that this was the boundary between Tibet and Nepal. Across the top of the pass was a long wall, mostly overgrown with grass, evidently at one time considered to be some kind of defence. Owing to the clouds being very low, we unfortunately had no view from the top, but just below us, on the Nepalese side, was a fine black lake, about half a mile long, with an island in the centre, which the Nepalese called Dungepokri. On the top were many interesting Alpine flowers, amongst them a charming white potentilla with a red centre; and a large cream-coloured primula, shading into deep orange. We also came across several new varieties of gentians. Here we rested for a couple of hours, hoping that the clouds might lift, but a nasty rain began to fall heavily. While we were waiting several coolies from Nepal passed by: from these we found out that the pass was closed by snow for five months in the year and that the trade market at Sakeding was closed by the end of October. We now turned our footsteps homeward, urged on by cold showers of rain. On the descent we were able to collect a few seeds. Autumn was approaching, though the trees had not yet begun to assume their autumn colours owing to the warm nights. That evening in the camp we had an enormous bonfire of birch, juniper and rhododendrons, which made the prettiest blaze imaginable, with flames of green, blue, violet and orange. The large fire also helped to keep away the leeches. Heavy rain fell again all night, and the thermometer did not descend below 55° Fahr. The morning, however, broke fine, and we started back again up the valley to Sakeding. The sun shone every now and then, giving us occasional glimpses of distant glaciers at the head of the valley. The walk through the forest, with the sunlight shining on the dark green leaves of the rhododendron and the dripping foliage, was very delightful.

The undergrowth consisted of wild roses, berberis with its necklaces of scarlet berries, wild currants of a great size—sour to the taste, but excellent when stewed—wild raspberries, light feathery bamboos, birch, willow and a most luxuriant vegetation of flowers and grasses. In one or two places the mountain ash were just beginning to show traces of colour. We soon left the leeches behind us and followed our old track through the forest beside the rushing waters of the Kama-chu. Enormous rocks which had fallen from above had in places almost blocked up the river. Often on these great boulders in the middle of the stream were growing the graceful Himalayan larch. On the steepest rock faces grew vegetation of every kind, thanks to the excessive moisture of the climate, and from every tree and from every bush hung long and picturesque lichens. Crested tits and bullfinches lived in great numbers in this forest and gave it quite a homelike appearance. The climb from the river had been a steep one, and we pitched our camp at Sakeding in a downpour of rain, but towards the evening the weather cleared up, allowing us fine views of great snow peaks which showed above the mists on the opposite sides of the valley. It was too far to go from Sakeding to Kharta in one day; we therefore decided to camp before crossing the Chog La. We passed our old camp by the green lake Ruddamlamtso, and I had a long chase after some ram chakor, but they were too clever for me and ran up the hill faster than I could follow them. The large moraines which converged in this valley were specially interesting, and threw much light on its past history. Each moraine had its own long line of boulders formed of different kinds of rock, according to the character of the mountains from which they had been carried down by the ice. It was not difficult to imagine the vast glaciers by which these lines of boulders had been deposited; glaciers which must at one time have completely blocked the valley and the disappearance of which has made room for the chain of lakes which now occupy the valley. We pitched our camp at a place called

Mendalongkyo—15,500 feet—in a pleasantly sheltered spot where a gurgling stream disappeared under an old moraine. In the afternoon Wollaston went out after rats, of which he secured a new variety. Our coolies had a great chase after a fat marmot, which they very nearly caught, but he got down into his hole just in time. Around the camp were quantities of a very beautiful pale blue gentian—a regular Eton blue colour. Wandering up the spur North-west of the camp I counted nine lakes in the next valley and four lakes in the one that we were in; as the rain began to fall again, I returned to camp.

The next morning, August 29, we began our homeward journey to Kharta. Getting up early, we climbed on to the high ridge North-west of the camp, from which we had a fair view; but unfortunately both Makalu and Mount Everest were hidden by clouds. We waited for a long time in hopes of a better view, but the clouds only grew thicker. We therefore followed the ridge above the Chog La. On the way I shot a Tibetan snow partridge (*Lerwa nivicola*), an extremely pretty bird with lovely markings. This was the first I had seen.

We now turned our backs upon the Kama Valley with much regret. We had explored many of these Himalayan valleys, but none seemed to me to be comparable with this, either for the beauty of its Alpine scenery, or for its wonderful vegetation. We shall not easily forget the smiling pastures carpeted with gentians and every variety of Alpine flower that rise to the very verge of icebound and snow-covered tracks, where mighty glaciers descend among the forests which clothe the lower slopes.

After crossing the Chog La, we went down once more into the valley of the lakes and then, crossing the Samchung La, descended to Kharta which we found bathed in sunshine.

CHAPTER VIII

THE UPPER KHARTA VALLEY AND THE 20,000 FOOT CAMP

During the early part of August Mallory and Bullock, after they had found that there was no possible means of attacking Mount Everest from the Kama Valley, crossed the Langma La and returned to the Kharta Valley. Up this valley they now proceeded until they reached the glaciers in which the Kharta River has its source. After exploring a number of valleys, they at last found one which led straight to Mount Everest. Accompanied by Major Morshead, who had joined them during their excursion, they made a long and tiring reconnaissance of this valley, and satisfied themselves that it afforded a practicable approach to the North-eastern ridge of Mount Everest. The slopes were fairly gentle, but were at that time covered with soft fresh snow, knee deep. Over these snow-covered glaciers, up which they had proceeded with great difficulty, they found a col from which it was possible to attack the mountain. Under the existing conditions of soft snow and warm weather it would have been quite impossible to take laden coolies along this route, and they therefore returned to Kharta to wait until the monsoon conditions had abated and the snow should have become hard and frozen.

On our return from the Kama Valley on August 29, we found Mallory and Bullock still at Kharta, waiting for the weather to improve. About this time it was showing distinct signs of improvement. The clouds were not so thick and there were many more bright intervals with blue skies. They therefore determined to start off on August 31, to form an advanced base camp up the Kharta Valley.

On September 1, much to the surprise of every one, Raeburn arrived back from Darjeeling. He reported very wet conditions throughout Tibet, the rivers everywhere being unfordable, and most of the bridges washed away. He also reported having seen five bags of our mails at Chushar. Our posts had latterly been very erratic, and for five weeks no mails had arrived. We did not know what had happened to them. We were sending in a couple of our own coolies every fortnight to Phari with our outgoing mail, and the first lot of these coolies had not yet returned, so that we were all without news of the outside world. Although it was the beginning of September, the night temperatures at Kharta were still much too high, ranging from 52° Fahr. to 47° Fahr. On September 3 Morshead and Wheeler left for the Upper Kharta Valley, intending to go slowly and to map and fill in the detail of the valley as they went along.

The tameness of the birds gave us many opportunities of studying their habits. A large family of redstarts lived in our garden at Kharta, and used to amuse me very much. The young birds were now fully fledged and spent most of the day in hopping in and out of my tent; they were not in the least degree afraid, and the mother would come and feed them actually inside my tent. On the terrace near the camp there were a number of prettily marked white rock pigeons which formed a welcome addition to our diet of Tibetan mutton, of which we were getting very tired.

On September 5 Wollaston, Raeburn and I, with twenty-six Tibetan coolies, and eleven of our own, started off to join the climbing party up the Kharta Valley. The first 7 miles of this valley I knew well, having traversed them many times before. The barley fields were now fast ripening, and were a beautiful golden colour. Curious to relate, the barley that grew at 14,000 feet was riper than that which grew at 12,000 feet. Two kinds of barley seemed to be grown here—the ordinary variety, and another with a red ear such as is, I believe, grown in the Shetlands. We rode past the tidy-looking monastery of Gandenchöfel, surrounded by its juniper trees, and after a steep climb past the entrance of the valley leading to the Langma La, descended on to some fine river terraces, on which were many prosperous farms and well-tilled fields. These extended for several more miles up the valley. We pitched our camp on a grassy flat a couple of miles above the last house, where willows, rhododendrons and junipers grew plentifully; the marshy ground was carpeted with gentians, one of the commonest being dark blue in colour with ten petals, and rather like a star in shape, the other being larger and of a pale Eton-blue colour. I managed to collect a certain number of seeds of both of these. We had a grand bonfire that evening, made of juniper and willow, the last that we were to have for a long time. The weather was disappointing and a drizzling rain fell all night with a temperature of 42° Fahr.

It was still raining when we started in the morning, so that there were no views. A white andromeda was still in flower on the hillsides, but the rhododendrons were all over. On the opposite side of the valley juniper alone flourished and grew to an altitude of nearly 17,000 feet. After going a couple of miles, we passed Morshead and Wheeler's tents pitched on an old yak camp. When we arrived, they were still having breakfast, as the weather was too bad to do any surveying. On leaving them we had a steep climb over grassy slopes, where the drizzling rain now changed to snow, and for the rest of the day it fell steadily. There appeared to be many branch valleys, and as our views in the mist were very curtailed, we were not at all certain as to whether we were going up the right valley—I only knew approximately the height of the place at which we were to camp. Therefore, on arriving at that height, I sent my coolies off in two different directions up two different valleys to see where Mallory and Bullock's camp might be. The mist lifted for a moment, and one of them luckily saw Mallory, whose camp was only a few hundred yards from us. We decided to call this our "Advanced base camp." It was pitched in some small grassy hollows at a height of 17,350 feet. The site was well sheltered from the winds, and was a regular Alpine garden. Gentians of three different kinds were growing there, including the lovely light-blue one. There was also a beautiful little white saxifrage with yellow and brown spots inside the flower, a delightful pink androsace, and dwarf delphiniums with their single deep-blue flowers. Here grew also the musk-scented hairy light-blue delphinium with its overpowering smell of musk. The latter flower, the Tibetans told me, was a great preventative of lice, and I noticed that our cooks and most of our servants had picked great bundles of it. They also told me that if a man habitually wears this flower about him during his lifetime, after his death when cut up and exposed to the birds, no bird or wolf will touch his flesh owing to the strong scent apparently left by the musk. A pretty pink aster grew here in great clusters, and a few blue poppies were still out. Acchu, our cook, and Gyalzen Kazi, who were coming along behind us, both missed their way and wandered several miles further up the valley before they found out their mistake, and when they eventually arrived in camp, were both suffering from severe headaches, due to the great height. During our stay at this camp we had plenty of time and many opportunities of observing bird and animal life. Some of the birds were very brilliantly coloured. There was a snow bunting with bright scarlet breast and head, also a beautiful redstart with red body and black and white wings. Overhead the great lammergeier, or bearded vulture, sailed in graceful circles, while the big black raven croaked on the rocks by the camp. Morning and evening we could hear the ramchakor (*Tetraogallus tibetanus*) calling on the opposite side of the valley, and with glasses we could see them chasing one another and running round in circles. Red foxes I met with on several occasions over 18,000 feet.

Mallory and Bullock, who had already been here for a few days, had spent their time in carrying wood and stores up to a higher camp further up the valley; they had been having a certain amount of trouble with their coolies, due to the Sirdar, who was always trying to create difficulties. I therefore sent him away on a job to Chushar to collect some of our stores which were supposed to have been detained there, and which would keep him busy for a number of days and prevent him from interfering with our coolies at a critical period. We had brought up with us six live sheep, and very lively these proved. Dukpa, Mallory's cook, let three of them escape, but luckily some coolies coming up the valley saw two of them, and after a great chase brought them back. The third they could not catch and eventually drove him under a cliff, where they killed him with stones and brought his carcass back to us. The weather continued very unsettled. During the night a couple of inches of snow fell, but until the temperature became colder and the sky cleared, it was no use trying to go up to the upper camp. I shot a ramchakor on the opposite side of the valley. They are the most tasty of the Tibetan birds, and are quite excellent eating.

On September 8, after a frosty night, Bullock, Mallory and I with three coolies, for the purpose of keeping fit, made a little excursion along a rocky ridge that lay to the South of us. On the top of the ridge there were a number of sharp rock pinnacles that had to be climbed. I found these gymnastics at a height of over 19,000 feet to be very exhausting, but Mallory did not seem to mind them in the least. There should have been a lovely view from here, but all we got was an occasional glimpse of glaciers and rocky peaks through the mist. The sun was trying to shine through the clouds and at first it was beautifully warm; but after a couple of hours snow began to fall, so we hurriedly descended on to the glacier below. Snow fell all the way back to camp, and by nightfall there were 3 inches of fresh snow round our tents. During the night the thermometer dropped to 21° Fahr., and the morning broke clear and frosty. I started off early to climb the hill behind the camp, from which there was a very extensive view, both Everest and Makalu being for the moment quite clear and free from cloud. To the

North extended a great range of snow peaks between 23,000 feet and 24,000 feet in height, rather uninteresting in appearance, and to the East stretched a great sea of accumulating cloud, out of which appeared the tops of Kanchenjunga and Jannu. The peak on which we stood was just under 20,000 feet; I spent several hours basking in the hot sunshine, which was rapidly melting the fresh snow. I was surprised to find growing at this height a tiny yellow saxifrage.

That evening eight coolies arrived with our long-expected mail, and the rest of the day was spent in reading letters and sorting out papers, for over two hundred letters and papers had arrived for me alone. There was again a sharp frost of 10° that night and the early morning was beautiful, but clouds came quickly drifting up the valley and obscured the fine views we had from the camp of Mount Everest and the rocky peaks to the North of the camp. On September 11, in spite of a warm night, Mallory and Bullock, being very optimistic, left for the upper camp, while Morshead and Wheeler rejoined us from their camp below, not having been able to do any work down there owing to bad weather. Snow fell steadily all the evening to a depth of about 3 inches. Next day was cloudy, but warm, and the snow disappeared again with extraordinary rapidity. I went out with a shotgun to try and shoot some ramchakor, and while after them saw a very fine grey wolf who was also stalking the ramchakor. He came up to within 50 yards of me, so that I was able to have a good look at him. He had a beautiful coat, and it was very unfortunate that I did not have a rifle with me. I wandered some way up a side valley to the foot of a glacier, but saw no signs of birds, as the wolf had evidently been there before me. In the afternoon Mallory and Bullock returned from the upper camp, having been driven down by the bad weather: another 5 inches of snow fell that evening, so that we were kept busy beating our tents to keep the ridge poles from breaking. On September 13, 14 and 15, snow fell on and off the whole time; but in spite of the bad weather I managed to shoot a burhel for food. Their meat is very much better than that of the tame sheep. On September 16 we had at last a fine day with a sharp frost at night. Wheeler at once seized this opportunity and took up a station on a hill-top on the opposite side of the valley, from which he was able to get some useful views. The next day, after 13° of frost in the night, Mallory, Morshead and I started off to climb Kama Changri, a peak to the South of the camp, that overhung the Kama Valley. We left the camp at 2 a.m., by the light of a full moon, which made the going as light as though it were day. We soon reached our view-point of a few days before, where, except for the distant roar of the stream far away below in the valley, there was no other sound, only an intense stillness. Never anywhere have I seen the moon or the stars shine so brightly. To the South, far away from us, there were constant flashes of lightning—the valleys in Tibet, the great gorges of the Arun, the wooded valleys of Nepal all lay buried under a white sea of clouds, out of which emerged the higher mountains like islands out of a fairy sea. In this bright moonlight, mountains like Kanchenjunga—100 miles away—stood out sharp and distinct. Here on this sharp ridge, at a height of 21,000 feet, with no obstruction to hide the view, sunrise came to us in all its beauty and grandeur. To the West, and close at hand, towered up Mount Everest, still over 8,000 feet above us; at first showing up cold, grey and dead against a sky of deep purple. All of a sudden a ray of sunshine touched the summit, and soon flooded the higher snows and ridges with golden light, while behind, the deep purple of the sky changed to orange. Makalu was the next to catch the first rays of the sun and glowed as though alive; then the white sea of clouds was struck by the gleaming rays of the sun, and all aglow with colour rose slowly and seemed to break against the island peaks in great billows of fleecy white.

Such a sunrise has seldom been the privilege of man to see, and once seen can never be forgotten. After sunrise the climbing became more unpleasant. We tried to follow the direct way up the mountain, but the snow was in bad condition and the slope very steep. We therefore crossed the glacier, putting on our snow-shoes, and followed easier snow slopes but bad owing to the soft snow. The going was very tiring; Mallory and Morshead appeared to feel the height very much. After six hours we reached the top, 21,300 feet, from which we had a most superb view. We looked straight down on to the Kama Valley. Makalu was immediately opposite us with its colossal precipices. Glaciers, cliffs of ice, rock peaks, fluted snow ridges and immense mountains towered all around us above a vast sea of clouds which stretched for hundreds of miles away to the plains of India. Here I was able to take many photographs, but no photograph can adequately portray the grandeur or the impressiveness of such a scene. We stopped on the top of Kama Changri for over three hours. It was extraordinarily warm; there was not a breath of air, and the sun seemed to shine with an intense heat. Clouds then began to roll up, and we returned to camp by an easier way down the glacier.

Next day, in spite of 13° of frost at night, snow and sleet fell all day again, and made us very depressed. In order to prevent our going to sleep too soon after dinner, four of us used to play bridge every night, and I do not suppose that bridge has often been played at so great a height.

On September 19, after a cold night with 16° of frost, Mallory, Bullock, Morshead and Wheeler started off for the 20,000-foot camp. The weather was now steadily growing colder every night. On September 20 we had 18° of frost, as well as a further fall of snow. During the night a very fine lunar halo was seen, but the morning broke clear. Wollaston, Raeburn and I started to join the remainder of the party at the 20,000-foot camp, leaving Gyalzen Kazi, our second interpreter, behind in charge of the advance base camp. It was very necessary to have some one here to whom we could send back for any extra stores or supplies that might be wanted, and who would be able to forward to us anything that might be sent up from Kharta. A four hours' walk brought us to the camp. I had a thorough feeling of lassitude all the way. It required, indeed, some effort to walk at all, and a strong effort, both of mind and body, to reach camp. On the way beautiful views of Mount Everest gave us encouragement. The foot of the Kharta Glacier descends to 19,000 feet. From that point on to the camp we travelled beside it. At first the glacier is cut up into wonderfully shaped "seracs," but as we got higher the surface became smoother. It was an exceptionally white glacier; there were no moraines on its surface, and it was covered everywhere with a fresh coating of thick snow. We found the camp on a terrace between two glaciers. That above the camp resembled the pictures of a Greenland ice cap. A thick coating of ice, to a depth of 50 to 60 feet, covered the gentle slopes above us, and came down to within a couple of hundred yards of the camp. The drainage from the melting ice percolated through the stony ground, so that on digging to a depth of 6 inches we came upon water. A couple of hundred feet below the camp was the big white glacier which descended from the Lhakpa La. The day was gloriously fine, and we obtained magnificent views of Mount Everest and the snowy chain to the South of us across the Kharta Glacier. Over the top of this snowy chain appeared the great rocky crests of Makalu. At an altitude of over 19,800 feet I saw a hare and heard several ramchakor calling. There grew close to the camp a few gentians with their curious square leaves, also a dwarf blue delphinium and a little white saxifrage. It was an extraordinary height at which to find flowers and their season of summer cannot last long. On arrival at the camp, we found only Wheeler and Bullock there, as Mallory and Morshead with fourteen coolies had gone on ahead to carry loads up to the Lhakpa La, which was to be our next camp. They returned in a very exhausted condition in the course of the afternoon. The snow, they reported, was in better condition than last time on the lower slopes; but as they got higher, they found it still very soft and powdery. These extra loads that they had taken up to this camp would enable the whole party to go up to it and to sleep there, if necessary, for several days. As the sun was setting behind Mount Everest, we were treated to a glorious view. The ring of clouds that surrounded it were all touched by the bright evening sunlight, while the mountain itself was in deep shadow except for great streamers of powdery fresh snow which were being blown off the whole length of its crests. We stood and watched this extraordinary sight for some time, devoutly hoping that the wind would soon die down. Unfortunately we were soon to experience what a strong wind meant at these heights.

On the following night we had 20° of frost, and the weather appeared to be getting rather more settled. We were now sufficiently high up to be above the ordinary clouds, and we could look down upon the great sea of them which overhung the Arun Valley and the greater part of Nepal. As the sun warmed the clouds, they used to rise higher, but they seldom arrived as far as our camp owing to a strong North-westerly wind always blowing in the upper regions of the air which drove them back again. Watching the movements of the clouds day by day gave me the impression that the Mount Everest group forms a dividing line between the two monsoon systems. The monsoon that causes so much rain in Sikkim comes from the Bay of Bengal, and these moist currents sweep up to Mount Everest, but it is only when the current is very strong that they pass beyond it. At this time of year this monsoon was still active, whereas the Arabian Sea monsoon—that is to say, the moist winds from the Arabian Sea—which had given us previously much rain and snow on the Western sides and slopes of Mount Everest, was now over, with the result that on the West side of Everest we had blue skies every day and no rain clouds, whereas on the East side the clouds and the moisture brought up by the Bengal monsoon still prevailed. During the course of the morning I climbed an easy hill to the East side of the camp and some 500 feet above it. We walked along at first just below the ice cap, which was very pretty with its long icicles gleaming in the sunlight. We then crossed on to the ice cap and found the snow in excellent condition, firm and crisp to the tread, so that it was a pleasure to walk along it. From the top of this hill, 20,500 feet, was a very fine view to the East, over the great sea of cloud which filled up all the valleys as far as the Massif of Kanchenjunga which towered up in the distance, and the more slender peak of Jannu. Amongst the Sikkim peaks I could also recognise Chomiomo and the Jonsong peak. To the South Makalu towered up above all the other mountains: while between it and Mount Everest, beyond the Southern watershed of the Kama Valley, showed up some of the great Nepalese peaks, among which we noted Chamlang, 24,000 feet. To the West of us Mount Everest showed up sharp and clear and very white after all the fresh snow that had fallen in the last month. From this side Mount Everest certainly looks its best, standing up as a solitary peak instead of being rather dwarfed by the high ridges that radiate from it. The weather remained fine all day, and it was a real pleasure to sit outside one's tent and bask in the sun. Though we were 20,000 feet, we had breakfast, lunch and tea out of doors in front of our tents, and we could not have been warmer or enjoyed pleasanter conditions if we had been down at 5,000 feet.

On September 22, leaving Raeburn behind, Mallory, Bullock, Morshead, Wheeler, Wollaston and myself started off to Lakhpa La camp. We left the 20,000-foot camp in 22° of frost at four o'clock in the morning, accompanied by twenty-six coolies, who were divided up into four parties, each of which was properly roped. It was a beautiful moonlight night, and the mountains showed up nearly as brightly as in the daytime. We rapidly descended the 200 feet from our terrace to the glacier, when we all "roped up." The snow on the glacier was in excellent condition, and as it was frozen hard we made good progress. Dawn overtook us on the broad flat part of the glacier, the first beams of the sun falling on the summit of Mount Everest, which lay straight in front of us, and changing the colour of the snow gradually from pink to orange, all the time with a background of deep purple sky, every detail showing up sharp and clear in the frosty air. We mounted gradually past Kartse, the white conical-shaped peak climbed by Mallory and Bullock a month ago from the Kama Valley. We wended our way without much difficulty through the ice-fall of the glacier, below some superbly fluted snow ridges that rose straight above us. Then followed a long and at times a somewhat steep climb over soft powdery snow to the top of the pass. Even at these heights we came across tracks in the snow. We were able to pick out tracks of hares and foxes, but one that at first looked like a human foot puzzled us considerably. Our coolies at once jumped to the conclusion that this must be "The Wild Man of the Snows," to which they gave the name of Metohkangmi, "the abominable snow man" who interested the newspapers so much. On my return to civilised countries I read with interest delightful accounts of the ways and customs of this wild man whom we were supposed to have met. These tracks, which caused so much comment, were probably caused by a large "loping" grey wolf, which in the soft snow formed double tracks rather like those of a barefooted man. Tibet, however, is not the only country where there exists a "bogey man." In Tibet he takes the form of a hairy man who lives in the snows, and little Tibetan children who are naughty and disobedient are frightened by wonderful fairy tales that are told about him. To escape from him they must run down the hill, as then his long hair falls over his eyes and he is unable to see them. Many other such tales have they with which to strike terror into the hearts of bad boys and girls.

I reached the top of the pass (22,350 feet) by 10.30 a.m., and was rewarded by a wonderful view of Mount Everest, now only a couple of miles away. From the pass there was a steep descent of about 1,200 feet to a glacier which after many wanderings finds its way into the Rongbuk Glacier. This valley had never been thoroughly investigated by Mallory and Bullock in their visit to the Rongbuk Valley. It does not, however, actually form the main Rongbuk Glacier, but stops several miles short of it, the entrance to the valley containing this huge glacier being both small and very insignificant. The bad weather that they had experienced in the Rongbuk Valley during the latter half of their stay there had made it impossible for Mallory and Bullock to explore this valley, or see what lay at its head.

We were now opposite the Chang La (North Col) which joins Mount Everest to Changtse (the North peak), and from this col was, so far as we were able to judge, the only route to the summit. The way from the glacier up to the Chang La looked steep and unpromising, and we doubted whether it would be possible to take laden coolies up, even to this point. I took as many photographs as I could, and as quickly as possible, for there was an icy wind blowing which almost froze my hands. This wind blew the fine powdery snow off all the crests of the ridges and it penetrated everywhere. We found a little hollow in the snow a few feet below the crest, and here we set to work to pitch our camp. There was not much shelter, but it was the only possible place. We had only brought small Alpine Meade and Mummery tents with us. Two of us occupied each tent. They were very small and uncomfortable, and in order to enter them we had to crawl through a narrow funnel almost as though we were entering a dog kennel. The effort of crawling in was very exhausting and caused us to remain out of breath for a considerable time afterwards. Even these small tents were with difficulty pitched owing to the strong winds: cooking was quite out of the question until dark when the wind temporarily lulled. We had brought up with us some Primus stoves and spirit lamps. No one, except perhaps Wheeler, was very expert with the Primus stove, and though no doubt under favourable conditions they would be easy to work, even at these heights, we were never very successful with them and were forced to rely upon the spirit stoves. After sunset we had a scratch meal of consommé, which we managed to warm up, followed by some cold ham and biscuits, after which we retired to bed. The moment the sun went down there were 25° of frost. Up till now I had felt no ill-effects from the rarefied air; I had not even had a headache and my appetite was good, though I owned to feeling rather lazy and it always needed an effort to concentrate one's thoughts. The coolies who had accompanied us up to this camp all seemed to be well and were very cheerful. The eiderdown sleeping-bags were a great comfort; they were our only means of keeping thoroughly warm with 34° of frost outside. But I cannot say that I felt comfortable or, in fact, that I slept at all, as the snow which at most times had been much too soft, seemed here to freeze into uncomfortable lumps and bumps underneath one's back, so that I could never get comfortable all night. The wind howled round our flimsy tents, and I do not think anyone, except perhaps Mallory, got any sleep that night. In the morning we were all suffering from bad headaches, due to the airlessness of these little tents, and I am sure that anyone camping at high altitudes ought to have a much larger type of tent in which to sleep if he is to avoid headaches. We blessed the early morning sun when it appeared and began to unfreeze us. I noticed then that our faces and hands were all a curious blue colour in the morning, due to what is called, I believe, cyanosis of the blood. With much difficulty Wheeler made us a little tea, which if not drunk at once, froze; Mallory thawed out some sardines which had all been frozen solid. There was luckily less wind than during the night, and as the sun rose higher, we all became more alive. The coolies, too, were at first all torpid and complained of bad headaches, but on getting into the fresh air, out of their small and stuffy tents, the headaches rapidly passed away. After consultation, we decided that there was no object—in fact, that it would be dangerous—for the whole party to go on, so we decided that it would be best for the expert Alpine climbers only, together with a few picked coolies, to attempt the Chang La. If weather conditions were favourable, they might, we thought, see how high they could get on Mount Everest itself. We therefore quickly sorted out and divided up the stores, and after seeing Mallory, Bullock and Wheeler off, unpitched our own tents, being satisfied that we could be of no use by remaining where we were, and that it would be best that we should return to our 20,000-foot camp and carry down with us as many stores as we could. We accomplished this without any difficulty, and arrived back during the course of the afternoon. The contrast here was extraordinary. We seemed to be in a totally different climate, and our larger tents and camp beds appeared to us to be the height of luxury. We spent a very comfortable night in spite of 22° of frost, and all slept soundly after our exertions, though once or twice during the night I was awakened by rats gnawing at the food which had been left out on the boxes in my tent. One of the coolies also started to say his prayers in a loud tone of voice at 1 a.m., but after a few winged words he relapsed into silence.

The next day was delightfully warm and sunny, though there had been during the night a good deal of lightning towards the South. The snow could be seen whirling off the crest of Mount Everest during the morning, and in the course of the afternoon the wind grew much stronger, and blew huge clouds of snow off the slopes of the mountain, and from all the surrounding ridges. We could see great wisps of snow being blown off the pass that we had just left, so that the climbing party must have been having a very cold time in their new camp. In the evening there was a curious false sunset in the East with fine purple and orange rays, while as usual the Kama and the Kharta Valleys were filled with a sea of cloud. Here, however, we seemed to be above and beyond the reach of the clouds. Next night there was again constant lightning to the South and

23° of frost, but the weather kept fine and sunny. On climbing a snow-covered hill to the West of the camp, about 21,000 feet, I had some superb views of Everest and Makalu with their appalling cliffs and beautifully-fluted snow slopes. A strong North-westerly gale still continued in the upper regions of the air above 22,000 feet, and every ridge of Everest was smothered with clouds of blown snow. I had a pleasant glissade down steep snow slopes back to the camp, where the climate was delicious and where I could bask in the sun at the entrance of my tent with a sun temperature of 173° Fahr. Earlier in the season we had often recorded temperatures of 195° and 197° Fahr. in the sun with the black bulb thermometer. During the afternoon we were able with our glasses to see black specks appearing on the top of the Lhakpa La. These were the Alpine climbers and their coolies returning after their strenuous efforts on Mount Everest. We watched them with the greatest interest descending the glacier and wondered how far they had been successful. They all arrived back safely in the course of the evening, having been extraordinarily lucky in not having had any casualties or frost-bites in spite of the Arctic gales. Mallory will, however, tell of their adventures in another chapter.

CHAPTER IX

THE RETURN TO KHARTA BY THE KAMA VALLEY

Winter was now rapidly approaching. Every night was growing steadily colder, and we were all anxious to get down to lower altitudes. Every one had been feeling the strain of life at these high altitudes. It had been, however, a great relief to us that all the party had got back to the 20,000-foot camp in safety, and that we had had no cases of sickness or frost-bite. The coolies had throughout worked most willingly and to the best of their ability. They had been well supplied with boots and socks, warm clothing of all kinds, cap comforters and fur gloves, as well as blankets, and for those who had slept at the higher camps, eiderdown sleeping-bags had been provided capable of holding four or five. Here at the 20,000-foot camp we did not have to depend on Primus stoves or spirit lamps, as while we were waiting at the advanced base camp we had daily sent up coolies with loads of wood for our future use, and even during our stay here the coolies who had been left behind under Gyalzen Kazi had been sending up further loads. We now divided our party into two: Mallory, Bullock, Raeburn and Morshead were to be responsible for taking all the stores back to Kharta, and for this purpose we had arranged with Chheten Wangdi and the Kharta Jongpen for a number of Tibetan coolies to help in the work of removal. The remainder of us, that is to say, Wollaston, Wheeler and myself, were to cross over a snow pass and return to Kharta *viâ* the Kama Valley. Wheeler was anxious to do this in order to complete his survey work, for up till now he had been unable to visit the Kama Valley. Wollaston had already seen the lower parts of the Kama Valley, but was very anxious to see the upper end, particularly after my descriptions of the scenery and the Alpine flowers that were to be met with there.

On September 26 the two parties started off in different directions. Taking with us fifteen coolies, all pretty heavily laden, we descended to the great Kharta Glacier, which it was necessary for us to cross. We were not at all certain as to the conditions we were likely to meet with on the other side of the pass. The climb from the Kharta Glacier to the Karpo La, 20,300 feet, was quite gentle, though the snow was very soft and powdery. On the North side of the pass we found the slopes to be a snow-covered glacier, but on the South side there was a very steep rocky descent which had to be faced. From the top of the pass we had a remarkably fine view into the Kama Valley which lay below us. Makalu, Pethangtse and Everest stood up clear above the clouds which floated along the bottom of the Kama Valley. Across the gaps between these peaks we could see other snow ranges in Nepal. Here at the top of the pass we were luckily just sheltered from the North-west and the gale, but on either side of us snow was being blown off the mountains in long white streamers. Our descent was down a very steep rocky rib. We began by roping ourselves together, but the coolies were all of them heavily laden and were, moreover, very clumsy on the rope, sending down so many loose stones that I found my position as foremost man quite untenable owing to the amount of débris and rocks which were dislodged above me. We therefore unroped, and Wollaston lowered the coolies one by one over the steepest part—a somewhat long proceeding—after which they were able independently to make their way down to the glacier below without mishap. We now put on the rope again, and so crossed the easy glacier which led down to the moraine on which I had been two months before. Wheeler branched off here and took up a position on one of the ridges. Here he found the gale very troublesome, his theodolite being nearly blown over several times. He managed, however, to take a number of readings and to get a good many photographs—sufficient to map the whole of the upper part of the Kama Valley. All that day the gale continued above 20,000 feet. Below this the valley was filled with clouds, over which at first we had magnificent views. As soon as we descended into the valley, we gradually became enveloped in the autumn mists, which lasted all the remainder of the way to Pethang Ringmo. This was the place where I had met the yak herds two months before when they were pasturing their yaks on the grassy uplands. They had left the place, and we were therefore no longer able to draw on them for butter and milk. I had, however, arranged for Wheeler's fat cook to be sent up from Kharta to this place to meet us and to bring with him some fresh meat and vegetables. These we found on arrival, the fat cook having only arrived an hour before. We all of us slept that night much better than we had been doing at the higher camps, and though even down here we had 14° of frost, I was delighted to find that my boots were not frozen as hard as nails, as they had been all the last week.

From this camp I determined to attempt an expedition which I had long desired to make. My ambition was to reach the ridge between Makalu and Everest, and from it to have a look right down into Nepal. Mallory and Bullock did not much encourage me in my project, and doubted whether it could be accomplished within the short time which was now available. I decided, nevertheless, to make the attempt. On the night of the 26th all our servants overslept themselves, and I had some difficulty in waking them next morning. We succeeded, however, after a hurried breakfast in making a start at 5.45 a.m., just as the first sunlight was touching the highest peak of Mount Everest. It was a most perfect autumn morning, without a cloud in the sky and with the ground underfoot white with hoar-frost. After going a mile up the valley, we had to cross the Kangshung Glacier—here about a mile wide and consisting of a great mass of ice hummocks, often 100 feet or more in height, mostly covered with boulders, with the ice showing every now and then below us in curious caverns and lakes. It took us an hour to cross this glacier, as the walking was very tiring up and down hill over loose stones all the time; luckily, however, many of the stones were frozen to the ice, which made the crossing easier than it might have been later in the day. We then climbed on to a spur, over 19,000 feet, which jutted out into the valley. From this we had marvellous views right away to Kanchenjunga in the East. On the opposite side Mount Everest stood out with every detail showing clearly in the autumn sunshine. Above us towered the perpendicular cliffs of Chomolonzo, opening out into a most astonishing series of peaks, the existence of which we had never suspected when looking at the mountain from the valley below. For once in a way the air was drier and the valleys below were not filled with cloud, so there was a prospect of our having clear views all day. Wheeler had come a short way along the ridge until he got a good view-point, when he stopped to set up his theodolite and camera for a station, after which he came along no further. I followed the crest of the ridge as far as I could, finding it at times very difficult and rocky and having to make many detours to get along. A descent of about 500 feet was followed by a climb of another 1,000 feet, at the end of which we found ourselves exactly opposite to the great amphitheatre of granite formed by Chomolonzo and Makalu and facing Westwards. So steep were these great white granite cliffs that no snow lodged on them. Above them were other cliffs of ice with rather gentler slopes; at their feet was a great glacier that filled up the whole of this basin and then swept down till it almost joined the Kangshung Glacier. I had taken with me as usual Ang Tenze and Nyima Tendu, the two coolies who always accompanied me, each of them carrying a camera. We now came to a glacier which it was necessary to cross, and therefore roped up once more. The snow by this time had become rather soft, and we were constantly breaking through the crust. The glare and heat of the sun on this glacier were very intense, and both Nyima and I were feeling very limp from the heat. Ang Tenze was extraordinarily active and did not seem to mind heat or height—a quite exceptionally gifted mountaineer. Having successfully crossed the glacier, we left the soft snow and found our way over some easy rocks and eventually reached the top of the ridge for which we were making, at a height of about 21,500 feet, and some 500 feet above the snow-covered pass to the East of us. From the top of the ridge we had a most glorious view looking across range upon range of snowy mountains in Nepal. Immediately below us was a large snow "névé," towards which glaciers descended from a number of snow-covered peaks. From this névé a great glacier swept round towards the Southern side of Makalu, apparently descending into a valley that ran parallel to the Kama Valley and on the South side of Makalu. Chamlang and other snow peaks to the South showed up very clearly, covered with snow and ice to very much lower elevations than any mountain on the North side of the Himalayas. On either side of us towered up Makalu and Everest, but seen from this point the huge cliffs of Chomolönzo presented by far the most astounding sight. From here I could see a few thousand feet of the Southern slopes of Mount Everest which we had been unable to see from any other point before. From the angle at which I saw them these appeared very steep, and even if it were possible and permissible to go into Nepal, it seems improbable that a practicable route lies up that face of the mountain. I spent a couple of hours up here taking photographs, enjoying the views, and eating my lunch in comfort, for the sun was hot and for once in a way there was no wind. To the South-west of us, across the névé, there appeared to be another easy pass which seemed to lead round to the South of Mount Everest, and Ang Tenze, who came from the Khombu Valley, said that he thought that he recognised some of the mountain

CHOMOLÖNZO.
from the alp below the Langma La, Kama Valley.

tops that he saw over this, and that if we crossed this pass, we should eventually descend into the Khombu Valley. He also told me that there were stories that once upon a time there was a pass from the Khombu Valley into the Kama Valley, and that this was probably the pass in question, but that it had been disused for a great number of years. To support his theory we found on the way down a kind of shelter built of stones and some pieces of juniper hidden under a big rock. This would have been too high up for any yak herds to camp, as it was above the grazing pastures, and seemed to prove that the spot might have been used as a halting-place for smugglers or people fleeing from the law before they crossed these passes. It had taken us six and a half hours from camp to get up to the top of this pass; and we had had no halts on the way beyond what were necessary to take photographs. The downward journey took us four hours. We tried another way by the side of the Makalu Glacier, desiring thereby to avoid the tiresome and rather difficult bit along the top of the ridge. This short cut proved, however, to be still more trying and wearisome. From the cliffs above there had been great rock falls down to the edge of the glacier, and for a couple of miles we had to jump from boulder to boulder and to clamber either up or down the whole time. There was still the Kangshung Glacier to cross, with more up and down hill work, the stones being much looser and more inclined to slip under foot than they were in the morning. Eventually we reached camp, just before dark, and feeling very tired. A cup of tea, however, with a little brandy in it, completely removed all fatigue. Wollaston had been able during the day to get some beautiful photographs of the snow-powdered cliffs of Chomolönzo, and also some interesting ones of the Kangshung Glacier. Besides these he had been able to collect a number of seeds. It is astonishing how quickly at these heights seeds ripen, and how short a time it is after flowering that they are fit for picking.

We had been very lucky in getting such a perfect day

in the Kama Valley, for fine days there were very few. After our one perfect day the weather changed again, and for the next three days we descended the Kama Valley in sleet and snow. The first morning our march was only to our old camp at Tangsham on a glacial terrace 1,000 feet above the valley. At first Everest was clear and all the mountains to the West, but heavy clouds came rolling up from the South-east and soon enveloped everything. On the way I managed to collect for Wollaston a number of the seeds of that lovely blue primula which I had found in flower here in August. I shot, too, a common snipe, which I was very surprised to meet at these altitudes. I flushed him beside a small spring close to the camp. During the afternoon it snowed and sleeted, and Wheeler came in very tired in the evening after having spent the whole of the day on a prominent peak, from which he had been unable to get a single photograph or to take any bearings. In spite of the snow that evening we had a cheery bonfire of juniper, willow and rhododendron. The next morning, though we were down at 15,000 feet, there were a couple of inches of fresh snow on the ground. The weather at first was very misty, and we had no views at all. We soon, however, descended below the snow, and the autumnal colours in the valley began to show. On the opposite side of it below the great black cliffs, the bushes were all shades of brown and gold. In the forests the rose bushes had turned a brilliant red, and the mountain ash showed every shade of scarlet and crimson, contrasting well with the shiny dark green leaves of the rhododendron. The golden colours of the birch and the dark junipers also made a beautiful combination of colour. Rain set in again steadily, and as snow was falling on the "field of marigolds" where we had intended to camp, we pitched our tents in the midst of a huge rock-fall—1,000 feet lower down. Our coolies did not pitch any tents for themselves, but preferred to scatter in twos and threes and to camp under the overhanging rocks which they found apparently warmer and more comfortable than the tents.

There had been a wonderful growth of vegetation among these huge boulders, many of them 40 feet to 50 feet in height, which had come down from the cliffs above. Wollaston and I spent most of the afternoon pottering round and collecting seeds of plants of different kinds. The next morning we had trouble in getting hold of the coolies; they were scattered among the rocks, and in spite of shouts, refused to budge until I went round with a big stick and poked them out of their holes. I crossed the Shao La in thick mist, though Wollaston and Wheeler, who came along an hour behind, had some beautiful glimpses of Makalu in the clouds and were able to get some photographs. After crossing the pass, we descended past several beautiful lakes and arrived in fine weather at Kharta in the afternoon. The autumn tints on the way down were again very beautiful, and most of the crops had already been gathered in. Mallory and Bullock had, we found, left Kharta, being in a great hurry to get back to civilisation again.

It was September 30 when we reached Kharta. We had now finished our reconnaissance. We had investigated all the valleys to the West, North-west, North, North-east and East of the mountain, and had eventually found that there was only one possible route of approach to the summit. The bad weather and the furious North-westerly gales had prevented our attaining any great height this year. The rainy season had begun some three weeks later than usual. The rains, they told us, had been much heavier than in most years in Tibet, and the wet season had lasted until very nearly the end of September, after which time a period of gales set in which made climbing at heights above 23,000 feet a physical impossibility. Undoubtedly the best time to try and climb the mountain would be before the monsoon breaks in May or early June. It might be possible, if the monsoon happened to end by the beginning of September, to tackle the mountain early in September, but after the middle of that month the chances of doing any good grow steadily weaker and the cold increases with great rapidity.

Whether it will be possible in any conditions to reach the summit I am very doubtful. We, however, had never intended to make a sustained effort to reach the top in 1921. The reconnaissance of the mountain and its approaches afforded us indeed no time to make such an effort, and we felt bound to investigate every valley that led up to it. The Everest Committee had already before we left for India in 1921 decided to send out a second Expedition in the following year, for the express purpose of climbing Mount Everest, and for this purpose had already then promised the leadership to Brig.-General C. G. Bruce, whose unrivalled knowledge of climbing and climatic conditions in the Himalayas specially fitted him for the work. Whether the task is capable of accomplishment I will not attempt to say, though I should think the chances are on the whole against success. If Mount Everest were 6,000, or even 5,000 feet lower, I think there can be no doubt that it could be climbed. There are no physical difficulties in the shape of the mountain which prevent it being climbed—the difficulties are all connected with its altitude. If the snow is soft and powdery, and the conditions are such as we met with so often; or if, again, there is difficult rock climbing in the last 2,000 or 3,000 feet of the climb, I do not think the summit will be reached. I cannot say what the effect will be if oxygen is taken to aid the human effort. I only know that cylinders of oxygen are very uncomfortable and heavy to carry, and that to wear a mask over the mouth and to climb so equipped would not seem to be very feasible or pleasant. Living at great heights, and trying to sleep at great heights, lowers the vitality enormously. Larger tents than those with which we were supplied might well be taken in order to prevent the depressing headaches that follow from sleeping in a confined and airless space. Among minor discomforts which count for much may be mentioned the difficulty of preparing good warm food, and for this purpose a coolie should be trained in cooking and in the use of the "Primus" and spirit stoves. This coolie should be a man accustomed to great heights, and he should accompany the party up to the highest camps in order to avoid the difficulties we had in connection with the preparation of our food and then having to live on such makeshifts as sardines and biscuits. I never lost my appetite at heights over 20,000 feet—I was always able to eat well, though not everything appealed to the palate. Sweet things were especially wanted. That it is possible to acclimatise the system to live at heights is true, but only to a certain extent—up to about 18,000 feet we could acclimatise ourselves very comfortably, and I know in my own case that after six months' living in Tibet, I was able to do far more than when I first came into the country, but at greater heights I think a prolonged stay permanently lowers the vitality. Sleeplessness is another great enemy at heights, and most of the party I found slept very poorly at the highest camp. Mallory, I think, was the only exception. It ought to be possible to pick out a few coolies capable of carrying loads able to go as far as any European can get. Some of them seem to feel the height much less than others, and I believe that an unladen native would be able to go much higher if he had the knowledge of ice and snow that Alpine climbers have, and would not improbably reach a greater height than any European. Twenty-nine thousand feet is, however, a tremendous height for anyone to attain, and I own that I am not at all sanguine that the summit will be reached, though I have no doubt that this year will see the Duke of the Abruzzi's record of 24,600 broken, and I shall not be at all surprised to see a height of 25,000 or 26,000 feet arrived at.

CHAPTER X

THE RETURN JOURNEY TO PHARI

Autumn had already come to Kharta. The willows and the poplars under which we were camped were fast shedding their leaves, which rustled on the ground, or blew into our tents, a warning that winter was not far off. Even here there were one or two degrees of frost every night. The days, however, were still warm and sunny. The next five days were fully occupied with strenuous work. Wheeler and I took alternate mornings and afternoons in the dark room. We had each taken a large number of photographs during the past month. These had to be developed before we started on our return journey to Darjeeling, and this would be our last opportunity. An account of our last month's doings and our final reconnaissance had to be written out for *The Times*, and this, together with many other letters, had to be sent off to Phari as soon as possible. Our stores, tents, Alpine equipment, had all to be collected and sorted out. Lists had to be made of all of them, and most of them had to be re-packed. The coolies were perpetually worrying us for money and advances of pay in order that they might be able to buy Tibetan clothing, or have money which they could spend on drink at Kharta, where it was apparently very cheap. Our cook and most of the coolies used constantly to return to camp in the evening blind drunk, and I had to see that the cook was never allowed near the kitchen under these conditions. On such an occasion my servant, Poo, would have to do the cooking in his place. The chang, or barley beer, that they got must have been a much stronger brew than what was given to us, as what we had did not appear intoxicating at all, but the interpreters told us that coolie beer was double strength.

The Jongpen was rather sad as the moment of our departure drew near. We invited him to lunch one day, and he seemed to appreciate the beauties of Scotch whisky, which he said was very much better than his own chang. We had to pay him a return visit the following day, when he gave us a great spread. Knowing that we were anxious to collect such curios as were available, he produced all kinds of things for our inspection. I bought from him a curious old Tibetan musket, elaborately decorated with silver, and fitted with a pair of antelope horns on which to rest it when firing. Some interesting copper and silver teapots we were also able to get from him, and I remember his showing Wollaston many pieces of finely embroidered Chinese silk. Both Hopaphema and the Jongpen had a very good idea of the value of money, and were not at all afraid of asking a stiff price for any of the curios which they produced. We managed, however, to pick up some interesting Chinese snuff bottles of carved agate, some with pictures painted inside. China cups of the Chienlung and Kanghe periods we were also able to get; there were, however, many things in the monasteries which we rather coveted, but which the Lamas would not sell. Their tables were very ornamentally carved with dragons and weird designs, all painted over in brilliant colours. The Jongpen had one such table, but unfortunately I found out that he had only borrowed it from the nearest monastery for the purpose of entertaining us, and therefore he could not sell it. We left behind us a good many stores which it was not worth while to bring along. Among them was a lot of acid hypo-sulphite of soda, which the Jongpen at once seized upon, and which he said he intended to make use of in washing his clothes, knowing that soda was used occasionally for this purpose. The Jongpen, of whom we had taken many photographs, and who had seen the results, was anxious to buy one of our cameras, and to develop and print everything himself. He imagined the whole process was very easy, and was extremely anxious to get hold of one of the Expedition's cameras, but we had to disappoint him in this. Nothing small would content him—he wanted the biggest of the lot, and was quite willing to exchange a sword or any other weapon for a camera. We, however, left behind with him three pairs of skis, which we had brought out with us, but which had never been unpacked. These skis had throughout our journeys been looked upon by the Tibetans with the greatest interest. They had heard about flying machines, and they thought that these were the framework of a flying machine which we had brought with us, and on which we intended to fly to the top of the mountains. Wherever we arrived there was always a great crowd assembled round these skis, discussing the various methods by which they could be put together and describing how the white man would then fly. I left them with the Jongpen and told him that they were very good exercise for him in the winter time, when the snow was deep, and that if he wanted to reduce his weight, which was already considerable, there could be no better method than by making use of them in the snow.

At last, on October 5, we managed to leave Kharta. There were no pack animals available; we had therefore to make use of coolies for our transport for the first march; it took 140 of them to carry all our loads. For some time the scene of confusion was very amusing. The Jongpen himself came down, and it was only owing to his help that by mid-day we got all the loads sorted out and put on the backs of the coolies. Before he was able to do this he had to have recourse to the system of drawing lots by putting garters on each load, a system which I have already described in a previous chapter. Before we left, the Jongpen and Hopaphema brought us presents of sheep and vegetables, and they and all the people of the valley seemed genuinely sorry that we were departing. Throughout our long stay at Kharta they had been most helpful and had done everything they could for our comfort. They were both of them very human, with a delightful sense of humour, and we quickly became great friends. It was with much regret that we turned our backs on Kharta.

We started off without a cloud in the sky, but with a strong South wind blowing. High up on the mountains we could see the snow still being blown off in white clouds. Our route lay up the valley of the Bhong-chu for about 10 miles until the river suddenly turned to the East to go through a deep and impassable gorge. We had then to follow the valley of the Zachar-chu for 4 miles to Lumeh, where we camped beside the great poplar trees. The bridge by which we had crossed the Zachar-chu in July no longer existed. It had been washed away in August, but now that the snows were no longer melting higher up, and the rainy season was over, the river was very much lower, and it was possible to ford it. The people at Lumeh were very pleased to see us again; we found tents pitched and food prepared for our reception. From here there were two routes open to us. We could either, by crossing two passes, drop down to Tsogo in the valley of the Bhong-chu, and after fording the river there, follow our previous route (of the outward journey) to Tingri, or we could cross a small pass just above Lumeh, meeting the Bhong-chu again immediately above the gorge, where there was a bridge across it. We chose the latter route, as it was probably a couple of days shorter and would take us through new country. On leaving Lumeh, for the first time for several days we had a cloudy morning, which was unfortunate, as from the top of the Quiok (Cuckoo Pass) we had hoped for a fine view. Our transport to-day consisted of yaks and donkeys, which came along very well. There was a steep climb of 2,000 feet to the top of the pass, 15,000 feet, where we just managed to get a glimpse of Makalu in the clouds, but Everest was hidden. We thought that this would be our last chance of a view of the Everest and Makalu group, but it turned out not to be so. By going over this pass we had avoided the curious and impassable gorge by which the Bhong-chu cuts through a high range of mountains.

It was only a little over 6 miles to the famous rope bridge at Gadompa. I could not help laughing when I first saw the bridge. It was such a comical, ramshackle-looking affair, and everything about it seemed torn and ragged and uneven. Two crooked wooden posts set up in piles of stones supported the ropes of raw hide which spanned the river. During the rainy season one of these posts and all the ropes had been buried deep under the water, but now that the river had dropped over 10 feet, the posts were out of the water. Between these two wooden posts were three raw hide ropes, very frail and much frayed, and looking as though they might break at any moment. On these ropes was laid a semi-circular piece of wood, like the framework of a saddle, to which were attached two leather thongs. The person or bale of goods that had to be pulled across was tied by these two thongs to the framework, and this was allowed to slide rapidly with its load down to the point at which the "bridge" sagged most—somewhere about the middle of the river—which here rushed along in a formidable rapid. If the Tibetans on the far side failed to pull up the passenger or load and he or it was left for a minute, either would certainly get the full benefit of one of the ice-cold waves of the rapids and get thoroughly soaked before reaching the far side. The Tibetans had great fun with our coolies in transit, and very few of them were allowed to get over dry. The villages on either side are exempt from the duty of producing transport, and have instead to make themselves responsible for working the bridge. On one side the operators were all women and on the other all men. It took an average of five minutes to get each load or person across, and we spent twelve hours before we got all our loads over. For part of the time I superintended while Wheeler went to get some dinner, and after dinner, owing to there being a certain amount of moonlight, Wheeler carried on until the last load was brought over at midnight. It was a very chilly proceeding, as the wind blew very cold, with a suspicion of snow every now and then. It was a weird experience to see the loads of baggage suddenly appearing out of the darkness and then being unloaded and transferred to the yaks, who apparently were able to find their way about in the dark. We got everything over in safety without losing anything except a few eggs, which I saw drop out during the passage across, and I felt very much relieved that we had had no accident.

That night we camped in a pleasant willow grove at the village of Kharkhung. In the morning we awoke to find fresh snow on the ground, but this speedily disappeared when the sun came out. Our new transport consisted of donkeys and some very wild yaks, which rapidly got rid of their loads. The march was only a short one of about 12 miles up the valley of the Bhong-chu. The valley was uninteresting and stony, with practically no undergrowth, and we eventually camped in a windy spot near the village of Lashar, nearly opposite to the sandy camp at Shiling where we had halted on our outward journey after crossing the quicksands. The night proved much colder here, with 18° of frost, but the wind luckily died down and the next morning was beautiful. We continued up the sandy valley of the Bhong-chu, which is here several miles wide, until we came to its junction with the Yaru, where we regained the route which we had followed on the outward journey. Just before leaving the main valley we found, on looking behind us, that we were in full sight of Mount Everest and its great South-eastern ridge, and also of the Lhakpa La where we had camped. This was our final view of Mount Everest, and knowing the geography of these peaks as we now did, this view gave us an added interest in them. We had climbed slowly and had not realised the great height which we had reached or the conspicuous position of our camp on the Lhakpa La which we now saw sharply defined against the horizon from a distance of 50 miles.

We rode up the gorge of the Yaru, and at the village of Rongme we met the Phari Jongpen's brother. He was busy collecting the harvest rents, which are a fixed percentage of the crops. I gave him some of the photographs that I had taken of him and his house on the way up and very soon after a big crowd collected around. The Tibetans are very quick at recognising persons in a photograph, and they at once picked out all the people by name in a group. I then rode on past his house to the village of Shatog, where we camped. On the way I shot a couple of snipe and also saw a number of teal, wild geese and kulan (grey crane), but they were very wild and I could not get near enough for a shot. Heron joined us here. He had been exploring some of the valleys to the North, but had found nothing interesting or remarkable, geologically, and he accompanied us back as far as Khamba Dzong. We were anxious to push on as fast as possible, and determined to do a double march from here to Tinki Dzong, which our transport drivers said they could do quite easily. We started on a beautiful day after a sharp frost at night, causing many of the ponds to be frozen over. We crossed the broad swampy plain to Chushar. Wheeler, going on ahead at first, had a shot at some geese, but did not succeed in getting anything. We crossed the Yaru River by a very deep ford, and then kept along the North side of it, past numerous ponds on which were swimming many bar-headed geese; these were, however, very wily and would not allow us to approach within shot. We now had a steep 3,000-foot climb to the Tinki Pass. On the way up I came across some partridges; they were terrible runners, but after a good chase I managed to collect two. They turned out to be the ordinary Tibetan partridge (*Perdrix hodgsoniæ*). I then rode on down to Tinki, to which place I had sent on Chheten Wangdi in order to make arrangements for our reception and to have transport ready for us on the following day. The two Jongpens rode out to meet us; the elder of the two had been at Tinki when we passed through on the way out, but the other one I had not seen before as he had been away. I had very pleasant recollections of our reception there before, and was delighted to see the elder Jongpen, who was a most pleasant and agreeable gentleman.

They presented us with a couple of hundred eggs, rice and some grain for the ponies, and had tents already pitched for us under the walls of the fort. Here the Jongpens came and sat talking with us for a long time. Our transport showed no signs of turning up, so we were very glad to make our dinner off the rice and eggs that had been given us. The bulk of the transport did not arrive till midnight. They had made every effort to stop at Chushar, and it was with great difficulty that Gyalzen Kazi had induced them to go on. The animal which was carrying Wheeler's kit died on the way, and his bedding did not arrive till noon the following day, another animal having been sent to bring it in. I had had my maximum and minimum thermometers exposed as usual under the fly of my tent, but during the night some wretch came and stole them. What good they could have been to him I cannot imagine, but it was very annoying and I hope he will drink the mercury. The weather had now changed again for the worse: all day there were heavy snow showers with snow falling on the mountains around and preventing any views. The march was only a short one to Lingga. The wild birds in the lake beside the fort were as tame as ever, the Brahminy ducks (ruddy sheldrake) almost waddling into our tents and not paying the slightest attention to us. On the water were swimming about thousands of duck, bar-headed geese and teal which the Jongpen's little dog used to have great fun in chasing. We were not able to follow our former route from Tinki to Lingga as the country had altered considerably. Most of the plain was now a broad lake several miles long, and we had to follow the North side of the water along the foot of the hills. On these big lakes were many duck, but they were very wild. I managed on the way, however, to shoot two bar-headed geese, a couple of Gargany teal and a pochard, which proved a very welcome addition to our bill of fare. One shot was a most extraordinary one. I was stalking some geese which were getting very restless and starting to fly away, when just in front of me got up two teal close together,

I fired at the teal and both fell to my shot, and at the same time, to my great surprise, a goose, which was in the direct line of fire, and about 40 yards away, also fell.

We found the people at Lingga busy thrashing. The thrashing time in Tibet is a favourite one for drinking, and often the whole village after a day's harvest will be completely incapacitated as the result of too great an indulgence in chang. Their thrashing floors consist of an area of about half an acre of hard beaten earth on which the barley is spread to a depth of 6 to 8 inches. Fifty or sixty yaks are then driven into this enclosure, followed by thirty people or more, beating drums, rattling kerosene oil tins, ringing bells and shouting and yelling in order to frighten the yaks, who, tail in air, are driven backwards and forwards over the barley. This they continue doing until every one is tired and hoarse, when the whole of the workers, both male and female, adjourn for a long drink of beer, after which the same process is repeated.

On October 11 we arrived at Khamba Dzong. We were having sharp frosts now every night, and the mountains, both to the North and South of us, were covered low down with a thick white coating of snow. It was not, however, unpleasantly cold, and the cloud effects were very beautiful. On the way I shot two goa—Tibetan gazelle—with good heads, and horns over 14 inches long. We had to halt here in order to rest our coolies. All day to the South there was a furious storm raging along the Himalayas, and when it cleared up in the evening there had evidently been a heavy snowfall. In the course of the afternoon we put up over Dr. Kellas's grave the stone which the Jongpen had had engraved for us during our absence. On it were inscribed in English and Tibetan characters his initials and the date of his death, and this marks his last resting-place.

Raeburn, Wheeler and Heron now left us, as they wanted to return to Darjeeling by the short way over the Serpo La and down the Teesta Valley. This route is only possible for small parties; with all our transport we were unable to return that way as the villages on the way and in the Teesta Valley are small and can supply but very few animals or coolies. Wollaston and I had therefore to return to Phari and then to follow the main trade route, along which it is always possible to pick up any amount of hired transport. We left Khamba Dzong on October 13 in 20° of frost. Kanchenjunga and the Everest group were just visible, but ominous clouds were rapidly coming up. Our march was the same as on the outward journey to Tatsang (Falcon's Nest)—a distance of about 21 miles. We rode through the fine limestone gorge behind the fort, shooting on the way several Tibetan partridge (*Perdrix hodgsoniœ*). On reaching the top of the pass, I climbed another thousand feet on to the ridge to the South of the pass, where I had a wonderful panorama of snowy peaks, both to the South and to the North. Snow storms appeared to be raging on either side and the wind was extremely cold. I came across a fine flock of burhel (*Ovis nahura*), and had an easy shot at a fine ram, but missed him hopelessly, and they never gave me another chance. A little further on I missed a gazelle. On the plain below were grazing numerous kiang (*Equus hemionus*), their reddish-chestnut coats being well shown off by their white bellies and legs. Their mane appears to be of a darker colour, which is continued as a narrow stripe down the back. On the same plain I cculd see also a large flock of nyan (*Ovis hodgsoni*), all fair-sized rams. I had a long chase after the latter, but they never allowed me to approach close to them. Snow began to fall now and a regular blizzard set in, the fine powdery snow being blown along the ground into our faces. While riding along in this storm, I saw two fine nyan which I stalked. My 2·75 rifle was rather small for such a large animal, and though the larger of the two was badly hit by the first shot, he went off as though he were untouched and gave me a long chase after him. It was only possible to get a glimpse of him every now and then in the blizzard, and whenever I lay down to try and get a shot, the fine powdery snow blown along the surface of the ground nearly blinded me, so that it took five more bullets before he finally expired. He was a magnificent old beast with a grand head and horns, well over 40 inches in length and of great thickness. The weight of the body was enormous. I had only Ang Tenze with me. With much difficulty we cut off the nyan's head and then tried to lift the carcass, which must have weighed well over 200 lb., on to one of the ponies. With the greatest trouble we eventually managed to get the carcass on to the pony's back, but the pony seemed gradually to subside on to the ground under the weight and was quite unable to move. While we were doing this, my pony took it into his head to run away, and though we made every attempt to catch him, he completely defeated us, and was last seen galloping away towards his home. I had therefore an 8 mile trudge through the snow to get back to camp, not arriving there till well after dark. Five of the coolies went back after dark to get the meat. They cut off as much as they could carry, and the remainder had to be left for the nuns, who sent out their servants to bring it in. I was cheered up, however, by getting an English mail and many letters. Among these was one from Sir Charles Bell from Lhasa, who wrote to ask the Expedition not to do any more shooting in Tibet, as the Tibetans did not approve of it; for the remainder of the time, therefore, the guns had to be put away.

During the night there were 32° of frost, and everything inside our tents was frozen solid in the morning; but the wind luckily died down, and the next day was a most beautiful one. We knew that there was a long march before us, so our transport was off by eight o'clock. At Tatsang we were already 16,000 feet, and we gradually climbed higher, spending most of the day between 17,000 and 18,000 feet. For several miles we rode across a snow-covered plain over which the tops of Pawhunri, Chomiomo, and Kanchenjhow appeared to the South. As we rose higher, the snow gradually deepened to 6 inches and made the going very heavy. We had to cross three spurs of Pawhunri by passes of over

17,500 feet. Here the snow had been blown by the wind into drifts over 2 feet deep. We had arranged to camp at a place called Lunghi, but on our arrival there found that the nomads, who ordinarily spent the summer there, had already left and were encamped some 4 miles further down the valley. In a side valley I found some of their tents where I was able to warm myself and get some hot milk before moving on down the valley, where we were told that preparations had been made to receive us. There was luckily a bright moon and we rode on down to the spot, where we found some Tibetan tents which had been pitched for us; their owners had, moreover, had the forethought to have great braziers of cow dung burning in these tents. The smell was not agreeable, but we sat and warmed ourselves, waiting for our transport, which did not arrive until eleven o'clock that night. It was a bitterly cold wait, as the wind got up and blew down the valley with 25° of frost behind it. We were very glad to see our transport and coolies when they arrived; they had really come along very well, as a march of 23 miles in soft snow and at a great height all the time is no light feat.

Breakfast the next morning was very comfortless, as the wind was still blowing with 28° of frost, and everything —boots and foodstuffs of all kinds—was frozen inside our tents. We looked forward with no little pleasure to finding ourselves inside once more and sitting in front of a fire out of the everlasting wind which makes Tibet so trying. The march was a fairly easy one of about 20 miles over gentle undulating country until we reached the West side of the Tang La; there was, however, a bitterly cold strong South wind which blew with great violence all day and penetrated through everything. Many of our coolies had much difficulty in coming along, as they were suffering from snow blindness and their feet were also very tender from the cold and the deep snow of the last few days. Chomolhari was a glorious sight all the way. We were gradually approaching it, and it seemed to rise directly from the plain in front of us. From its summit and from its ridges great streamers of snow were being blown off and the gale—apparently from the North-west—still continued. Nearly every day since we left Kharta we saw along the higher peaks of the Himalayas the snow being blown off in great wisps, showing that a strong North-westerly current of air sets in at great heights after the monsoon is over. After reaching Darjeeling we noticed the same thing; every day, from Kanchenjunga and Kabru, could be seen the same great wisps of wind-blown snow. That night at Phari we were once more in a bungalow and out of the wind, and able to spend a very comfortable and pleasant evening reading our letters and papers in front of a fire which, though still mostly yak dung, was in a fireplace. October 16 we spent resting at Phari. Our coolies were much exhausted by the three days' march from Khamba Dzong, in which we had covered 65 miles, most of the time at considerable heights and in deep snow. We had returned by the short way, which the people of Phari had told us in the spring was impassable, and over which they would not go, sending us instead around by the long way to Dochen, which took us six days instead of three.

Phari is a place unfortunately too near civilisation. The Tibetans there have lost their good manners, such as we had been accustomed to meet in the more distant and out-of-the-way parts of the country. Much trade passes through the town, and the people there are too well off. They had an idea that the Expedition was a kind of milch cow out of which money could be extracted to their hearts' content. Of this view we had to disabuse them, and in consequence found them all very tiresome. The transport turned up the following morning, but they refused to load up unless they were paid in full beforehand and at a most exorbitant rate. This I refused to do, telephoning at the same time to the trade agent at Yatung. I sent for the Jongpen, and both Jongpens turned up. I rather imagine that they were at the bottom of this trouble, for one of them owed the Expedition some money; he had also, when forwarding on stores to us, seized the opportunity to charge five times the ordinary rate, on the pretext that he had supplied some of his own mules. After long arguments I eventually induced them to accept part of the payment, the remainder to be paid at Yatung, whereupon the Jongpens gave orders for the animals to be loaded. It was not, however, until the afternoon that we were able to leave Phari and to start on our downward march to Yatung.

CHAPTER XI

BACK TO CIVILISATION

When we turned our backs on Phari and started to march down the Chumbi Valley, we had left the real Tibet behind us. I could not somehow look upon the Chumbi Valley as being a part of Tibet. Its characteristics, its houses, its people, its vegetation, are all so different from the greater part of Tibet. There are not the same cold winds that freeze the very marrow, nor are there the wide plains and the undulating hills with their extensive views.

In spite of all discomforts, there is a very great charm and fascination about travelling in Tibet. Is it partly because it is an unknown country, and the unknown is always fascinating, or is it rather because of the innate beauty of the country itself, with its landscapes so free from all restraint and a horizon often 150 to 200 miles distant? Never anywhere have I seen a country so full of colour as is Tibet. There is not enough vegetation to hide the rocks and the stones. The foreground as well as the distant view is wonderfully full of colour and variety. Contrasts are one of the charms of life, and probably in this lies the secret of the charm and attractiveness of Tibet. It is essentially a country of contrasts. The climate, above all, has contrasts of its own. The sun is burningly hot, but in the shade the cold may be intense. To such a pitch can the extremes of heat and cold arrive, that a man may suffer from sunstroke and frost-bite at one and the same time.

The Tibetans themselves are a strong, well-built and hardy race—Mongolian in type. The women usually put a mixture of grease and soot on their faces to protect them against the glare of the fresh snow or the biting winds, for even they, with their thick skins, do not seem to get used to the severity of the changes. How much more does the European suffer when he travels in Tibet and seems to need a fresh skin almost every day. The soot mixture does not add to the beauty of the women, though I came across some who were not bad looking. Many of the people are nomads, living in tents all the year round and moving about from camp to camp pasturing their herds of yaks and their flocks of sheep. It is curious that even in the winter-time they can find grazing places, but the secret lies in the fact that the slopes face the South in the regions where the wind blows strongest, so that the surface is usually bare. The snowfall in winter in most parts of Tibet is not heavy, and the climate being so dry, the snow is powdery, and the wind blows it along and forms great drifts in the hollows, leaving the exposed slopes usually clear. On these the herds, or flocks of sheep, obtain sufficient nourishment from such scattered patches of frozen grass or lichens as they are able to find. Of all the animals that the Tibetans have, the yak is the most useful. His long black hair, which reaches to the ground under his belly, is woven into tents or ropes. The milk, after they have drunk what they want, is turned into butter and cheese, of which they produce great quantities. When old, he is killed and his flesh is dried, providing meat for a long time. His hide supplies leather of every kind. It is always used untanned, for no tanning is ever done in Tibet and any tanned skins always come up from India. The yak dung is in many places the only fuel to be got and is most carefully picked up. To the present generation of young children the yak is probably familiar from that delightful rhyme in "The Bad Child's Book of Beasts":—

> As a friend to the children, commend me the Yak—
> You will find it exactly the thing;
> It will carry and fetch, you can ride on its back
> Or lead it about with a string.

The Tartar who dwells on the plains of Tibet,
  A desolate region of snow,
Has for centuries made it a nursery pet,
  And surely the Tartar should know.

Then tell your papa where the Yak can be got,
  And if he is awfully rich,
He will buy you the creature—or else he will not;
  I cannot be positive which.

The traveller in Tibet can easily live on such supplies as can be drawn from the country. The Tibetan is always hospitable and will provide sheep, milk, cheese and butter almost everywhere. Vegetables, however, of any kind are very scarce, though in the summer a species of spinach can be got in some places. Living, as the Tibetans do, far away from all outside influences, their customs and manners have not changed, and are the same as they were several hundred years ago. I can fully sympathise with their present desire for seclusion and their eagerness not to be exploited by foreigners. They sent a few years ago some young Tibetan boys to Rugby to be educated in different professions. These boys have now returned again to Lhasa, and with their aid, and with the aid of others who are being sent out into the world to learn, they hope to be able to develop the resources of their own country at leisure, in their own way, and by themselves, without being exploited commercially by foreigners.

The staple food of the Tibetans is tsampa (parched barley). This is ground up and either milk or tea is added, forming it into a kind of dough. This is put in a little bag, which they carry about with them when travelling, and is often their only food for several days. Tsampa can be obtained everywhere in Tibet, though it is easier to get it in the villages than from the tents of the nomads. Tea can, of course, be obtained everywhere, and, as I have described before, is mixed with salt and butter, churned up with great violence, and then poured into teapots. At every camp, and at every house, will be met fierce dogs.

These dogs guard the flocks, or the nomad camps, and rather resemble large collies; as a rule, they are black and very fierce. The Tibetans were, however, always very good in tying them up before we approached their camps. In many of the houses we found tied up just outside the door another kind of dog, a huge brute of the mastiff type, always extremely savage and ready, if he had not been tied up, to tear the intruder to pieces. The peasants are still treated as serfs, though only in a mild form. For all Government officials, when on tour, they have to supply free transport and supplies of all kinds, so that official visits are not popular. At first the villagers were afraid that we might follow the example of the Tibetan officials and were much relieved to find that we did not do so.

I cannot leave the subject of Tibet without a few words about the monasteries. These are divided into two great schools, the Red Cap School and the Yellow Cap School. The former was founded by the Buddhist Saint, Padma Sambhava or Guru Rimpoche, in A.D. 749. They are the older of the two monastic sects, but their morals are much looser than those of the Yellow Sect, and the Lamas or monks of this sect are often married. In one monastery belonging to the Red Sect near Kharta, the Lamas and their wives were all living together. The Yellow Cap, or Gelukpa Sect, was founded in the fifteenth century by Tsong Kapa, who instituted a very much stricter moral code, and this sect looks down very much upon the Red Caps. The State religion of the country is Buddhism. By the middle of the seventeenth century, after a series of reincarnations, Nawang Lobsang had made himself master of Tibet and transferred his capital to Lhasa. He accepted the title of Dalai Lama (Ocean of Learning) from the Chinese, hence the Dalai Lama at Lhasa, by this doctrine of political reincarnation, has absorbed all the political power in the country into his own hands, although the Tashi Lama at Tashilumpo is in theory his senior and superior in spiritual matters. The old simple creed of the Buddhists can scarcely be recognised nowadays and is overlaid with devil worship in all its forms, supernatural agencies abounding everywhere. The top of a pass, a mountain, a river, a bridge, a storm; each will have its own particular god who is to be worshipped and propitiated. In many of the larger monasteries, too, they have oracles who are consulted far and wide and supposed to be able to foretell the future. These often acquire considerable power and influence by methods not unlike those resorted to in ancient Greece. It has been estimated that a fifth of the whole population of Tibet has entered monastic life. The conditions probably much resemble those which prevailed in mediæval Europe. The monasteries contain nearly all the riches of the country. They own large estates; they are the source of all learning, and all the arts and crafts seem to take their inspiration from articles for use in the monasteries. The ordinary Tibetan, surrounded as he is by the various spirits which occupy every valley and mountain top, is very superstitious. He therefore has inside his house his prayer wheel and his little shrine, before which he offers up incense daily. His Mani walls or mendongs, covered with inscribed stones or carved figures of Buddha, are alongside the paths he daily uses; on the top of the mountains or passes, in addition to these prayer-covered stones, flutter rags printed over with prayers. All these are intended to propitiate the evil spirits. In places where there are particularly malignant devils, it may be necessary to build several Chortens in order to keep them in subjection, and these Chortens are filled with several thousands of prayers and sacred figures stamped in the clay.

The country is divided up into districts, each under its own Jongpen, who is responsible direct to Lhasa or Shigatse and has yearly to send the revenue collected to headquarters. A certain percentage of the crops is collected every year, and in a year of good harvest the Jongpen is able to make a certain amount of money for himself in addition to what he has to send to Lhasa. Our visit to the Kharta Valley was an unexpected windfall for the Kharta Jongpen, as I fancy that much of the money that we paid out to the different villages for supplies or coolie hire eventually found its way into his pocket and was not likely to find its way to Lhasa. This may possibly have accounted for his pleasure in entertaining us and his desire to keep us there as long as possible. The Tibetans, however, everywhere have good manners and are invariably most polite—a pleasant characteristic. Although they are all Buddhists, and accordingly object to the taking of life, they do not in the least mind killing their sheep or their yaks for food, but they objected to our shooting wild sheep or gazelles or wild birds for food. I could have understood this objection better had they been vegetarians and not killed their sheep for eating purposes, but a real vegetarian, except in the strictest monasteries, is very rare in Tibet.

There was a great fascination in roaming through the country as we did. It was the fascination of the unknown, this travelling in regions where Europeans had never travelled before, and where they had never even been seen. The people had exaggerated notions of our ferocity, and were full of fears as to what we might be like and as to what we might do. In these out-of-the-way parts they had heard vaguely of the fighting in 1904, and they imagined that our visit might be on the same lines. They imagined, too, that all Europeans were cruel and seized what they wanted without payment. They were therefore much surprised when they found that we treated them fairly and paid for everything that we wanted at very good rates. The Expedition may, I venture to think, take credit to itself for having certainly done a great deal of good in promoting more friendly relations between the Tibetans and ourselves, and in giving them a better understanding of what an Englishman is. Their ignorance of the outside world was at times astounding. Tibetan officials and traders were an exception, but it was seldom that the ordinary Tibetan ever left the valley in which he was born and bred, with the result that except for the wildest rumours, they knew nothing of the outside world. For long-distance journeys, the Tibetans used ambling mules or ponies, which were capable of going long distances and keeping up a speed of about 5 miles an hour. To our idea, the Tibetan saddle with its high wooden framework is very uncomfortable, but on the top of their saddles they would put their bedding, spreading over it a brilliant and often beautifully coloured carpet as a saddle cloth. On the top of this the rider would sit perched, and, with a good ambling pony, could get along very comfortably.

I always enjoyed travelling and moving about in Tibet. It hardly has the climate of Tennyson's Island Valley of Avilion—" Where falls not hail or rain or snow, nor ever wind blows loudly"—for we used to get samples of nearly all of these almost every day. But no matter how barren nor how bare the immediate surroundings were there was a sense of exhilaration and freedom in the air. There was never a sense of being confined in a narrow space. There was always some distant view where the colours would be continually changing. In the summer-time the climate was not unpleasant, and there was always the pleasure of finding some new and beautiful flower, oftentimes springing up out of the driest sand. Wherever there was water, there was sure to be vegetation and many bright-coloured flowers with every kind of wild-bird life. The shrill whistle of the marmot would often alone break the silence of the scene. Animal life in some form was almost always visible, whether it was the wild kiang roaming on the plains, or the gazelle, or the wild sheep, there was always something of interest to watch. The little mouse hares which lived in great colonies would constantly dodge in and out of their holes and the song of the larks could always be heard.

By the end of October the climate was beginning to get very cold, the thermometer descending at times to Zero Fahrenheit, so that we were quite ready to leave the country, being anxious to get warm again, if only for a short time. There was sorrow in our hearts, however, at parting with the friendly and hospitable folk whom we had encountered, and at leaving behind us the familiar landscapes with the transparent pale blue atmosphere that is so hard to describe, and the distant views of range upon range of snowy mountains often reflected in the calm waters of some blue coloured lake. The attractions of Tibet may yet be strong enough to draw us back again once more. Many years ago the same attraction impelled me to cross the Himalayan mountains and to visit another part of Tibet, but my excursion was, I am afraid, not favourably regarded by the Indian Government and my leave was stopped for six months. The same attraction, however, still exists for this land of many colours with its lonely sunsets full of beauty, with its nights where the eager stars gleam bright as diamonds, and where the full moon shines upon the nameless mountains covered with snow and still as death.

As we turned our backs upon the country we left winter behind us, and descending the Chumbi Valley once more found ourselves in autumnal surroundings. The Himalayan larch were all of a beautiful golden colour; the birch were all turning brown, and the berberis were a brilliant scarlet. Red currants and the scarlet haws of the rose were still on the bushes. The currants were no longer sour to eat raw, and we picked many of them on the way down. Our pockets, too, were filled with seeds of rhododendrons and other flowers. On the way I was met by the native officer commanding the garrison at Yatung, which was now found by the 90th Punjabis. As I passed their quarters, the guard turned out, presenting arms very smartly, and all the detachment came out and saluted. They were certainly a very well-trained detachment. Once more the Macdonald family most kindly sent over a generous meal, besides presents of every sort and kind of European vegetable. From Yatung we obtained forty-five mules for our transport. These came along very much faster than the yaks and the donkeys that we had been using. Here Gyalzen Kazi, one of our interpreters, left us to return to his home at Gangtok. I was very sorry to lose him. He had been a pleasant companion and had been of great assistance to the Expedition. He was always most willing to undertake any difficult or unpleasant job there might be, and I never heard a murmur or grumble from him of any kind during the whole time that he was with us. Our march was only a short one of 11 miles to Langra, where there was a Tibetan rest-house built in the Chinese style and rather reminding me of our rest-house at Tingri. It was a most perfect autumnal day, with scarcely a cloud in the sky. The woods everywhere were very beautiful, the dark silver fir trees showing up the scarlet and yellow of the bushes and the gold of the larch. Our cook, Acchu, was drunk again, but Poo prepared us a good meal instead. The next morning, to our surprise, on looking out we found a couple of inches of fresh snow on the ground and the snow was still falling steadily. The mules, nevertheless, were all loaded up in good time, and I followed on foot to the top of the Jelep Pass, snow falling steadily all the way—a fine granular snow. At the top of the pass the wind was blowing keenly, driving the snow into our faces. Besides the 6 inches of fresh snow here, there was a good deal of the old snow that had fallen a week or more ago, and in some places formed drifts several feet deep. It is seldom that a clear view is ever obtained on the Jelep Pass. It rained when we came over in May and it snowed now, and twice before, when I have crossed it, it rained all the time. Snow fell all the way down to Gnatong, where there were already a couple of inches of slush. The next morning was luckily fine, as we were to do a long march to Rongli—a distance of only 18 miles, but with a descent of 9,500 feet. The first few miles we walked through the fresh snow, but in the afternoon we were wandering among the sweet scents of a tropical jungle with orchids still flowering on the trees and ripe oranges in the garden of our bungalow. We had jumped from winter to summer in a few hours. The Tibetan mules came along excellently, doing the march in just over eight

MEMBERS OF THE EXPEDITION.

Standing: WOLLASTON. HOWARD-BURY. HERON. RAEBURN.
Sitting: MALLORY. WHEELER. BULLOCK. MORSHEAD.

hours, a very different proceeding to our Government mules on the way up, which we were compelled to discard at Sedongchen. We reached Darjeeling on October 25. Lord Ronaldshay was unfortunately away on tour on his way to Bhutan, and as he had travelled via Gangtok, we had missed seeing him on the way. The next few days we spent in getting rid of the remainder of our stores, selling anything perishable that we could, getting tents dried and mended, and storing everything else in view of a second Expedition. We here said good-bye to our other interpreter, Chheten Wangdi, who had served us most faithfully throughout the Expedition, and it was with the greatest regret that we took leave of him on the railway station at Darjeeling.

Our Expedition had accomplished all that it had set out to do. All the approaches to Mount Everest from the North-west, North, North-east and East had been carefully reconnoitred and a possible route to the top had been found up the North-east ridge. Climatic conditions alone had prevented a much greater height being attained. Friendly relations had been established with the Tibetan officials and people wherever we went. Our travels had taken us through much unexplored and new country wherein we had discovered some magnificent and undreamt-of valleys where primeval forests existed such as we had never imagined to find in Tibet and where deep filled glens with the richest semi-tropical vegetation descended as low as 7,000 feet. Many beautiful flowers were discovered in these Alpine valleys, and we were able to collect a quantity of seeds from these which I hope may help to enrich and to beautify our gardens at home. A new part of the country has been opened up to human knowledge. It has been photographed and described. The surveyors have made an original survey at a scale of 4 miles to the inch of an area of some 12,000 square miles; a detailed photographic survey of 600 square miles of the environs of Mount Everest has been worked out, and, besides this, the maps of another 4,000 square miles of country have been revised. Dr. Heron, our indefatigable geologist, himself travelled over the greater part of this area, and has carefully investigated the geology of the whole region. That the Expedition was able to accomplish so much in such a short time was due to the hearty co-operation and keenness of all the members of the party. We were a happy family and, to use a rowing expression, we all "pulled together." Such success as we attained is entirely due to their strenuous and ceaseless efforts, and I can only express my gratitude to them for the unselfish way in which they helped and assisted me on every occasion.

The Expedition of 1921 is over; many problems have been solved, much new country has been brought within our ken, and many new beauties have been revealed, but the soul of man is never content with what has been attained. The solution of one problem only brings forward fresh problems to be solved, so this Expedition into unknown country brings within the realms of possibility further travels and further problems to be solved. There is much that yet remains to be done, much that remains to be discovered; and though we may not be privileged to discover a new race of hairy snow men, yet there is a wild and uncharted country full of beauty and interest that awaits those who dare face the discomfort and hardships of travelling in Tibet —discomforts which are soon forgotten and leave behind them only the memories of very wonderful scenes and places which the passing of time can never efface.

Let us probe the silent places, let us seek what luck betide us,
  Let us journey to a lonely land I know;
There's a whisper in the night wind, there's a star, a gleam to guide us,
  And the wild is calling, calling, let us go.

R. W. S.

THE RECONNAISSANCE OF THE MOUNTAIN

By

GEORGE H. LEIGH-MALLORY

CHAPTER XII

THE NORTHERN APPROACH

As a matter of history it has been stated already in an earlier chapter of this book that the highest mountain in the world attracted attention so early as 1850. When we started our travels in 1921, something was already known about it from a surveyor's point of view; it was a triangulated peak with a position on the map; but from the mountaineer's point of view almost nothing was known. Mount Everest had been seen and photographed from various points on the Singalila ridge as well as from Kampa Dzong; from these photographs it may dimly be made out that snow lies on the upper part of the Eastern face at no very steep angle, while the arête bounding this face on the North comes down gently for a considerable distance. But the whole angle subtended at the great summit by the distance between the two of these view-points which are farthest apart is only 54°. The North-west sides of the mountain had never been photographed and nothing was known of its lower parts anywhere. Perhaps the distant view most valuable to a mountaineer is that from Sandakphu, because it suggests gigantic precipices on the South side of the mountain so that he need have no regrets that access is barred in that direction for political reasons.

The present reconnaissance began at Kampa Dzong, no less than 100 miles away, and in consequence of misfortunes which the reader will not have forgotten was necessarily entrusted to Mr. G. H. Bullock and myself, the only representatives of the Alpine Club now remaining in the Expedition. It may seem an irony of fate that actually on the day after the distressing event of Dr. Kellas' death we experienced the strange elation of seeing Everest for the first time. It was a perfect early morning as we plodded up the barren slopes above our camp and rising behind the old rugged fort which is itself a singularly impressive and dramatic spectacle; we had mounted perhaps a thousand feet when we stayed and turned, and saw what we came to see. There was no mistaking the two great peaks in the West: that to the left must be Makalu, grey, severe and yet distinctly graceful, and the other away to the right—who could doubt its identity? It was a prodigious white fang excrescent from the jaw of the world. We saw Mount Everest not quite sharply defined on account of a slight haze in that direction; this circumstance added a touch of mystery and grandeur; we were satisfied that the highest of mountains would not disappoint us. And we learned one fact of great importance: the lower parts of the mountain were hidden by the range of nearer mountains clearly shown in the map running North from the Nila La and now called the Gyanka Range, but it was possible to distinguish all that showed near Everest beyond them by a difference in tone, and we were certain that one great rocky peak appearing a little way to the left of Everest must belong to its near vicinity.

It was inevitable, as we proceeded to the West from Kampa Dzong, that we should lose sight of Mount Everest; after a few miles even its tip was obscured by the Gyanka Range, and we naturally began to wonder whether it would not be possible to ascend one of these nearer peaks which must surely give us a wonderful view. I had hopes that we should be crossing the range by a high pass, in which case it would be a simple matter to ascend some eminence near it. But at Tinki we learned that our route would lie in the gorge to the North of the mountains where the river Yaru cuts its way through from the East to join the Arun.

From Gyanka Nangpa, which lies under a rocky summit over 20,000 feet high, Bullock and I, on June 11, made an early start and proceeded down the gorge. It was a perfect morning and for once we had tolerably swift animals to ride; we were fortunate in choosing the right place to ford the river and our spirits were high. How could they be otherwise? Ever since we had lost sight of Everest the Gyanka Mountains had been our ultimate horizon to the West. Day by day as we had approached them our thoughts had concentrated more and more upon what lay beyond. On the far side was a new country. Now the great Arun River was to divulge its secrets and we should see Everest again after nearly halving the distance. The nature of the gorge was such that our curiosity could not be satisfied until the last moment. After crossing the stream we followed the flat margin of its right bank until the cliffs converging to the exit were towering above us. Then in a minute we were out on the edge of a wide sandy basin stretching away with complex undulations to further hills. Sand and barren hills as before—but with a difference; for we saw the long Arun Valley proceeding Southwards to cut through the Himalayas and its western arm which we should have to follow to Tingri; and there were marks of more ancient river beds and strange inland lakes. It was a desolate scene, I suppose; no flowers were to be seen nor any sign of life beyond some stunted gorse bushes on a near hillside and a few patches of coarse brown grass, and the only habitations were dry inhuman ruins; but whatever else was dead, our interest was alive.

After a brief halt a little way out in the plain, to take our bearings and speculate where the great mountains should appear, we made our way up a steep hill to a rocky crest overlooking the gorge. The only visible snow mountains were in Sikkim. Kanchenjunga was clear and eminent; we had never seen it so fine before; it now seemed singularly strong and monumental, like the leonine face of some splendid musician with a glory of white hair. In the direction of Everest no snow mountain appeared. We saw the long base tongues descending into the Arun Valley from the

Gyanka Range, above them in the middle distance an amazingly sharp rock summit and below a blue depth most unlike Tibet as we had known it hitherto. A conical hill stood sentinel at the far end of the valley, and in the distance was a bank of clouds.

Our attention was engaged by the remarkable spike of rock, a proper aiguille. As we were observing it a rift opened in the clouds behind; at first we had merely a fleeting glimpse of some mountain evidently much more distant, then a larger and clearer view revealed a recognizable form; it was Makalu appearing just where it should be according to our calculations with map and compass.

We were now able to make out almost exactly where Everest should be; but the clouds were dark in that direction. We gazed at them intently through field glasses as though by some miracle we might pierce the veil. Presently the miracle happened. We caught the gleam of snow behind the grey mists. A whole group of mountains began to appear in gigantic fragments. Mountain shapes are often fantastic seen through a mist; these were like the wildest creation of a dream. A preposterous triangular lump rose out of the depths; its edge came leaping up at an angle of about 70° and ended nowhere. To the left a black serrated crest was hanging in the sky incredibly. Gradually, very gradually, we saw the great mountain sides and glaciers and arêtes, now one fragment and now another through the floating rifts, until far higher in the sky than imagination had dared to suggest the white summit of Everest appeared. And in this series of partial glimpses we had seen a whole; we were able to piece together the fragments, to interpret the dream. However much might remain to be understood, the centre had a clear meaning as one mountain shape, the shape of Everest.

It is hardly possible of course from a distance of 57 miles to formulate an accurate idea of a mountain's shape. But some of its most remarkable features may be distinguished for what they are. We were looking at Everest from about

North-east and evidently a long arête was thrust out towards us. Some little distance below the summit the arête came down to a black shoulder, which we conjectured would be an insuperable obstacle. To the right of this we saw the sky line in profile and judged it not impossibly steep. The edge was probably a true arête because it appeared to be joined by a col to a sharp peak to the North. From the direction of this col a valley came down to the East and evidently drained into the Arun. This was one fact of supreme importance which was now established and we noticed that it agreed with what was shown on the map; the map in fact went up in our esteem and we were inclined hereafter to believe in its veracity until we established the contrary. Another fact was even more remarkable. We knew something more about the great peak near Everest which we had seen from Kampa Dzong; we knew now that it was not a separate mountain; in a sense it was part of Everest, or rather Everest was not one mountain but two; this great black mountain to the South was connected with Everest by a continuous arête and divided from it only by a snow col which must itself be at least 27,000 feet high. The black cliffs of this mountain, which faced us, were continuous with the icy East face of Everest itself.

A bank of cloud still lay across the face of the mountain when Bullock and I left the crest where we were established. It was late in the afternoon. We had looked down into the gorge and watched our little donkeys crossing the stream. Now we proceeded to follow their tracks across the plain. The wind was fiercely blowing up the sand and swept it away to leeward, transforming the dead flat surface into a wriggling sea of watered silk. The party were all sheltering in their tents when we rejoined them. Our camp was situated on a grassy bank below which by some miracle a spring wells out from the sand. We also sought shelter. But a short while after sunset the wind subsided. We all came forth and proceeded to a little eminence near at hand; and as we looked down the valley there was Everest calm in the stillness of evening and clear in the last light.

I have dwelt upon this episode at some length partly because in all our travels before we reached the mountain it is for me beyond other adventures unforgettable; and not less because the vision of Everest inhabiting our minds after this day had no small influence upon our deductions when we came to close quarters with the mountain. We made other opportunities before reaching Tingri to ascend likely hills for what we could see; notably from Shekar Dzong we made a divergence from the line of march and from a hill above Ponglet, on a morning of cloudless sunrise, saw the whole group of mountains of which Everest is the centre. But no view was so instructive as that above Shiling and we added little to the knowledge gained that day.

On June 23, after a day's interval to arrange stores, the climbing party set forth from Tingri Dzong. We were two Sahibs, sixteen coolies, a Sirdar, Gyalzen and a cook Dukpa. The process of selecting the coolies had been begun some time before this; the long task of nailing their boots had been nearly completed on the march and we were now confident that sixteen of the best Sherpas with their climbing boots, ice axes and each a suit of underwear would serve us well. The Sirdar through whom coolies had been engaged in the first instance seemed to understand what was wanted and to have sufficient authority, and Dukpa, though we could not expect from him any culinary refinements, had shown himself a person of some energy and competence who should do much to reduce the discomforts of life in camp. Our equipment was seriously deficient in one respect: we were short of words. A few hours spent in Darjeeling with a Grammar of Tibetan had easily convinced me that I should profit little in the short time available by the study of that language. It had been assumed by both Bullock and myself that our experienced leaders would give the necessary orders for organisation in any dialect that might be required we had found little opportunity since losing them to learn a language, and our one hope of conversing with the Sirdar was a vocabulary of about 150 words which I had written down in a notebook to be committed to memory on the march and consulted when occasion should arise.

The task before us was not likely to prove a simple and straightforward matter, and we had no expectation that it would be quickly concluded. It would be necessary in the first place to find the mountain; as we looked across the wide plains from Tingri and saw the dark monsoon clouds gathered in all directions we were not reassured. And there would be more than one approach to be found. We should have to explore a number of valleys radiating from Everest and separated by high ridges which would make lateral communication extremely difficult; we must learn from which direction various parts of the mountain could most conveniently be reached. And beyond all investigation of the approaches we should have to scrutinise Mount Everest itself. Our reconnaissance must aim at a complete knowledge of the various faces and arêtes, a correct understanding of the whole form and structure of the mountain and the distribution of its various parts; we must distinguish the vulnerable places in its armour and finally pit our skill against the obstacles wherever an opportunity of ascent should appear until all such opportunities were exhausted. The whole magnitude of the enterprise was very present in our minds as we left Tingri. We decided that a preliminary reconnaissance should include the first two aims of finding the approaches to Mount Everest and determining its shape, while anything in the nature of an assault should be left to the last as a separate stage of organisation and effort. In the result we may claim to have kept these ends in view without allowing the less important to prey upon the greater. So long as a doubt remained as to the way we should choose we made no attempt to climb the peak; we required ourselves first to find out as much as possible by more distant observations.

Mount Everest, as it turned out, did not prove difficult to find. Almost in the direct line from Tingri are two great peaks respectively 26,870 and 25,990 feet high—known to the Survey of India as M_1 and M_2 and to Tibetans as Cho-Uyo and Gyachung Kang. They lie about W.N.W. of Everest. We had to decide whether we should pass to the South of them, leaving them on our left, or to the North. In the first case we surmised that we might find ourselves to the South of a western arête of Everest, and possibly in Nepal, which was out of bounds. The arête, if it existed, might perhaps be reached from the North and give us the view we should require of the South-western side, in which case one base would serve us for a large area of investigation and we should economise time that would otherwise be spent in moving our camp round from one side to another. Consequently we chose the Northern approach. We learned from local knowledge that in two days we might reach a village and monastery called Chöbuk, and from there could follow a long valley to Everest. And so it proved. Chöbuk was not reached without some difficulty, but this was occasioned not by obstacles in the country but by the manners of Tibetans. At Tingri we had hired four pack animals. We had proceeded 2 or 3 miles across the plain when we perceived they were heading in the wrong direction. We were trusting to the guidance of their local drivers and felt very uncertain as to where exactly we should be aiming; but their line was about 60° to the South of our objective according to a guesswork compass bearing. An almost interminable three-cornered argument followed. It appeared that our guides intended to take five days to Chöbuk. They knew all about "ca' canny." In the end we decided to take the risk of a separation; Gyalzen went with the bullocks and our tents to change transport at the village where we were intended to stay the night, while the rest of us made a bee line for a bridge where we should have to cross the Rongbuk stream. At the foot of a vast moraine we waited on the edge of the "maidan," anxiously hoping that we should see some sign of fresh animals approaching; and at length we saw them. It was a late camp that evening on a strip of meadow beside the stream, but we had the comfort of reflecting that we had foiled the natives, whose aim was to retard our progress; and in the sequel we reached our destination with no further trouble.

On June 25 we crossed the stream at Chöbuk. Tibetan bridges are so constructed as to offer the passenger ample opportunities of experiencing the sensation of insecurity and contemplating the possibilities of disaster. This one was no exception. We had no wish to risk our stores, and it was planned that the beasts should swim. They were accordingly unladen and driven with yell and blow by a willing crowd, until one more frightened than the rest plunged into the torrent and the others followed. We now found ourselves on the right bank of the Rongbuk stream, and knew we had but to follow it up to reach the glacier at the head of the valley. An hour or so above Chöbuk we entered a gorge with high red cliffs above us on the left. Below them was a little space of fertile ground where the moisture draining down from the limestone above was caught before it reached the stream—a green ribbon stretched along the margin with grass and low bushes, yellow-flowering asters, rhododendrons and juniper. I think we had never seen anything so green since we came up on to the tableland of Tibet. It was a day of brilliant sunshine, as yet warm and windless. The memory of Alpine meadows came into my mind. I remembered their manifold allurements; I could almost smell the scent of pines. Now I was filled with the desire to lie here in this "oasis" and live at ease and sniff the clean fragrance of mountain plants. But we went on, on and up the long valley winding across a broad stony bay; and all the stony hillsides under the midday sun were alike monotonously dreary. At length we followed the path up a steeper rise crowned by two chortens between which it passes. We paused here in sheer astonishment. Perhaps we had half expected to see Mount Everest at this moment. In the back of my mind were a host of questions about it clamouring for answer. But the sight of it now banished every thought. We forgot the stony wastes and regrets for other beauties. We asked no questions and made no comment, but simply looked.

It is perhaps because Everest presented itself so dramatically on this occasion that I find the Northern aspect more particularly imaged in my mind, when I recall the mountain. But in any case this aspect has a special significance. The Rongbuk Valley is well constructed to show off the peak at its head; for about 20 miles it is extraordinarily straight and in that distance rises only 4,000 feet, the glacier, which is 10 miles long, no more steeply than the rest. In consequence of this arrangement one has only to be raised very slightly above the bed of the valley to see it almost as a flat way up to the very head of the glacier from which the cliffs of Everest spring. To the place where Everest stands one looks along rather than up. The glacier is prostrate; not a part of the mountain; not even a pediment; merely a floor footing the high walls. At the end of the valley and above the glacier Everest rises not so much a peak as a prodigious mountain-mass. There is no complication for the eye. The highest of the world's great mountains, it seems, has to make but a single gesture of magnificence to be lord of all, vast in unchallenged and isolated supremacy. To the discerning eye other mountains are visible, giants between 23,000 and 26,000 feet high. Not one of their slenderer heads even reaches their chief's shoulder; beside Everest they escape notice—such is the pre-eminence of the greatest.

Considered as a structure Mount Everest is seen from the Rongbuk Valley to achieve height with amazing simplicity. The steep wall 10,000 feet high is contained between two colossal members—to the left the North-eastern arête, which leaves the summit at a gentle angle and in a distance of about half a mile descends only 1,000 feet before turning more sharply downwards from a clearly defined shoulder; and to the right the North-west arête (its true direction is about W.N.W.), which comes down steeply from the summit but makes up for the weaker nature of this support by immense length below. Such is the broad plan. In one respect it is modified. The wide angle between the two main arêtes involves perhaps too long a face; a further support is added. The Northern face is brought out a little below the North-east shoulder and then turned back to meet the crest again, so that from the point of the shoulder a broad arête leads down to the North and is connected by a snow col at about 23,000 feet with a Northern wing of mountains which forms the right bank of the Rongbuk Glacier and to some extent masks the view of the lower parts of Everest. Nothing could be stronger than this arrangement and it is nowhere fantastic. We do not see jagged crests and a multitude of pinnacles, and beautiful as such ornament may be we do not miss it. The outline is comparatively smooth because the stratification is horizontal, a circumstance which seems again to give strength, emphasising the broad foundations. And yet Everest is a rugged giant. It has not the smooth undulations of a snow mountain with white snow cap and glaciated flanks. It is rather a great rock mass, coated often with a thin layer of white powder which is blown about its sides, and bearing perennial snow only on the gentler ledges and on several wide faces less steep than the rest. One such place is the long arm of the North-west arête which with its slightly articulated buttresses is like the nave of a vast cathedral roofed with snow. I was, in fact, reminded often by this Northern view of Winchester Cathedral with its long high nave and low square tower; it is only at a considerable distance that one appreciates the great height of this building and the strength which seems capable of supporting a far taller tower. Similarly with Everest; the summit lies back so far along the immense arêtes that big as it always appears one required a distant view to realise its height; and it has no spire though it might easily bear one; I have thought sometimes that a Matterhorn might be piled on the top of Everest and the gigantic structure would support the added weight in stable equanimity.

On June 26 we pitched our tents in full view of Everest and a little way beyond the large monastery of Chöyling which provides the habitations nearest to the mountain, about 16 miles away. After three days' march from the Expedition's headquarters at Tingri we had found the object of our quest and established a base in the Rongbuk Valley, which was to serve us for a month.

The first steps in a prolonged reconnaissance such as we were proposing to undertake were easily determined by topographical circumstances. Neither Bullock nor I was previously acquainted with any big mountains outside the Alps; to our experience in the Alps we had continually to refer, both for understanding this country and for estimating the efforts required to reach a given point in it. The Alps provided a standard of comparison which alone could be our guide until we had acquired some fresh knowledge in the new surroundings. No feature of what we saw so immediately challenged this comparison as the glacier ahead of us; in so narrow a glacier it was hardly surprising that the lower part of it should be covered with stones, but higher the whole surface was white ice, and the white ice came down in a broad stream tapering gradually to a point when it was lost in the waste of the brown grey. What was the meaning of this? Even from a distance it was possible to make out that the white stream contained pinnacles of ice. Was it all composed of pinnacles? Would they prove an insuperable obstacle? In the Alps the main glaciers are most usually highways, the ways offered to the climber for his travelling. Were they not to prove highways here?

Our first expedition was designed to satisfy our curiosity on this head. Allowing a bountiful margin of time for untoward contingencies we set forth on June 27 with five coolies at 3.15 a.m., and made our way up the valley with a good moon to help us. To be tramping under the stars toward a great mountain is always an adventure; now we were adventuring for the first time in a new mountain country which still held in store for us all its surprises and almost all its beauties. It was not our plan at present to make any allowance for the special condition of elevation; we expected to learn how that condition would tell and how to make allowances for the future. We started from our camp at 16,000 feet—above the summit of Mont Blanc—just as we should have left an Alpine hut 6,000 feet lower, and when we took our first serious halt at 7 a.m. had already crossed the narrow end of the glacier. That short experience—an hour or so—was sufficient for the moment. The hummocks of ice covered with stones of all sizes—like the huge waves of a brown angry sea—gave us no chance of ascending the glacier; one might hopefully follow a trough for a little distance but invariably to be stopped by the necessity of mounting once more to a crest and descending again on the other side. Nevertheless, we were not dissatisfied with our progress. We were now in a stream bed between the glacier and its left bank and above the exit of the main glacier stream, which comes out on this side well above the snout. The watercourse offered an opportunity of progress; it was dry almost everywhere and for a bout of leaping from boulder to boulder we were usually rewarded by a space of milder walking on the flat sandy bed. Our pace I considered entirely satisfactory as we went on after breakfast; unconsciously I was led into something like a race by one of the coolies who was pressing along at my side. I noticed that though he was slightly built he seemed extremely strong and active, compact of muscle; but he had not yet learnt the art of walking rhythmically and balancing easily from stone to stone. I wondered how long he would keep up. Presently we came to a corner where our stream bed ended and a small glacier-snout was visible above us apparently descending from the North-west. We gathered on a high bank of stones to look out over the glacier. I observed now that the whole aspect of the party had changed. The majority were more than momentarily tired, they were visibly suffering from some sort of malaise. It was not yet nine o'clock and we had risen barely 2,000 feet, but their spirits had gone. There were grunts instead of laughter.

The glacier's left bank which we were following was now trending to the right. To the South and standing in front of the great North-west arm of Everest was a comparatively small and very attractive snow peak, perhaps a little less than 21,000 feet high. We had harboured a vague ambition to reach its shoulder, a likely point for prospecting the head of the Rongbuk Glacier. But between us and this objective was a wide stretch of hummocky ice which had every appearance of being something more than a mere bay of the main glacier. We suspected a western branch and proceeded to confirm our suspicion. After a rough crossing below the glacier above us we were fortunate enough to find another trough wider than the first and having a flat sandy bottom where we walked easily enough. Presently leaving the coolies to rest on the edge of the glacier Bullock and I mounted a high stony shoulder, and from there, at 18,500 feet, saw the glacier stretching away to the West, turning sharply below us to rise more steeply than before. Cloud prevented us from distinguishing what appeared to be a high mountain ridge at the far end of it.

It was evident that nothing was to be gained at present by pushing our investigations further to the West. Our curiosity was as yet unsatisfied about those white spires of ice to which our eyes had constantly returned. We declined the alternative of retracing our steps and without further delay set about to cross the glacier. It was now eleven o'clock and we were under no delusion that the task before us would be other than arduous and long. But the reward in interest and valuable information promised to be great, for, by exploring the glacier's right bank during our descent we should learn all we wanted to know before making plans for an advance. And we hoped to be in before dark.

The stone-covered ice on which we first embarked compared favourably with that of our earlier experience before breakfast. The sea, so to speak, was not so choppy; the waves were longer. We were able to follow convenient troughs for considerable distances. But at the bottom of a trough which points whither it will it is impossible to keep a definite direction and difficult to know to what extent one is erring. An hour's hard work was required to bring us to the edge of the white ice. Our first question was answered at a glance. It had always seemed improbable that these were séracs such as one meets on an Alpine icefall, and clearly they were not. We saw no signs of lateral crevasses. The shapes were comparatively conical and regular, not delicately poised but firmly based, safely perpendicular and not dangerously impending. They were the result not of movement but of melting, and it was remarkable that on either side the black ice looked over the white, as though the glacier had sunk in the middle. The pinnacles resembled a topsy-turvy system of colossal icicles, icicles thrust upwards from a common icy mass, the whole resting on a definable floor. The largest were about 50 feet high.

We were divided from this fairy world of spires by a deep boundary moat and entered it on the far side by what may be described as a door but that it had no lintel. An alley led us over a low wall and we had reached the interior. A connected narrative of our wanderings in this amazing country could hardly be true to its disconnected character. The White Rabbit himself would have been bewildered here. No course seemed to lead anywhere. Our idea was to keep to the floor so far as we were able; but most usually we were scrambling up a chimney or slithering down one, cutting round the foot of a tower or actually traversing along an icy crest. To be repeatedly crossing little cols with the continued expectation of seeing a way beyond was a sufficiently exciting labour; it was also sufficiently laborious since the chopping of steps was necessary almost everywhere; but fatigue was out of sight in the enchanted scene, with the cool delight of little lakes, of the ice reflected in their unruffled waters and of blue sky showing between the white spires. We had but one misadventure, and that of no consequence—it was my fate when crossing the frozen surface of one little lake to suffer a sudden immersion: the loss of dignity perhaps was more serious than the chilling of ardour, for we soon came upon a broadening alley and came out from our labyrinth as suddenly as we entered it, to lie and bask in the warm sun.

Our crossing of the white ice after all had taken little more than two hours, and we might well consider ourselves fortunate. But it must be remembered that we were far from fresh at the start and now the reaction set in. The stone-covered glacier on this side, besides being a much narrower belt was clearly not going to give us trouble, and after an ample halt we started across it easily enough. On the right bank we had noticed many hours before above the glacier a broad flat shelf, presumably an old moraine, and a clear mark along the hillside away down to a point below the snout. This was now our objective and no doubt once we had gained it our troubles would be ended. But in the first place it had to be gained. In the Alps it has often seemed laborious to go up hill towards the end of a day: it was a new sensation to find it an almost impossible exertion to drag oneself up a matter of 150 feet. And further exertions were to be required of us. A little way down the valley a glacier stream came in on our right; we had observed this before and hopefully expected to follow our terrace round and rejoin it on the far side of the gully. But it was late in the afternoon and the stream was at its fullest. We followed it down with defeated expectations; it always proved just too dangerous to cross. Finally it formed a lake at the edge of the glacier before disappearing beneath it and obliged us to make a detour on the ice once more. I suppose this obstacle was mild enough; but again an ascent was involved, and after it at least one member of the party seemed incapable of further effort. Another halt was necessary. We were now down to about 17,000 feet and at the head of a long passage at the side of the glacier, similar to that we had ascended in the morning on the other bank. Those who suffer from altitude on a mountain have a right to expect a recovery on the descent. But I saw no signs of one yet. It was a long painful hour balancing from boulder to boulder along the passage, with the conscious effort of keeping up the feat until we came out into the flat basin at the glacier end. Then as we left the glacier behind us the day seemed to come right. One obstacle remained, a stream which had been crossed with difficulty in the morning and was now swollen to a formidable torrent. It was carried with a rush—this was no moment for delay. Each man chose his own way for a wetting; for my part, after a series of exciting leaps on to submerged stones I landed in the deepest part of the stream with the pick of my axe dug into the far bank to help me scramble out. After this I remember only of the last 4 miles the keen race against the gathering darkness; fatigue was forgotten and we reached camp at 8.15 p.m., tired perhaps, but not exhausted.

It has seemed necessary to give an account of this first expedition in some detail in order to emphasise certain conditions which governed all our movements from the Rongbuk Valley. We now knew how to get about. Flat though the glacier might be, it was no use for travelling in any part we had seen, not a road but an obstacle. The obstacle, however, had not proved insurmountable, and though the crossing had been laborious and long, we were not convinced that it need be so long another time; careful reconnaissance might reveal a better way, and we had little doubt that both the main glacier and its Western branch could be used freely for lateral communication if we chose. It would not always be necessary in organising an expedition to be encamped on one side of the glacier rather than the other. And we had discovered that it was not a difficult matter to make our way along the glacier sides; we could choose either a trough or a shelf.

We had also been greatly interested by the phenomena of fatigue. The most surprising fact when we applied our standard of comparison was that coming down had proved so laborious; Bullock and I had each discovered independently that we got along better when we remembered to breathe hard, and we already suspected what we afterwards established—that it was necessary to adopt a conscious method of breathing deeply for coming down as for going up. Another inference, subsequently confirmed on many occasions, accused the glacier. The mid-day sun had been hot as we crossed it and I seemed to notice some enervating influence which had not affected me elsewhere. It was the glacier that had knocked me out, not the hard work alone but some malignant quality in the atmosphere, which I can neither describe nor explain; and in crossing a glacier during the day I always afterwards observed the same effect; I might feel as fit and fresh as I could wish on the moraine at the side but only once succeeded in crossing a glacier without feeling a despairing lassitude.

I shall now proceed to quote from my diary:

June 28.—A slack day in camp. It is difficult to induce coolies to take any steps to make themselves more comfortable. We're lucky to have this fine weather. The mountain appears not to be intended for climbing. I've no inclination to think about it in steps to the summit. Nevertheless, we gaze much through field-glasses. E. is, generally speaking, convex, steep in lower parts and slanting back to summit. Last section of East arête * should go; but rocks up to the shoulder are uninviting. An arête must join up here, coming down towards us and connecting

* It had not yet been established that the true direction of this arête is North-east.

up with first peak to N.* There's no true North arête to the summit, as we had supposed at first. It's more like this:

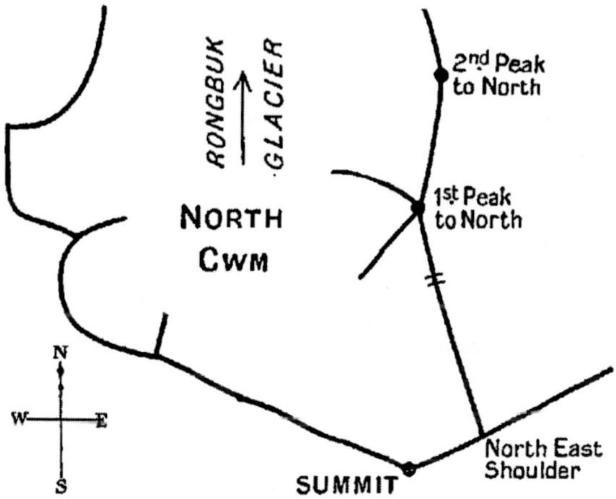

G. H. B. thinks little of the North-west arm. But I'm not so sure; much easy going on that snow if we can get to it and rocks above probably easier than they look—steep but broken. Are we seeing the true edge? I wish some folk at home could see the precipice on this side—a grim spectacle most unlike the long gentle snow slopes suggested by photos. Amusing to think how one's vision of the last effort has changed; it looked like crawling half-blind up easy snow, an even slope all the way up from a camp on a flat snow shoulder; but it won't be that sort of grind; we'll want climbers and not half-dazed ones; a tougher job than I bargained for, sanguine as usual.

E. is a rock mountain.

Obviously we must get round to the West first. The Western glacier looks as flat as this one. Perhaps we shall

* i.e. the North Peak (Changtse).

be able to walk round into another cwm* on the far side of North-west buttress.

June 29.—Established First Advanced Camp.

The start late, about 8 a.m., an hour later than ordered. Loads must be arranged better if anything is to be done efficiently. Gyalzen's response to being hustled is to tie knots or collect tent pegs—with no idea of superintending operations. An exciting day with destination unfixed. We speculated that the shelf on the left bank would resemble that on right. A passage on stone-covered glacier unavoidable and bad for coolies—perhaps to-day's loads were too heavy for this sort of country. From breakfast place of 27th I went on with Gyalzen, following up a fresh-water stream to the shelf; good going on this shelf for forty minutes, with no sign of more water, and I decided to come back to the stream. Just as we were turning I saw a pond of water and a spring, an ideal place, and it's much better to be further on. Real good luck. Wind blows down the glacier and the camp is well sheltered. Only crab that we lose the sun early—4 p.m. to-day; but on the other hand it should hit us very soon after sunrise.

Coolies in between 3.30 and 4.30. Dorji Gompa first, stout fellow, with a big load. They seem happy and interested. . . . It should now be possible to carry reconnaissance well up the main glacier and to the basin Westwards without moving further—once we get accustomed to this elevation.

June 30.—A short day with second† party, following the shelf to a corner which marks roughly the junction of the main glacier with its Western branch. A clearing day after a good night; we found a good way across to the opposite corner, about an hour across, and came back in leisurely fashion. Neither B. nor I felt fit.

* Cwm, combe or corry—the rounded head of a valley.

† The coolies had been divided into three parties which were to spend four or five days in the advanced camp by turns to be trained in the practice of mountaineering while the rest supplied this camp from our base.

CHAPTER XIII

THE NORTHERN APPROACH—*continued*

The reader will gather from these notes some idea of the whole nature of our problem and the subjects of our most anxious thoughts. The camp established on June 25 lasted us until July 8. Meanwhile the idea was growing, the vision of Everest as a structural whole, and of the glaciers and lower summits to North and West. This idea resembled the beginning of an artist's painting, a mere rough design at the start, but growing by steps of clearer definition in one part and another towards the precise completion of a whole. For us the mountain parts defined themselves in the mind as the result of various expeditions. We set out to gain a point of view with particular questions to be answered; partial answers and a new point of view stimulated more curiosity, other questions, and again the necessity to reach a particular place whence we imagined they might best be answered. And at the same time another aim had to be kept in mind. The coolies, though mountain-men, were not mountaineers. They had to be trained in the craft of mountaineering, in treading safely on snow or ice in dangerous places, in climbing easy rocks and most particularly in the use of rope and ice-axe—and this not merely for our foremost needs, but to ensure that, whenever we were able to launch an assault upon Mount Everest, and all would be put to the most exhausting test, they should have that reserve strength of a practised balance and ordered method on which security must ultimately depend.

On July 1 I set out with five coolies to reach the head of the great cwm under the North face of Mount Everest. The snow on the upper glacier was soft and made very heavy going. Bad weather came up and in a race against the clouds we were beaten and failed to find out what happened to the glacier at its Western head under the North-west arête. My view of the col lying between Everest and the North Peak (Changtse)—the North Col as we now began to call it, or in Tibetan Chang La—was also unsatisfactory; but I saw enough to make out a broken glacier running up eastwards towards the gap with steep and uninviting snow slopes under the pass. I was now sure that before attempting to reach this col from the Rongbuk Glacier, if ever we determined to reach it, we should have to reconnoitre the other side and if possible find a more hopeful alternative; moreover, from a nearer inspection of the slopes below the North-west arête I was convinced that they could be chosen for an attack only as a last resort; if anything were to be attempted here, we must find a better way up from the East.

I had vaguely hoped to bring the party home sufficiently fresh to climb again on the following day. But the fatigue of going in deep snow for three hours up the glacier, though we had been no higher than 19,100 feet, had been too great, and again we had noticed only a slight relief in coming down; it was a tired party that dragged back over the glacier crossing and into camp at 6.15 p.m., thirteen hours after starting.

July 3 was devoted to an expedition designed chiefly to take coolies on to steeper ground and at the same time to explore the small glacier which we had observed above us on the first day to the North-west; by following up the terrace from our present camp we could now come to the snout of it in half an hour or less. After working up the glacier we made for a snow col between two high peaks. On reaching a bergschrund we found above its upper lip hard ice, which continued no doubt to the ridge. While Bullock looked after the party below I cut a staircase slanting up to a small island of rock 100 feet away; from that security I began to bring the party up. We had now the interesting experience of seeing our coolies for the first time on real hard ice; it was not a convincing spectacle, as they made their way up with the ungainly movements of beginners; and though the last man never left the secure anchorage of the bergschrund, the proportion of two Sahibs to five coolies seemed lamentably weak, and when one man slipped from the steep steps at an awkward corner, though Bullock was able to hold him, it was clearly time to retire. But the descent was a better performance; the coolies were apt pupils, and we felt that with practice on the glacier the best of them should become safe mountaineers. And on this day we had reached a height of 21,000 feet * from our camp at 17,500 feet. I had the great satisfaction of observing that one could cut steps quite happily at this altitude. The peak lying to the North of the col, which had been our objective on this day, attracted our attention by its position; we thought it should have a commanding view over all this complicated country, and after a day in camp very pleasantly spent in receiving a visit from Colonel Howard-Bury and Dr. Heron, set out on July 5 determined to reach its summit. The start was made at 4.15 a.m. in the first light, an hour earlier than usual; we proceeded up the stone shoots immediately above our camp and after a halt for photography at the glorious moment of sunrise had made 2,500 feet and reached the high shoulder above us at 7 a.m. This place was connected with our peak by a snowy col which had now to be reached by a long traverse over a South-facing slope. Though the angle was not steep very little snow was lying here, and where the ice was peeping through it was occasionally necessary to cut steps. I felt it was a satisfactory performance to reach the col at 9.30 a.m.; the coolies had come well, though one of them was burdened with the quarter-plate camera; but evidently their efforts had already tired them. Ahead of

* Calculated from the readings of two aneroids, allowing a correction for the height of the camp as established later by Major Wheeler.

us was a long, curving snow arête, slightly corniced and leading ultimately to a rocky shoulder. We thought that once this shoulder was gained the summit would be within our reach. Shortly after we went on two coolies dropped out, and by 11.30 a.m. the rest had given up the struggle. It was fortunate that they fell out here and not later, for they were able to make their way down in our tracks and regain the col below in safety. The angle steepened as we went on very slowly now, but still steadily enough, until we reached the rocks, a frail slatey structure with short perpendicular pitches. From the shoulder onwards my memories are dim. I have the impression of a summit continually receding from the position imagined by sanguine hopes and of a task growing constantly more severe, of steeper sides, of steps to be cut, of a dwindling pace, more frequent little halts standing where we were, and of breathing quicker but no less deep and always conscious; the respiratory engine had to be kept running as the indispensable source of energy, and ever as we went on more work was required of it. At last we found ourselves without an alternative under an icy wall; but the ice was a delusion; in the soft flaky substance smothering rocks behind it we had strength left to cut a way up to the crest again, and after a few more steps were on the summit itself.

It was now 2.45 p.m. The aneroid used by Bullock, which, after comparison with one of Howard-Bury's was supposed to read low, registered 23,050 feet,* and we puffed out our chests as we examined it, computing that we had risen from our camp over 5,500 feet. The views both earlier in the day and at this moment were of the highest interest. To the East we had confirmed our impression of the North Peak as having a high ridge stretching eastwards and forming the side of whatever valley connected with

* The survey established the height of this peak as 22,520 feet, and our subsequent experience suggests that aneroid barometers habitually read too high when approaching the upper limit of their record.

the Arun River in this direction; the upper parts of Everest's North face had been clearly visible for a long time, and we could now be certain that they lay back at no impossibly steep angle, more particularly above the North col and up to the North-east shoulder. All we had seen immediately to the West of the mountain had been of the greatest interest, and had suggested the idea that the crinkled summit there might be connected not directly with Mount Everest itself, but only by way of the South peak. And finally we now saw the connections of all that lay around us with the two great triangulated peaks away to the West, Gyachung Kang, 25,990 and Cho-Uyo, 26,870 feet. While complaining of the clouds which had come up as usual during the morning to spoil our view we were not dissatisfied with the expansion of our knowledge and we were elated besides to be where we were. But our situation was far from perfectly secure. The ascent had come very near to exhausting our strength; for my part I felt distinctly mountain-sick; we might reflect that we should not be obliged to cut more steps, but we should have to proceed downwards with perfect accuracy of balance and a long halt was desirable. However, the clouds were now gathering about us, dark thunder-clouds come up from the North and threatening; it was clear we must not wait; after fifteen minutes on the summit we started down at three o'clock. Fortune favoured us. The wind was no more than a breeze; a few flakes of snow were unnoticed in our flight; the temperature was mild; the storm's malice was somehow dissipated with no harm done. We rejoined the coolies before five o'clock and were back in our camp at 7.15 p.m., happy to have avoided a descent in the dark.

Our next plan, based on our experience of this long mountain ridge, was to practise the coolies in the use of crampons on hard snow and ice. But snow fell heavily on the night of the 6th; we deferred our project. It was the beginning of worse weather; the monsoon was breaking in earnest. And though crampons afterwards came up to our camps wherever we went they were not destined to help us, and in the event were never used.

On July 8 we moved up with a fresh party of seven coolies, taking only our lightest tents and no more than was necessary for three nights, in the hope that by two energetic expeditions we should reach the Western cwm which, we suspected, must exist on the far side of the North-west arête, and learn enough to found more elaborate plans for exploring this side of the mountain should they turn out to be necessary. Again we were fortunate in finding a good camping ground, better even than the first, for the floor of this shelf was grassy and soft, and as we were looking South across the West Rongbuk Glacier we had the sun late as well as early. But we were not completely happy. A Mummery tent may be well enough in fair weather, though even then its low roof suggests a recumbent attitude; it makes a poor dining-room, even for two men, and is a cold shelter from snow. Moreover, the cold and draught discouraged our Primus stove—but I leave to the imagination of those who have learned by experience the nausea that comes from the paraffin fumes and one's dirty hands and all the mess that may be. It was chiefly a question of incompetence, no doubt, but there was no consolation in admitting that. In the morning, with the weather still very thick and the snow lying about us we saw the error of our ways. Is it not a first principle of mountaineering to be as comfortable as possible as long as one can? And how long should we require for these operations in such weather? It was clear that our Second Advanced Camp must be organised on a more permanent basis. On the 9th therefore I went down to the base and moved it up on the following day so as to be within reach of our present position by one long march. The new place greatly pleased me; it was much more sheltered than the lower site and the tents were pitched on flat turf where a clear spring flowed out from the hillside and only a quarter of an hour below the end of the glacier. Meanwhile Bullock brought up the Whymper tents and more stores from the First Advanced Camp, which was now established as a half-way house with our big 80-foot tent standing in solemn grandeur to protect all that remained there. On July 10 I was back at the Second Advanced Camp and felt satisfied that the new arrangements, and particularly the presence of our cook, would give us a fair measure of comfort.

But we were still unable to move next day. The snow-fall during the night was the heaviest we had yet seen and continued into the next day. Probably the coolies were not sorry for a rest after some hard work; and we reckoned to make a long expedition so soon as the weather should clear. Towards evening on the 10th the clouds broke. Away to the South-west of us and up the glacier was the barrier range on the frontier of Nepal, terminated by one great mountain, Pumori, over 24,000 feet high. To the West Rongbuk Glacier they present the steepest slopes on which snow can lie; the crest above these slopes is surprisingly narrow and the peaks which it joins are fantastically shaped. This group of mountains, always beautiful and often in the highest degree impressive, was now to figure for our eyes as the principal in that oft-repeated drama which seems always to be a first night, fresh and full of wonder whenever we are present to watch it. The clinging curtains were rent and swirled aside and closed again, lifted and lowered and flung wide at last; sunlight broke through with sharp shadows and clean edges revealed—and we were there to witness the amazing spectacle. Below the terrible mountains one white smooth island rose from the quiet sea of ice and was bathed in the calm full light of the Western sun before the splendour failed.

With hopes inspired by the clearing views of this lovely evening, we started at 5.30 a.m. on July 12 to follow the glacier round to the South and perhaps enter the Western cwm. The glacier was a difficult problem. It looked easy enough to follow up the medial moraine to what we called the Island, a low mountain pushed out from the frontier ridge into the great sea of ice. But the way on Southwards from there would have been a gamble with the chances of success against us. We decided to cross the glacier directly to the South with a certainty that once we had reached the moraine on the other side we should have a clear way before us. It was exhilarating to set out again under a clear sky, and we were delighted to think that a large part of this task was accomplished when the sun rose full of warmth and cheerfulness. The far side was cut off by a stream of white ice, so narrow here that we expected with a little good fortune to get through it in perhaps half an hour. We entered it by a frozen stream leading into a bay with high white towers and ridges above us. A side door led through into a further bay which took us in the confidence of success almost through the maze. With some vigorous blows we cut our way up the final wall and then found ourselves on a crest overlooking the moraine with a sheer ice-precipice of about 100 feet below us.

The only hope was to come down again and work round to the right. Some exciting climbing and much hard work brought us at length to the foot of the cliffs and on the right side. The performance had taken us two and a half hours and it was now nearly ten o'clock. Clouds had already come up to obscure the mountains, and from the point of view of a prolonged exploration the day was clearly lost. Our course now was to make the best of it and yet get back so early to camp that we could set forth again on the following day. We had the interest, after following the moraine to the corner where the glacier bends Southwards, of making our way into the middle of the ice and finding out how unpleasant it can be to walk on a glacier melted everywhere into little valleys and ridges and covered with fresh snow. We got back at 3 p.m.

On July 13, determined to make good, we started at 4.15 a.m. With the knowledge gained on the previous day and the use of 250 feet of spare rope we were able to find our way through the ice pinnacles and reached the far moraine in less than an hour and a half; and we had the further good fortune when we took to the snow to find it now in such good condition that we were able to walk on the surface without using our snow-shoes. As we proceeded up the slopes where the snow steepened the weather began to thicken and we halted at 8 a.m. in a thick mist with a nasty wind and some snow falling. It was a cold halt. We were already somewhat disillusioned about our glacier, which seemed to be much more narrow than was to be expected if it were really a high-road to the Western cwm, and as we went on with the wind blowing the snow into our faces so that nothing could be clearly distinguished we had the sense of a narrowing place and a perception of the even surface being broken up into large crevasses on one side and the other. At 9.30 we could go no further. For a few hundred yards we had been traversing a slope which rose above us on our left, and now coming out on to a little spur we stood peering down through the mist and knew ourselves to be on the edge of a considerable precipice. Not a single feature of the landscape around us was even faintly visible in the cloud. For a time we stayed on with the dim hope of better things and then reluctantly retired, baffled and bewildered.

Where had we been? It was impossible to know; but at least it was certain there was no clear way to the West side of Everest. We could only suppose that we had reached a col on the frontier of Nepal.

A further disappointment awaited us when we reached camp at 1 p.m. I had made a simple plan to ensure our supply of gobar* and rations from the base camp. The supplies had not come up and it was not the sort of weather to be without a fire for cooking.

I shall now proceed to quote my diary:—

July 14. — A day of rest, but with no republican demonstrations. Very late breakfast after some snow in

* In the Rongbuk Valley there was no wood and our supply of yak dung had to come up from Chöbuk.

the night. Piquet after tiffin and again after dinner was very consoling. The little streams we found here on our arrival are drying up; it seems that not much snow can have fallen higher.

July 15.—Started 6 a.m. to explore the glacier to West and North-west. A very interesting view just short of the Island; the South peak appearing. Fifty minutes there for photos; then hurried on in the hope of seeing more higher up and at a greater distance. It is really a dry glacier here but with snow frozen over the surface making many pitfalls. We had a good many wettings in cold water up to the knees. The clouds were just coming up as we halted on the medial moraine. I waited there in hope of better views, while Bullock took on the coolies. They put on snow-shoes for the first time and seemed to go very well in them. Ultimately I struggled across the glacier, bearing various burdens, to meet them as they came down on a parallel moraine. Snow-shoes seemed useful, but very awkward to leap in. Bullock went a long way up the glacier, rising very slightly towards the peak Cho-Uyo, 26,870 feet. Evidently there is a flat pass over into Nepal near this peak, but he did not quite reach it.

The topographical mystery centres about the West Peak. Is there an arête connecting this with the great rock peak South of Everest or is it joined up with the col we reached the day before yesterday? The shape of the West cwm and the question of its exit will be solved if we can answer these questions. Bullock and I are agreed that the glacier there has probably an exit on the Nepal side. It all remains extremely puzzling. We saw the North col quite clearly to-day, and again the way up from there does not look difficult.

A finer day and quite useful. Chitayn * started out with us and went back. He appears to be seedy, but has been quite hopeless as Sirdar down in the base camp and is without

* A useful coolie with experience in the Indian Army. I had used him as second Sirdar.

authority. It is a great handicap having no one to look after things down there. Chitayn is returning to Tingri to-morrow. I hope he will cheer up again.

July 16.—I made an early start with two coolies at 2.45 a.m. and followed the medial moraine to the Island. Reached the near summit at sunrise about 5.30. Difficult to imagine anything more exciting than the clear view of all peaks. Those near me to the South-west quickly bathed in sun and those to the South and East showing me their dark faces. To the left of our col of July 13 a beautiful sharp peak stood in front of the gap between Everest and the North Peak, Changtse. Over this col I saw the North-west buttress of Everest hiding the lower half of the West face which must be a tremendous precipice of rock. The last summit of the South Peak, Lhotse, was immediately behind the shoulder; to the right (i.e. West) of it I saw a terrible arête stretching a long distance before it turned upwards in my direction and towards the West Peak. This mountain dropped very abruptly to the North, indicating a big gap on the far side of our col. There was the mysterious cwm lying in cold shadow long after the sun warmed me! But I now half understand it. The col under the North-west buttress at the head of the Rongbuk Glacier is one entrance, and our col of July 13, with how big a drop one knows not, another.

I stayed till 7 a.m. taking photos, a dozen plates exposed in all. The sky was heavy and a band of cloud had come across Everest before I left.

Back to breakfast towards 9 a.m. A pleasant morning collecting flowers, not a great variety but some delicious honey scents and an occasional cheerful blue poppy.

July 17.—More trouble with our arrangements. The Sirdar has muddled the rations and the day is wasted. However, the weather is bad, constant snow showers from 1 to 8 p.m., so that I am somewhat reconciled to this reverse.

July 18.—Yesterday's plan carried out—to move up a camp with light tents and make a big push over into the

West cwm; eight coolies to carry the loads. But the loads have been too heavy. What can be cut out next time? I cannot see many unnecessary articles. Heavy snow showers fell as we came up and we had rather a cheerless encampment, but with much heaving of stones made good places for the tents. A glorious night before we turned in. Dark masses of cloud were gathered round the peak above us; below, the glacier was clear and many splendid mountains were half visible. The whole scene was beautifully lit by a bright moon.

July 19.—Started 3 a.m.; still some cloud, particularly to the West. The moon just showed over the mountains in that direction which cast their strange black shadows on the snowfield. One amazing black tooth was standing up against the moonlight. No luck on the glacier and we had to put on snow-shoes at once. An exciting walk. I so much feared the cloud would spoil all. It was just light enough to get on without lanterns after the moon went down. At dawn almost everything was covered, but not by heavy clouds. Like guilty creatures of darkness surprised by the light they went scattering away as we came up and the whole scene opened out. The North ridge of Everest was clear and bright even before sunrise. We reached the col at 5 a.m., a fantastically beautiful scene; and we looked across into the West cwm at last, terribly cold and forbidding under the shadow of Everest. It was nearly an hour after sunrise before the sun hit the West Peak.

But another disappointment—it is a big drop about 1,500 feet down to the glacier, and a hopeless precipice. I was hoping to get away to the left and traverse into the cwm; that too quite hopeless. However, we have seen this Western glacier and are not sorry we have not to go up it. It is terribly steep and broken. In any case work on this side could only be carried out from a base in Nepal, so we have done with the Western side. It was not a very likely chance that the gap between Everest and the South Peak could be reached from the West. From what we have seen now I do not much fancy it would be possible, even could one get up the glacier.

We saw a lovely group of mountains away to the South in Nepal. I wonder what they are and if anything is known about them. It is a big world!

* * * * *

With this expedition on July 19 our reconnaissance of these parts had ended. We proceeded at once to move down our belongings; on July 20 all tents and stores were brought down to the base camp and we had said good-bye to the West Rongbuk Glacier.

So far as we were concerned with finding a way up the mountain, little enough had been accomplished; and yet our growing view of the mountain had been steadily leading to one conviction. If ever the mountain were to be climbed, the way would not lie along the whole length of any one of its colossal ridges. Progress could only be made along comparatively easy ground, and anything like a prolonged sharp crest or a series of towers would inevitably bar the way simply by the time which would be required to overcome such obstacles. But the North arête coming down to the gap between Everest and the North Peak, Changtse, is not of this character. From the horizontal structure of the mountain there is no excrescence of rock pinnacles in this part and the steep walls of rock which run across the North face are merged with it before they reach this part, which is comparatively smooth and continuous, a bluntly rounded edge. We had still to see other parts of the mountain, but already it seemed unlikely that we would find more favourable ground than this. The great question before us now was to be one of access. Could the North col be reached from the East and how could we attain this point?

At the very moment when we reached the base camp I received a note from Colonel Howard-Bury telling us that his departure from Tingri was fixed for July 23 and that he would be sleeping at Chöbuk in the valley below us two days later on his way to Kharta. It was now an obvious plan to synchronise our movements with his.

Besides the branch which we had already explored the Rongbuk Glacier has yet another which joins the main stream from the East about 10 miles from Everest. It had always excited our curiosity, and I now proposed to explore it in the initial stages of a journey across the unknown ridges and valleys which separated us from Kharta. I calculated that we should want eight days' provisions, and that we should just have time to organise a camp in advance and start on the 25th with a selected party, sending down the rest to join Howard-Bury. And it was an integral part of the scheme that on one of the intervening days I should ascend a spur to the North of the glacier where we proposed to march in order to obtain a better idea of this country to the East. But we were now in the thickest of the monsoon weather; the 21st and 22nd were both wet days and we woke on the 23rd to find snow all around us nearly a foot deep; it had come down as low as 16,000 feet. It was hardly the weather to cut ourselves adrift and wander among the uncharted spurs of Everest, and we thought of delaying our start. Further it transpired that our organisation was not running smoothly—it never did run smoothly so long as we employed, as an indispensable Sirdar, a whey-faced treacherous knave whose sly and calculated villainy too often, before it was discovered, deprived our coolies of their food, and whose acquiescence in his own illimitable incompetence was only less disgusting than his infamous duplicity. It was the hopeless sense that things were bound to go wrong if we trusted to this man's services—and we had no one else at that time through whom it was possible to order supplies from the natives—that turned the scale and spoilt the plan. Even so, in the natural course of events, I should have obtained my preliminary view. But on the night of the 22nd I received from Howard-Bury an extremely depressing piece of news, that all my photos taken with the quarter-plate camera had failed—for the good reason that the plates had been inserted back to front, a result of ignorance and misunderstanding. It was necessary as far as possible to repair this hideous error, and the next two days were spent in a photographic expedition. And so it came about that we saw no more until a much later date of the East Rongbuk Glacier. Had our plan been carried out even in the smallest part by a cursory survey of what lay ahead, I should not now have to tell a story which is lamentably incomplete in one respect. For the East Rongbuk Glacier is one way, and the obvious way when you see it, to the North Col. It was discovered by Major Wheeler before ever we saw it, in the course of his photographic survey; but neither he, nor Bullock, nor I have ever traversed its whole length.

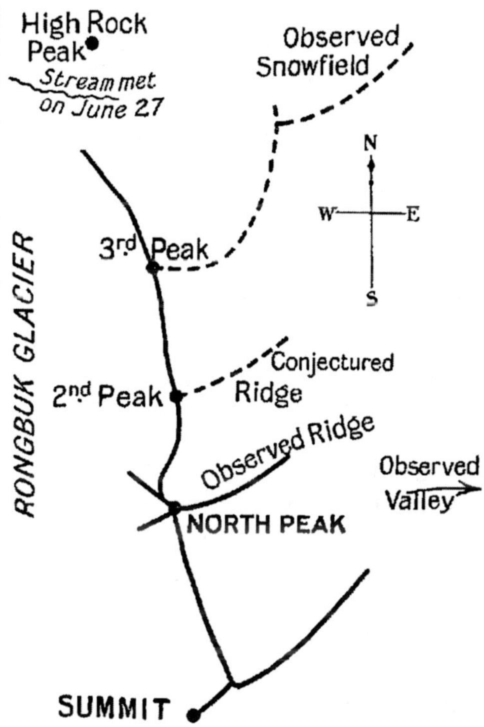

We should have attached more importance, no doubt, in the early stages of reconnaissance, to the East Rongbuk Glacier had we not been deceived in two ways by appearances. It had been an early impression left in my mind, at all events, by what we saw from Shiling, that a deep valley came down to the East as the R.G.S. map suggests, draining into the Arun and having the North-east arête of Everest as its right bank at the start. Further, the head of this valley seemed to be, as one would expect, the gap between Everest and the first peak to the North which itself has also an Eastern arm to form the left bank of such a valley. The impression was confirmed not only by an excellent view from a hill above Ponglet (two days before Tingri and about 35 miles North of Everest), but by all nearer and more recent views of the mountains East of the Rongbuk Glacier. The idea that a glacier running parallel to the Rongbuk started from the slopes of Everest itself and came so far to turn Westward in the end hardly occurred to us at this time. From anything we had seen there was no place for such a glacier, and it was almost unimaginable that the great mountain range running North from the North Col, Chang La, was in no part a true watershed. We saw the East Rongbuk Glacier stretching away to the East and perceived also a bay to the South. But how, if this bay were of any importance, could the glacier stream be so small? We had found it too large to cross, it is true, late in the afternoon of our first expedition, but only just too large; and again it seems now an unbelievable fact that so large an area of ice should give so small a volume of water. The glacier streams are remarkably small in all the country we explored, but this one far more surprisingly small than any other we saw.

It was some measure of consolation in these circumstances to make use of a gleam of fine weather. When the bad news arrived on July 22 about the failure of my photographs we had ceased to hear the raindrops pattering on the tent, but could feel well enough when we pushed up the roof that snow was lying on the outer fly. It was a depressing evening. I thought of the many wonderful occasions when I had caught the mountain as I thought just at the right moment, its moments of most lovely splendour—of all those moments that would never return and of the record of all we had seen which neither ourselves nor perhaps anyone else would ever see again. I was not a cheerful companion. Moreover, from the back of my mind I was warned, even in the first despair of disappointment, that I should have to set out to repair the damage so far as I was able, and I hated the thought of this expedition. These were our days of rest after a month's high-living; we were off with one adventure and on with another; tents, stores, everything had been brought down to our base and we had said good-bye to the West Rongbuk Glacier. The clouds were still about us next morning and snow lay on the ground 9 inches deep. But by midday much of the snow had melted at our level and the clouds began to clear. At 2 p.m. we started up with the Mummery tents and stores for one night. I made my way with one coolie to a spot some little distance above our First Advanced Camp. As we pushed up the stormy hillside the last clouds gathered about Everest, and lingering in the deep North cwm were dispersed and the great white-mantled mountains lay all clear in the light of a glorious evening. Before we raced down to join Bullock my first dozen plates had been duly exposed; whatever the balance of hopes and fears for a fine morning to-morrow something had been done already to make good.

My ultimate destination was the Island which I had found before to command some of the most splendid and most instructive views. I was close up under the slopes of this little mountain before sunrise next morning. It has rarely been my lot to experience in the course of a few hours so much variety of expectation, of disappointment and of hope deferred, before the issue is decided. A pall of cloud lying like a blanket above the glacier was no good omen after the clear weather; as the sun got up a faint gleam on the ice encouraged me to go on; presently the grey clouds began to move and spread in all directions until I was enveloped and saw nothing. Suddenly the frontier crest came out and its highest peak towering fantastically above me; I turned about and saw to the West and North-west the wide glacier in the sun—beyond it Gyachung Kang and Cho-Uyo, 26,870 to 25,990 feet: but Everest remained hidden, obscured by an impenetrable cloud. I watched the changing shadows on the white snow and gazed helplessly into the grey mass continually rolled up from Nepal into the deep hollow beyond the glacier head. But a breeze came up from the East; the curtain was quietly withdrawn; Everest and the South Peak stood up against the clear blue sky. The camera was ready and I was satisfied. A few minutes later the great cloud rolled back and I saw no more.

Meanwhile Bullock had not been idle. He paid a visit to the North cwm, more successful than mine in July, for he reached the pass leading over into Nepal under the North-west arête and had perfectly clear views of Chang La, of which he brought back some valuable photos. But perhaps an even greater satisfaction than reckoning the results of what we both felt was a successful day was ours, when we listened in our tents that evening at the base camp to the growling of thunder and reflected that the fair interval already ended had been caught and turned to good account.

In snow and sleet and wind next morning, July 25, our tents were struck. We turned our backs on the Rongbuk Glacier and hastened along the path to Chöbuk. The valley was somehow changed as we came down, and more agreeable to the eye. Presently I discovered the reason. The grass had grown on the hillside since we went up. We were coming down to summer green.

CHAPTER XIV

THE EASTERN APPROACH

The new base at Kharta established by Colonel Howard-Bury at the end of July was well suited to meet the needs of climbers, and no less agreeable, I believe, to all members of the Expedition. At the moderate elevation of 12,300 feet and in an almost ideal climate, where the air was always warm but never hot or stuffy, where the sun shone brightly but never fiercely, and clouds floated about the hills and brought moisture from the South, but never too much rain, here the body could find a delicious change when tired of the discipline of high-living, and in a place so accessible to traders from Nepal could easily be fed with fresh food. But perhaps after life in the Rongbuk Valley, with hardly a green thing to look at and too much of the endless unfriendly stone-shoots and the ugly waste of glaciers, and even after visions of sublime snow-beauty, a change was more needed for the mind. It was a delight to be again in a land of flowery meadows and trees and crops; to look into the deep green gorge only a mile away where the Arun goes down into Nepal was to be reminded of a rich vegetation and teeming life, a contrast full of pleasure with Nature's niggardliness in arid, wind-swept Tibet; and the forgotten rustle of wind in the willows came back as a soothing sound full of grateful memories, banishing the least thought of disagreeable things.

The Kharta base, besides, was convenient for our reconnaissance. Below us a broad glacier stream joined the Arun above the gorge; it was the first met with since we had left the Rongbuk stream; it came down from the West and therefore, presumably, from Everest. To follow it up was an obvious plan as the next stage in our activities. After four clear days for idleness and reorganisation at Kharta we set forth again on August 2 with this object. The valley of our glacier stream would lead us, we supposed, to the mountain; in two days, perhaps, we should see Chang La ahead of us. A local headman provided by the Jongpen and entrusted with the task of leading us to Chomolungma would show us where it might be necessary to cross the stream and, in case the valley forked, would ensure us against a bad mistake.

The start on this day was not propitious. We had enjoyed the sheltered ease at Kharta; the coolies were dilatory and unwilling; the distribution of loads was muddled; there was much discontent about rations, and our Sirdar was no longer trusted by the men. At a village where we stopped to buy tsampa some 3 miles up the valley I witnessed a curious scene. As the tsampa was sold it had to be measured. The Sirdar on his knees before a large pile of finely ground flour was ladling it into a bag with a disused Quaker Oats tin. Each measure-full was counted by all the coolies standing round in a circle; they were making sure of having their full ration. Nor was this all; they wanted to see as part of their supplies, not only tsampa and rice, but tea, sugar, butter, cooking fat and meat on the Army scale. This was a new demand altogether beyond the bargain made with them. The point, of course, had to be clearly made, that for their so-called luxuries I must be trusted to do my best with the surplus money (100 tankas or thereabouts) remaining over from their allowances after buying the flour and rice. These luxury supplies were always somewhat of a difficulty; the coolies had been very short of such things on the Northern side—we had no doubt that some of the ration money had found its way into the Sirdar's pockets. It would be possible, we hoped, to prevent this happening again. But even so the matter was not simple. What the coolies wanted was not always to be bought, or at the local price it was too expensive. On this

PETHANG-TSE.

occasion a bountiful supply of chillies solved our difficulty. After too many words, and not all in the best temper, the sight of so many of the red, bright, attractive chillies prevailed; at length my orders were obeyed; the coolies took up their loads and we started off again.

With so much dissatisfaction in the air it was necessary for Bullock and me to drive rather than lead the party. In a valley where there are many individual farms and little villages, the coolies' path is well beset with pitfalls and with gin. Without discipline the Sahib might easily find himself at the end of a day's march with perhaps only half his loads. It was a slow march this day; we had barely accomplished 8 miles, when Bullock and I with the hindmost came round a shoulder on the right bank about 4 p.m. and found the tents pitched on a grassy shelf and looking up a valley where a stream came in from our left. The Tibetan headman and his Tibetan coolies who were carrying some of our loads had evidently no intention of going further, and after some argument I was content to make the stipulation that if the coolies (our own as well as the Tibetans) chose to encamp after half a day's march, they should do a double march next day.

The prospect was far from satisfactory: we were at a valley junction of which we had heard tell, and the headman pointed the way to the left. Here indeed was a valley, but no glacier stream. It was a pleasant green nullah covered with rhododendrons and juniper, but presented nothing that one may expect of an important valley. Moreover, so far as I could learn, there were no villages in this direction: I had counted on reaching one that night with the intention of buying provisions, more particularly goats and butter. Where were we going and what should we find? The headman announced that it would take us five more days to reach Chomolungma: he was told that he must bring us there in two, and so the matter was left.

If the coolies behaved badly on this first day, they certainly made up for it on the second. The bed of the little valley which we now followed rose steeply ahead of us, and the path along the hill slopes on its left bank soon took us up beyond the rhododendrons. We came at last for a mid-day halt to the shores of a lake. It was the first I had seen in the neighbourhood of Everest; a little blue lake, perhaps 600 yards long, set on a flat shelf up there among the clouds and rocks, a sympathetic place harbouring a wealth of little rock plants on its steep banks; and as our present height by the aneroid was little less than 17,000 feet, we were assured that on this Eastern side of Everest we should find Nature in a gentler mood. But we were not satisfied with our direction; we were going too much to the South. Through the mists we had seen nothing to help us. For a few moments some crags had appeared to the left looming surprisingly big; but that was our only peep, and it told us nothing. Perhaps from the pass ahead of us we should have better fortune.

At the Langma La when we reached it we found ourselves to be well 4,000 feet above our camp of the previous night. We had followed a track, but not always a smooth one, and as we stayed in hopes of a clearing view, I began to wonder whether the Tibetan coolies would manage to arrive with their loads; they were notably less strong than our Sherpas and yet had been burdened with the wet heavy tents. Meanwhile we saw nothing above our own height. We had hoped that once our col was crossed we should bear more directly Westward again; but the Tibetan headman when he came up with good news of his coolies, pointed our way across a deep valley below us, and the direction of his pointing was nearly due South. Everest, we imagined, must be nearly due West of Kharta, and our direction at the end of this second day by a rough dead reckoning would be something like South-west. We were more than ever mystified. Fortunately our difficulties with the coolies seemed to be ended. Two of our own men stayed at the pass to relieve the Tibetans of the tents and bring them quickly on. Grumblings had subsided in friendliness, and all marched splendidly on this day. They were undepressed with the gloomy circumstance of again encamping in the rain.

In the Sahibs' tent that night there took place a long and fragmentary conversation with the headman, our Sirdar acting as interpreter. We gained one piece of information: there were two Chomolungmas. It was not difficult to guess that, if Everest were one, the other must be Makalu. We asked to be guided to the furthest Chomolungma.

The morning of August 4 was not more favourable to our reconnaissance. We went down steeply to the valley bed, crossed a stream and a rickety bridge, and wound on through lovely meadows and much dwarf rhododendron till we came to the end of a glacier and mounted by its left bank. Towards mid-day the weather showed signs of clearing; suddenly on our left across the glacier we saw gigantic precipices looming through the clouds. We guessed they must belong in some way to Makalu. We were told that this was the first Chomolungma, while the valley we were now following would lead us to the other. It was easy to conclude that one valley, this one, must come up on the North side of Makalu all the way to Everest. But we saw no more. In a few moments the grey clouds blowing swiftly up from below had enveloped us, rain began to fall heavily, and when eventually we came to broad meadows above the glaciers, where yaks were grazing and Tibetan tents were pitched, we were content to stop. At least we should have the advantage here of good butter and cream from this dairy farm. There was indeed no point in going farther; we had no desire to run our heads against the East face of Everest; we must now wait for a view.

The weather signs were decidedly more hopeful as I looked out of our tent next morning, and we decided at once to spend the day in some sort of reconnaissance up the valley. Presently away at the head of it we saw the clouds breaking about the mountain-sides. Everest itself began to clear; the great North-east arête came out, cutting the sky to the right; and little by little the whole Eastern face was revealed to us.

As I recall now our first impression of the amazing scenery around us, I seem chiefly to remember the fresh surprise and vivid delight which, for all we had seen before, seemed a new sensation. Even the map of the Kama Valley, now that we have it, may stir the imagination. Besides Everest itself the crest of the South Peak, 28,000 feet high, and its prodigious South-east shoulder overlook the Western end; while Makalu, 12 miles from Everest, thrusts out Northwards a great arm and another peak to choke the exit; so that whereas the frontier ridge from Everest to Makalu goes in a South-easterly direction, the Kangshung Glacier in the main valley runs nearly due East. In this spacious manner three of the five highest summits in the world overlook the Kama Valley.

And we now saw a scene of magnificence and splendour even more remarkable than the facts suggest. Among all the mountains I have seen, and, if we may judge by photographs, all that ever have been seen, Makalu is incomparable for its spectacular and rugged grandeur. It was significant to us that the astonishing precipices rising above us on the far side of the glacier as we looked across from our camp, a terrific awe-inspiring sweep of snow-bound rocks, were the sides not so much of an individual mountain, but rather of a gigantic bastion or outwork defending Makalu. At the broad head of the Kama Valley the two summits of Everest are enclosed between the North-east arête and the South-east arête bending round from the South Peak; below them is a basin of tumbled ice well marked by a number of moraines and receiving a series of tributaries pouring down between the buttresses which support the mountain faces in this immense cirque. Perhaps the astonishing charm and beauty here lie in the complications half hidden behind a mask of apparent simplicity, so that one's eye never tires of following up the lines of the great arêtes, of following down the arms pushed out from their

SUMMIT OF MAKALU.

great shoulders, and of following along the broken edge of the hanging glacier covering the upper half of this Eastern face of Everest so as to determine at one point after another its relation with the buttresses below and with their abutments against the rocks which it covers. But for me the most magnificent and sublime in mountain scenery can be made lovelier by some more tender touch; and that, too, is added here. When all is said about Chomolungma, the Goddess Mother of the World, and about Chomo Uri, the Goddess of the Turquoise Mountain, I come back to the valley, the valley bed itself, the broad pastures, where our tents lay, where cattle grazed and where butter was made, the little stream we followed up to the valley head, wandering along its well-turfed banks under the high moraine, the few rare plants, saxifrages, gentians and primulas, so well watered there, and a soft, familiar blueness in the air which even here may charm us. Though I bow to the goddesses I cannot forget at their feet a gentler spirit than theirs, a little shy perhaps, but constant in the changing winds and variable moods of mountains and always friendly.

The deviation from our intended line of approach involved by entering the Kama Valley was not one which we were likely to regret. In so far as our object was to follow up a glacier to the North Col we were now on the wrong side of a watershed. A spur of mountains continues Eastwards from the foot of Everest's North-east arête; these were on our right as we looked up the Kama Valley; the glacier of our quest must lie on the far side of them. But the pursuit of this glacier was not our sole object. We had also to examine both the East face and North-east arête of our mountain and determine the possibilities of attack on this side. A plan was now made to satisfy us in all ways. We chose as our objective a conspicuous snowy summit, Carpo-ri, on the watershed and apparently the second to the East from the foot of the North-east arête. Could we climb it we should not only see over into the valley North of us and up to Chang La itself, we hoped, but also examine, from the point most convenient for judging the steepness of its slopes, the whole of the Eastern side of Mount Everest.

On August 6 the Whymper tents were taken up, and a camp was made under a moraine at about 17,500 feet, where a stream flows quietly through a flat space before plunging steeply down into the valley. In this sheltered spot we bid defiance to the usual snowstorm of the afternoon; perhaps as night came on and snow was still falling we were vaguely disquieted, but we refused to believe in anything worse than the heavens' passing spite, and before we put out our candles the weather cleared. We went out into the keen air; it was a night of early moons. Mounting a little rise of stones and faintly crunching under our feet the granular atoms of fresh fallen snow we were already aware of some unusual loveliness in the moment and the scenes. We were not kept waiting for the supreme effects; the curtain was withdrawn. Rising from the bright mists Mount Everest above us was immanent, vast, incalculable—no fleeting apparition of elusive dream-form: nothing could have been more set and permanent, stedfast like Keats's star, "in lone splendour hung aloft the night," a watcher of all the nights, diffusing, it seemed universally, an exalted radiance.

It is the property of all that is most sublime in mountain scenery to be uniquely splendid, or at least to seem so, and it is commonly the fate of the sublime in this sort very soon to be mixed with what is trivial. Not infrequently we had experience of wonderful moments; it is always exciting to spend a night under the stars. And such a situation may be arranged quite comfortably; lying with his head but just within the tent a man has but to stir in his sleep to see, at all events, half the starry sky. Then perhaps thoughts come tumbling from the heavens and slip in at the tent-door; his dozing is an ecstasy: until, at length, the alarm-watch sounds; and after? . . . Mean considerations din it all away, all that delight. On the morning of August 7 the trivial, with us, preponderated. Something more than the usual inertia reigned in our frozen camp at 2 a.m. The cook was feeling unwell; the coolies prolonged their minutes of grace after the warning shout, dallied with the thought of meeting the cold air, procrastinated, drew the blankets more closely round them, and—snored once more. An expedition over the snow to the outlying tents by a half-clad Sahib, who expects to enjoy at least the advantage of withdrawing himself at the last moment from the friendly down-bag, is calculated to disturb the recumbency of others; and a kick-off in this manner to the day's work is at all events exhilarating. The task of extricating our frozen belongings, where they lay and ought not to have lain, was performed with alacrity if not with zeal; feet did not loiter over slippery boulders as we mounted the moraine, and in spite of the half-hour lost, or gained, we were well up by sunrise. Even before the first glimmer of dawn the snow-mantled, slumbering monsters around us had been somehow touched to life by a faint blue light showing their form and presence—a light that changed as the day grew to a pale yellow on Everest and then to a bright blue-grey before it flamed all golden as the sun hit the summit and the shadow crept perceptibly down the slope until the whole mountain stood bare and splendid in the morning glory. With some premonition of what was in store for us we had already halted to enjoy the scene, and I was able to observe exactly how the various ridges and summits caught the sun. It was remarkable that while Everest was never, for a moment, pink, Makalu was tinged with the redder shades, and the colour of the sky in that direction was a livid Chinese blue red-flushed. Its bearing from us was about South-east by South, and its distance nearly twice that of Everest, which lay chiefly to the South-west.

The first crux of the expedition before us would evidently be the ascent of a steep wall up to the conspicuous col lying East of our mountain. The least laborious way was offered by an outcrop of rocks. The obstacle looked decidedly formidable and the coolies had little or no experience of rock-climbing. But it proved a pleasure reminiscent of many good moments once again to be grasping firm granite and to be encouraging novices to tread delicately by throwing down an occasional stone to remind them of the perils of clumsy movements. The coolies, as usual, were apt pupils, and after agreeable exertions and one gymnastic performance we all reached the col at 9 a.m. with no bleeding scalps.

We had already by this hour taken time to observe the great Eastern face of Mount Everest, and more particularly the lower edge of the hanging glacier; it required but little further gazing to be convinced—to know that almost everywhere the rocks below must be exposed to ice falling from this glacier; that if, elsewhere, it might be possible to climb up, the performance would be too arduous, would take too much time and would lead to no convenient platform; that, in short, other men, less wise, might attempt this way if they would, but, emphatically, it was not for us.

Our interest was rather in the other direction. We had now gained the watershed. Below us on the far side was a glacier flowing East, and beyond it two important rock peaks, which we at once suspected must be two triangulated points each above 23,000 feet. Was this at last the valley observed so long ago from the hill above Shiling, more than 50 miles away, to point up towards the gap between Changtse and Everest? As yet we could not say. The head of the glacier was out of sight behind the Northern slopes of our mountain. We must ascend further, probably to its summit, to satisfy our curiosity—to see, we hoped, Changtse and its relation to this glacier, and perhaps the Chang La of our quest.

The task before us was not one which had suggested from a distant view any serious difficulties. The angle of sight from our breakfast-place on the col to the next white summit West of us was certainly not very steep. But no continuous ridge would lead us upwards. The East face in front of us and the South face to our left presented two bands of fortification, crowned each by a flat emplacement receding a considerable distance, before the final cone. We knew already that the snow's surface, despite a thin crust, could not hold us, and counted on snow-shoes to save labour at the gentler angles. But the escarpments in front of us were imposing. The first yielded to a frontal attack pushed home with a proper after-breakfast vigour. The second when we reached it was a more formidable obstacle. The steepness of the Eastern slope was undeniable and forbidding and the edge of its junction with the South side was defined by a cornice. On that side, however, lay the only hope.

We had first to traverse a broad gully. The powdery snow lay deep; we hesitated on the brink. Here, if anywhere, the unmelted powdery substance was likely to avalanche. Confidence was restored in sufficient measure by contemplating an island of rock. Here lay a solution. By the aid of its sound anchorage the party was secured across the dangerous passage. With his rope adequately belayed by a coolie, though the manner was hardly professional, the leader hewed at the cornice above his head, fixed a fist-and-axe hold in the crest and struggled over. Such performances are not accomplished at heights above 20,000 feet without the feeling that something has been done. Appearances suggested the necessity of establishing the whole party firmly above the cornice before proceeding many steps upward, and the first man had the diversion of observing at his leisure the ungraceful attitudes and explosive grunts of men strong indeed, but unaccustomed to meet this kind of obstacle. But with the usual menace of clouds, which even now were filling the head of the Kama Valley, it was no season for delay; and it was no place to be treated lightly. The angle was quite as steep as we liked; on the slopes to our left again we should evidently be exposed to the danger of an avalanche. It was necessary to avoid treading on our frail cornice and no less important to keep near the edge. Here a foot of powdery snow masked a disintegrated substance of loose ice. Nothing less than a vigorous swinging blow had any other effect than to bury the pick and require a fourfold effort to pull it out again. Luckily one or even two such blows usually sufficed to make a firm step. But 400 feet of such work seemed an ample quantity. If was a relief at length to reach level snow, to don our rackets again and to follow a coolie bursting with energy now sent first to tread a path. At 12.15 p.m. we reached the far edge of this flat shoulder lying under the final slopes of our mountain and at the most 500 feet below the summit.

No one without experience of the problem could guess how difficult it may be to sit down on a perfectly flat place with snow-shoes strapped to the feet. To squat is clearly impossible; and if the feet are pushed out in front the projection behind the heel tends to tilt the body backwards so that the back is strained in the mere effort to sit without falling. The remedy of course is to take off the snow-shoes; but the human mountaineer after exhausting efforts is too lazy for that at an elevation of 21,000 feet. He prefers not to sit; he chooses to lie—in the one convenient posture under the circumstances—flat upon his back and with his toes and snow-shoes turned vertically upwards. On this occasion the majority of the party without more ado turned up their toes.

The situation, however, was one of the greatest interest. We were still separated from Mount Everest by a spur at our own height turning Northwards from the foot of the North-east arête and by the bay enclosed between this and its continuation Eastward to which our mountain belonged. But the distance from the North-east arête was small enough and we were now looking almost directly up its amazing crest. If any doubts remained at this time as to that line of attack, they now received a *coup de grâce*. Not only was the crest itself seen to be both sharp and steep, suggesting an almost infinite labour, but the slopes on either hand appeared in most places an impracticable alternative; and leading up to the great rock towers of the North-east shoulder, the final section, the point of a cruel sickle, appeared effectually to bar further progress should anyone have been content to spend a week or so on the lower parts. To discern so much required no prolonged study; to the right (North) the country was more intricate. The summit of Changtse was eventually revealed, as the clouds cleared off, beyond, apparently a long way beyond, the crest of the spur in front of us. To the extreme right, looking past the final slopes of the white cone above us was a more elevated skyline and

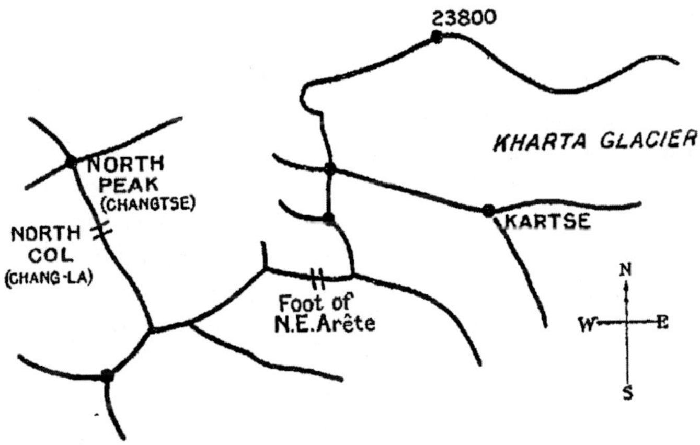

DIAGRAM SHOWING THAT THE KHARTA GLACIER DOES NOT LEAD TO THE NORTH COL.

below it the upper part of the glacier, the lower end of which we had seen earlier in the day descending Eastward. But its extreme limit was not quite visible. We had still to ask the question as to where exactly it lay. Could this glacier conceivably proceed in an almost level course up to Chang La, itself? Or was it cut off much nearer to us by the high skyline which we saw beyond it? Was it possible, as in the second case must be, that this skyline was continuous with the East arête of Changtse, the whole forming the left bank of the glacier? If no answer was absolutely certain, the probability at least was all on one side—on the wrong side alike for our present and our future plans. We could hardly doubt that the glacier-head lay not far away under Chang La, but here near at hand under another col; beyond this must be the glacier of our quest, turning East, as presumably it must turn beyond the skyline we saw now, and beyond the rock peaks which we had observed to the North of us when first we reached the watershed.

One more effort was now required so that we might see a little more. Chang La itself was still invisible. Might we not see it from the summit of our mountain? And was it not in any case an attractive summit? An examination of the various pairs of upturned toes where the prostrate forms were still grouped grotesquely in the snow was not encouraging. But the most vigorous of the coolies was with us, Nyima, a sturdy boy of eighteen, who from the very start of the Expedition had consistently displayed a willing spirit in every emergency. To my demand for volunteers he responded immediately, and soon persuaded a second coolie, Dasno, who had been going very strongly on this day, to accompany him. As the three of us started off the clouds suddenly boiled up from below and enveloped us completely. A few minutes brought us to the foot of the steepest slopes; we took off our snow-shoes and crossed a bergschrund, wading up to our thighs. Dasno had already had enough and fell out. But the conical shape of our peak was just sufficiently irregular to offer a defined blunt edge where two surfaces intersected. Even here the snow was deep enough to be a formidable obstacle at that steep angle; but the edge was safe from avalanches. As we struggled on I glanced repeatedly away to the left. Presently through a hole in the clouds all was clear for a moment to the West; again I saw Changtse, and now my eyes followed the line of its arête descending towards Everest until the col itself was visible over the spur in front of us. The view was little enough; the mere rim appeared; the wall or the slopes below it, all that I most wanted to see, remained hidden. We struggled on to the top, in all nearly an hour's work of the most exhausting kind. The reward was in the beauty of the spot, the faintly-defined edges of clean snow and the convex surfaces bent slightly back from the steepness on every side to form the most graceful summit I have seen. To the North-east we saw clearly for a minute down the glacier. The rest was cloud, a thin veil, but all too much, inexorably hiding from us Changtse and Chang La.

A disappointment? Perhaps. But that sort of suffering cannot be prolonged in a mind sufficiently interested. Possibly it is never a genuine emotion; rather an automatic reaction after too sanguine hopes. And such hopes had no part in our system. We counted on nothing. Days as we found them were not seldom of the disappointing kind; this one had been of the best, remarkably clear and fine. If we were baffled that was no worse than we expected. To be bewildered was all in the game. But our sensation was something beyond bewilderment. We felt ourselves to be foiled. We were unpleasantly stung by this slap in the face. We had indeed solved all doubts as to the East face and North-east arête, and had solved them quickly. But the way to Chang La, which had seemed almost within our grasp, had suddenly eluded us, and had escaped, how far we could not tell. Though its actual distance from our summit might be short, as indeed it must be, the glacier of our quest appeared now at the end of a receding vista; and this was all our prospect.

Our next plans were made on the descent. With the relaxation of physical effort the feeling of dazed fatigue wears off and a mind duly strung to activity may work well enough. The immediate object was to reach our tents not too late to send a coolie down to the base camp the same evening; on the following morning a reinforcement of four men would enable us to carry down all our loads with sufficient ease, and with no delay we should move the whole party along the next stage back towards Langma La—and thus save a day. The main idea was simple. It still seemed probable that the elusive glacier drained ultimately Eastwards, in which case its waters *must* flow into the Kharta stream; thither we had now to retrace our steps and follow up the main valley as we had originally intended; it might be necessary to investigate more valleys than one, but there sooner or later a way would be found. Only, time was short. At the earliest we could be back in the Kharta Valley on August 9. By August 20 I reckoned the preliminary reconnaissance should come to an end, if we were to have sufficient time before the beginning of September for rest and reorganisation at Kharta—and such was the core of our plan.

These projects left out of account an entirely new factor. In the early stages of the reconnaissance I had taken careful note of the party's health. One or two of the coolies had quickly fallen victims to the high altitudes; but the rest seemed steadily to grow stronger. Nothing had so much surprised us as the rapid acclimatisation of the majority, and the good effects, so far as they appeared, of living in high camps. Both Bullock and myself left the Rongbuk Valley feeling as fit as we could wish to feel. All qualms about our health had subsided. For my part I was a confirmed optimist, and never imagined for myself the smallest deviation from my uniform standard of health and strength. On August 7, as we toiled over the nevé in the afternoon, I felt for the first time a symptom of weariness beyond muscular fatigue and beyond the vague lassitude of mountain-sickness. By the time we reached the moraine I had a bad headache. In the tent at last I was tired and shivering and there spent a fevered night. The next morning broke with undeniable glory. A photograph of our yesterday's conquest must be obtained. I dragged myself and the quarter-plate camera a few steps up to the crest of the moraine—only to find that a further peregrination of perhaps 300 yards would be necessary for my purpose: and 300 yards was more than I could face. I was perforce content with less interesting exposures and returned to breakfast with the dismal knowledge that for the moment at all events I was *hors de combat.* We learned a little later that Colonel Howard-Bury had arrived the night before in our base camp. It was easily decided to spend the day there with him—the day I had hoped to save; after the long dragging march down the green way, which on the ascent had been so pleasant with butterflies and flowers, I was obliged to spend it in bed.

Three days later, on August 11, our tents were pitched in a sheltered place well up the Kharta Valley, at a height of about 16,500 feet. Two tributary streams had been passed by, the first coming in from the North as being clearly too small to be of consequence, and the second from the South, because wherever its source might be, it could not be far enough to the North. Ahead of us we had seen that the valley forked; we must follow the larger stream and then no doubt we should come soon enough to the glacier of our quest and be able at last to determine whether it would serve us to approach Chang La. August 12, a day of necessary idleness after three long marches, was spent by the coolies in collecting fuel, of which we were delighted to observe a great abundance, rhododendron and gobar all about us, and, only a short way down the valley, the best we could hope for, juniper. The last march had been too much for me, and again I was obliged to keep my bed with a sore throat and swollen glands.

It seemed certain that the next two days must provide the climax or anticlimax of our whole reconnaissance. The mystery must surely now be penetrated and the most important discovery of all be made. A competition with my companion for the honour of being first was, I hope, as far from my thoughts as ever it had been. From the start Bullock and I had shared the whole campaign and worked and made our plans together, and neither for a moment had envied the other the monopoly of a particular adventure. Nevertheless, after all that had passed, the experience of being left out at the finish would not be agreeable to me;

I confess that not to be in at the death after leading the hunt so long was a bitter expectation. But the hunt must not be stopped, and on the morning of August 13, from the ungrateful comfort of my sleeping-bag, I waved farewell to Bullock. How many days would he be absent before he came to tell his story, and what sort of story would it be? Would he know for certain that the way was found? or how much longer would our doubts continue?

It was impossible to stay in bed with such thoughts, and by the middle of the morning I was sitting in the sun to write home my dismal tale. A hint from one of the coolies interrupted my meditations; I looked round and now saw, to my great surprise and unfeigned delight, the approaching figure of Major Morshead. I had long been hoping that he might be free to join us; and he arrived at the due moment to cheer my present solitude, to strengthen the party, and to help us when help was greatly needed. Moreover, he brought from Wollaston for my use a medical dope; stimulated by the unusual act of drug-taking, or possibly by the drug itself, I began to entertain a hope for the morrow, a feeling incommunicably faint but distinguishably a hope.

Meanwhile Bullock, though he had not started early, had got off soon enough in the morning to pitch his tents if all went well some hours before dark, and in all probability at least so far up as to be within view of the glacier snout. As the night was closing in a coolie was observed running down the last steep sandy slope to our camp. He brought a chit from Bullock: "I can see up the glacier ahead of me and it ends in another high pass. I shall get to the pass to-morrow morning if I can, and ought to see our glacier over it. But it looks, after all, as though the most unlikely solution is the right one and the glacier goes out into the Rongbuk Valley."

Into the Rongbuk Valley! We had discussed the possibility. The glacier coming in there from the East remained unexplored. But even if we left out of account all that was suggested by the East arête of Changtse and other features of this country, there remained the unanswerable difficulty about the stream, the little stream which we had but just failed to cross in the afternoon of our first expedition. How could so little water drain so large an area of ice as must exist on this supposition?

In any case we were checked again. The mystery deepened. And though the interest might increase, the prospect of finding a way to Chang La, with the necessary margin of time before the end of the month, was still receding, and, whether or no the unexpected should turn out to be the truth, the present situation suggested the unpleasant complication of moving our base once more somewhere away to the North.

On the following day with the gathering energy of returning health I set forth with Morshead: we walked in a leisurely fashion up the valley rejected by Bullock and had the surprising good fortune of a clear sky until noon. I soon decided that we were looking up the glacier where we had looked down on the 7th, as Bullock too had decided on the previous day: at the head of it was a high snow col and beyond that the tip of Changtse. What lay between them? If a combe existed there, as presumably it did, the bed of it must be high: there could hardly be room, I thought, for a very big drop on the far side of the col. Might not this, after all, be a sufficiently good approach, a more convenient way perhaps than to mount the glacier from its foot, wherever that might be? The near col, so far as I could judge, should easily be reached from this side. Why not get to the col and find out what lay beyond it? The time had come to abandon our object of finding the foot of a glacier in order to follow it up; for we could more easily come to the head of it and if necessary follow it down.

I was sanguine about this new plan, which seemed to have good prospects of success and might obviate the difficulties and inconvenience of shifting the base (possibly again to the Rongbuk side, which I had no desire to revisit) and, as I still felt far from fit, I was in some hopes now that two more days would bring us to the end of our present labours. Bullock very readily agreed to the proposal. He brought no positive information from the col which he had reached, though he inclined to the idea that the water crossed at Harlung on our journey to Kharta, a moderate stream, but perhaps too clear, might provide the solution of our problem. A fresh bone was now thrown into our stew. A letter arrived from Howard-Bury with an enclosure from Wheeler, a sketch map of what he had seen more particularly East of the Rongbuk Glacier, on which the Eastern branch, with its Western exit, was clearly marked where we now know it to be. It was, unfortunately, a very rough map, professedly nothing more, and was notably wrong in some respects about which we had accurate knowledge. We were not yet convinced that the head of the East Rongbuk Glacier was really situated under the slopes of Everest, and not perhaps under the Eastern arm of Changtse. Still, we had some more pickings to digest. Our business was to reach the nearer pass, and I felt sure that once we had looked over it to the other side whatever doubts remained could be cleared up in subsequent discussion with Wheeler. Meanwhile, I hoped, we should have discovered one way to Chang La, and a sufficiently good one.

It took us in the sequel not two but four days to reach the pass which was ultimately known as Lhakpa La (Windy Gap). The story may serve as a fair illustration of the sort of difficulty with which we had to contend. It was arranged on the 15th that we should meet Bullock's coolies at the divide in the valley; they were bringing down his camp and we could all go on together: but our messenger succeeded in collecting only half their number and much delay was caused in waiting for the others. From here we followed the Western stream, a stony and rather fatiguing walk of two hours or so (unladen) up to the end of the glacier, and then followed a moraine shelf on its left bank,

I hoped we should find an easy way round to the obvious camping place we had previously observed from the Carpo-ri. But the shelf ended abruptly on steep stony slopes, clouds obscured our view, and after our misfortunes in the morning we were now short of time, so that it was necessary to stay where we were for the night. A thick layer of mist was still lying along the valley when we woke, and we could see nothing, but were resolved, nevertheless, to reach the col if possible. We went up, for the best chance of a view, to the crest of the hill above us, and followed it to the summit (6.30 a.m.). The view was splendid, and I took some good photographs; but the drop on the far side was more serious than our hopes had suggested. We tried to make the best of things by contouring and eventually halted for breakfast on the edge of the glacier a long way North of the direct line at 8.45 a.m. Before we went on we were again enveloped in mist, and after stumbling across the glacier in snow-shoes to the foot of an icefall, we turned back at 11 a.m. By that time we were a tired party and could not have reached the col; and even had we reached it, we should have seen nothing. Still we felt when we found our tents again that with all we had seen the day had not been lost, and we determined, before renewing our attempt on Lhakpa La, to push on the camp. There was still time to send a message down to the Sirdar so as to get up more coolies and supplies and move forward next day. From this higher camp we hoped that the col might be reached at an early hour, and in that case it would be possible for a party to cross it and descend the glacier on the other side.

The first coolies who came up in the morning brought a message from the Sirdar to the effect that supplies were short and he could send none up. The rations were calculated to last for another three days, but their distribution had been muddled. However, enough was subsequently sent up to carry us over into the next day, though it was necessary of course to abandon our project of a more distant reconnaissance. Our camp was happily established in the usual snowstorm. The weather, in fact, was not treating us kindly. Snow was falling in these days for about eight to ten hours on the average and we were relieved at last to see a fine morning.

On August 18, with the low moon near setting, the three of us with one coolie set forth on the most critical expedition of our whole reconnaissance. Failure on this day must involve us in a lamentable delay before the party could again be brought up for the attack; at the earliest we should be able to renew the attempt four days later, and if in the end the way were not established here the whole prospect of the assault in September would be in jeopardy. We scaled the little cliff on to the glacier that morning with the full consciousness that one way or another it was an imperative necessity to reach the col. The first few steps on the glacier showed us what to expect; we sank in to our knees. The remedy was, of course, to put on rackets—which indeed are no great encumbrance, but a growing burden on a long march and on steep slopes most difficult to manage. We wore them for the rest of the day whenever we were walking on snow. About dawn the light became difficult; a thin floating mist confused the snow surfaces; ascents and descents were equally indistinguishable, so that the errant foot might unexpectedly hit the slope too soon or equally plunge down with sudden violence to unexpected depths. Crevasses forced, or seemed to force, us away to the right and over to the rocks of the left bank. We were faced with one of those critical decisions which determine success or failure. It seemed best to climb the rocks and avoid complications in the icefall. There was an easy way through on our left which we afterwards used; but perhaps we did well; ours was a certain way though long, and we had enough trudging that day; the rocks, though covered with snow to a depth of several inches, were not difficult, and a long traverse brought us back to the glacier at about 8.30 a.m.

Our greatest enemy as we went on was not, after all, the

deep powdery snow. The racket sank slightly below the surface and carried a little snow each step as one lifted it; the work was arduous for the first man. But at a slow pace it was possible to plod on without undue exhaustion. The heat was a different matter. In the glacier-furnace the thin mist became steam, it enveloped us with a clinging garment from which no escape was possible, and far from being protected by it from the sun's fierce heat, we seemed to be scorched all the more because of it. The atmosphere was enervating to the last degree; to halt even for a few minutes was to be almost overwhelmed by inertia, so difficult it seemed, once the machinery had stopped and lost momentum, to heave it into motion again. And yet we must go on in one direction or the other or else succumb to sheer lassitude and overpowering drowsiness. The final slopes, about 700 feet at a fairly steep angle, undoubtedly called for greater efforts than any hitherto required of us.

The importance of breathing hard and deeply had impressed itself upon us again and again. I had come to think of my own practice as a very definite and conscious performance adopted to suit the occasion. The principles were always the same—to time the breathing regularly to fit the step, and to use not merely the upper part of the lungs, but the full capacity of the breathing apparatus, expanding and contracting not the chest only, but also the diaphragm, and this not occasionally but with every breath whenever the body was required to work at high pressure. Probably no one who has not tried it would guess how difficult it is to acquire an unconscious habit of deep breathing. It was easy enough to set the machine going in the right fashion; it was another task to keep it running. The moment attention to their performance was relaxed, the lungs too would begin to relax their efforts, and often I woke from some day-dream with a feeling of undue fatigue, to find the cause of my lassitude only in the lungs' laziness. The best chance of keeping them up to their work, I found, was to impose a rhythm primarily upon the lungs and swing the legs in time with it.

The practice employed for walking uphill under normal conditions is exactly contrary, in that case the rhythm is consciously imposed on the legs and the rest of the body takes care of itself.

During the various expeditions of our reconnaissance I came to employ two distinct methods of working the legs with the lungs. As soon as conscious breathing was necessary it was my custom deliberately to inhale on one step and exhale on the next. Later, at a higher elevation, or when the expenditure of muscular energy became more exhausting, I would both inhale and exhale for each step, in either case timing the first movement of lifting the leg to synchronise with the beginning, so to speak, of the breathing-stroke. On this occasion as we pushed our way up towards Lhakpa La I adopted a variation of this second method, a third stage, pausing a minute or so for the most furious sort of breathing after a series of steps, forty or thirty or twenty, as the strength ebbed, in order to gain potential energy for the next spasm of lifting efforts. Never before had our lungs been tested quite so severely. It was well for us that these final slopes were no steeper. It was difficult and tiring enough as it was to prevent the rackets sliding, though without them we could not possibly have advanced in such snow. But happily the consequences of a slip were not likely to be serious. We were able to struggle on without regarding dangers, half-dazed with the heat and the glare and with mere fatigue, occasionally encouraged by a glimpse of the skyline above us, a clean edge of snow where the angle set back to the pass, more often enveloped in the scorching mist which made with the snow a continuous whiteness, so that the smooth slope, even so near as where the foot must be placed next, was usually indistinguishable. We had proceeded a considerable distance and I was satisfied with our progress, when the leader broke the monotony; he was seen to hesitate in the act of stepping up, to topple over and fall headlong downwards. This time he had guessed wrong; his foot had hit unexpectedly against the steepening slope. Somehow he had passed in extreme fatigue from the physical state of stable equilibrium; he had become such a man as you may "knock down with a feather," and this little misadventure had upset his balance. Mere surprise gave him strength to stop his slide. He raised himself, disgusted, to his feet again and after sundry gruntings the party went on.

Some little way further up Major Morshead, who was walking last in the party, with one brief exclamation to tell us what he intended, quietly untied the rope and remained where he was in his steps, unable to go further.

At length we found ourselves on flatter ground; the pass was still invisible, how far ahead of us we could not guess. Unexpectedly we came upon the brink of a crevasse. We worked round it, vaguely wondering whether after all our pains we were to meet with many troubles of this sort. And then after a few more steps we were visibly on some edge of things; we had reached the col itself.

Some twenty minutes later, as we sat on the snow gazing most intently at all that lay about us, Bullock and I were surprised by a shout. A moment later Major Morshead rejoined us, to the great rejoicing of all three.

It was about 1.15 p.m. when the first two of us had reached Lhakpa La; the clouds, which had been earlier only a thin veil, rent occasionally to give us clear glimpses, had thickened perceptibly during the last hour, so that we had now no hope of a clear view. In a sense, despite our early start from a high camp, we were too late. Little was to be seen above our level. The slopes of Everest away on our left, were visible only where they impinged upon the glacier. But we were not actually in cloud on the col. The South-facing rocks of Changtse presented their profile, steep and jagged, an imposing spectacle so far up as we could see; between them and Everest we looked down on a broad bay, the smooth surface of which was only occasionally broken by large crevasses. The descent to it from where we were could also be seen well enough, and we judged it perfectly simple and not much more than 800 feet.* The East ridge of Changtse had no existence for us; we looked across at what presumably were the splayed-out slopes supporting it. Below them was a narrow glacier (it grew when we crossed it to broader dimensions), shaping its course somewhat to the West of North, joined after losing its white snow-covering by another and cleaner glacier coming steeply down from the left, then apparently bending with this confluent to the right, and finally lost to view. We could see no more; the mountain sides, which must hem it in on the North, remained completely hidden, and for all we had seen the exit of this glacier was still a mystery.

Another great question remained unsolved. We had been able to make out the way across the head of the glacier towards the wall under Chang La; and the way was easy enough. But the wall itself, in spite of some fleeting glimpses and partial revelations, we had never really seen. We conjectured its height should be 500 feet or little more; and it was probably steep. It had been impossible to found an opinion as to whether the col were accessible. Nevertheless, I held an opinion, however flimsy the foundations. I had seen the rim of the col from both sides, and knew that above it on either hand were unserrated edges. When we added to whatever chances might be offered by the whole extent of the wall, which was considerable, the possibilities of finding a way to the col by the slopes of Everest to the South or by those of Changtse to the North, I felt we had enough in our favour. I was prepared, so to speak, to bet my bottom dollar that a way could be found, and was resolved that before we turned homewards this year we must get up from the East. When I thought of the 4,000 feet on the other side, the length combined with the difficulties, the distance that would necessarily separate us there from

* It turned out to be a full 1,200 feet.

North-east of Mount Everest and Chang La
from Lhakpa La.

any convenient base and all the limitations in our strength, I could have no reasonable doubt that here to the East lay the best chance of success.

It remained to determine by which of two possible routes we should reach the glacier-head between Lhakpa La and Chang La. Presuming that Wheeler was right we could use the old base at the foot of the Rongbuk Glacier which was only one stage, though a very long one, from Chöbuk, and proceed simply enough by two rough marches and one which should be easier to a camp at the foot of the wall or possibly to the col itself. On the East we could use as an advanced base a place two easy marches from Kharta; from there I reckoned one long day and two easy ones, provided the snow were hard, to Chang La. Against this route was the loss of height in crossing Lhakpa La; and for it the convenience of a good encampment on stones at 20,000 feet, better than anything we might expect to find at a similar elevation on the other side. So far the pros and cons. were evenly balanced. But there was one great and perhaps insuperable obstacle in working from the Rongbuk Valley. We had always found difficulties there in obtaining an adequate supply of fuel. There is no wood at Chöbuk or for some distance below it. A few small bushes grow in a little patch of vegetation by the riverside an hour higher up. But it is a very niggardly supply, and when I thought of the larger scale of the preparations we should now have to make, it became clear that we should have to rely on gobar, which, besides being a more extravagant fuel in the sense that it gives less fire for a given weight than wood, is also difficult to get in the Rongbuk Valley, for little enough is to be found there, and the monastery at Chöyling is a large consumer. On the other hand, in the Kharta Valley we were in a land of plenty. Gobar and rhododendron were to be had within a stone's throw of our present advanced base camp, and a little lower was an abundance of juniper. Food supplies also were better here; fresh vegetables and eggs, luxuries never seen on the other side, could easily be obtained from Kharta, and even the sheep in this region could be praised at the expense of the Rongbuk breed, which was incomparably skinny; lurking in the thigh of one recently killed we had actually discovered a nugget of fat.

And presuming Wheeler were wrong? In any case we knew enough of the country to be sure that a valley further to the North would offer us little better than the Rongbuk Valley, for it must be situated in the drier area unvisited by the monsoon currents from the Arun. The conclusion was drawn as we came down from Lhakpa La more swiftly than the reader of these arguments might suppose. We had now found a way to approach Chang La—not an ideal way, because it would involve a descent, and not one that could be used immediately; but good enough for our purpose. If laden coolies could not be brought to the Lhakpa at present over so much soft snow they might find the march to their liking later; for good snow at angles not too steep involves far less labour than rougher ground; and might we not expect the snow to harden before long? The whole plan of campaign had been founded upon the belief that September would be the best month for climbing, and our greatest efforts, some sort of an assault upon the mountain, were timed to take place then. We must now proceed upon the assumption that what the wise men prophesied about the matter would come true; and they promised a fine September. About the beginning of the month the monsoon would come to an end; then we should have a succession of bright, clear days to melt the snow and cold, starry nights to freeze it hard. At worst the calm spell would only be broken by a short anger. In September, perhaps a fortnight hence, on these same slopes where now we toiled we should find a solid substance beneath our feet and an easy way.

The abiding thought, therefore, after the first rush downwards on the steep slopes below the col contained a measure of solid satisfaction. We had now brought to an end our preliminary reconnaissance. Ahead of us was a new phase in our operations, and one which should hold in store for us the finest adventure of all, the climax of all reconnoitring expeditions, that advance which was to bring us as near to the summit as our strength would take us. As we plodded on, retracing our steps, some little satisfaction was highly acceptable. To the tired party even descent seemed laborious. We reached the edge of the glacier where we had come on to it at 5.30 p.m. But the march from there to our lower camp was both long and rough. Major Morshead, who had not been trained with Bullock and me to the pace of such expeditions, had kept up so far in the gamest fashion; but he was now much exhausted. The day ended with a series of little spurts, balancing over the snow-sprinkled boulders along and along the valley, in the dim misty moonlit scene, until at 2 o'clock in the morning we reached our lower camp, twenty-three hours after the early start.

On August 20 we went down to Kharta for ten days' rest and reorganisation. The party was gathering there for the assault, in which all were to help to the best of their powers. Col. Howard-Bury and Mr. Wollaston were there; Dr. Heron came in on the following day, and a little later Major Wheeler. A conversation with this officer, who had been working in the Rongbuk Valley since Bullock and I had left it, was naturally of the highest interest, and he now confirmed what his sketch-map had suggested: that the glacier on to which we had looked down from Lhakpa La drained into the Rongbuk Valley. But this certain knowledge could have no bearing on our plans; we remained content with the way we had found and troubled our heads no more for the present about the East Rongbuk Glacier.

CHAPTER XV

THE ASSAULT

In the agreeable climate of Kharta we were sufficiently occupied with the results of photography and preparations for the future; and there was time besides for unmixed idleness, which we knew how to appreciate. Our thoughts turned often to the weather. Local lore confirmed our expectations for September, and we looked each day for signs of a change. It was arranged, in hope if not in confidence, to move up on the first signs of improvement. Already before we came down to Kharta our Advanced Base Camp had been moved up; it was now situated at about 17,300 feet on a convenient grassy plateau and only a reasonable stage below our 20,000-foot camp, where some light tents and stores had also been left. At these two camps we had, in fact, left everything which we should not absolutely require at Kharta, so that few mountaineering stores would have to be carried forward from the Base when we came up again. Our first task would be to supply the Advanced Base with food and fuel, and a start had already been made by collecting here a pile of wood, nominally thirty loads. Transport in any case was not likely to be a difficulty in the early stages. Local coolies could easily be hired, and Howard-Bury was to follow us up after a short interval with all available strength to help in every possible way.

The first object which our plans must include was, of course, to reach Chang La; by finding the way to this point we should establish a line of attack and complete a stage of our reconnaissance. Secondly we must aim at reaching the North-east Shoulder. In so far as it was an object of reconnaissance to determine whether it was possible to climb

Mount Everest, our task could never be complete until we had actually climbed it; but short of that it was important to have a view of the final stage, and could we reach the great shoulder of the arête we should at least be in a better position to estimate what lay between there and the summit. Finally we saw no reason to exclude the supreme object itself. It would involve no sacrifice of meaner ends; the best would not interfere with the good. For if it should turn out that the additional supplies required for a longer campaign were more than our coolies could carry, we would simply drop them and aim less high.

In organising the assault we had first to consider how our camps could be established, at Lhakpa La or perhaps better beyond it at a lower elevation, at Chang La, and finally as high as possible, somewhere under the shoulder, we thought, at about 26,500 feet. From the camp on Chang La we should have to carry up ten loads, each of 15 lb., which would provide tents enough, and sleeping-sacks and food for a maximum of four Sahibs and four coolies; sixteen coolies were allowed for this task; twelve therefore would have to return on the day of their ascent and sleep at Chang La, and on the assumption that they would require an escort of Sahibs who must also sleep at this camp, four small tents must remain there, making six in all to be carried up to this point. The lower end of the ladder must be so constructed as to support this weight at the top. It was comparatively a simple matter to provide the earlier camps. The first above the advanced base—that at 20,000 feet—could be filled before we moved up to sleep there, the coolies returning on the same day whenever they carried up loads. And the same plan could be adopted for the second at Lhakpa La; only one journey there, I calculated, would be required before we started in force from the 20,000-foot camp to go straight ahead without delay. The crux would lie in the stage from Lhakpa La to Chang La. At the most we should have twenty-three coolies, sixteen who had been all along with the climbing party, three whom Wheeler had partially trained, and four more Sherpas, the maximum number being determined by the supply of boots. But it would not be necessary to carry on all the loads from Lhakpa La ; and return journeys could be made from Chang La both by those who were not to stay there and by the twelve already mentioned who might fetch supplies if necessary on the final day of the assault. This plan was never executed in its later stages, and we cannot know for certain whether it would have held good. But it may be conjectured, in view of our experience, that the weakest link would have broken ; either an extra day would have been spent between Lhakpa La and Chang La, or, if we had reached Chang La according to programme with the minimum of supplies, the coolies would not have been brought to this point a second time and the climbing party would have been cut off from its reserves. And, granted the most favourable conditions for the attempt, in asking the coolies to carry loads of 30 lb. on two consecutive days at these high altitudes, we were probably expecting too much of them. It must be concluded, if this opinion is correct, that we had not enough coolies for what we intended.

On the last day of August, Bullock and I were established once again at our Advanced Base. The weather had not yet cleared, though it was showing some signs of change. But it had been neccssary to move up for the coolies' sake. At Kharta, where they found little to amuse them and no work to employ their time, they had sought diversion with the aid of liquor and become discontented and ill-affected. They were badly in need of a routine, which at the Advanced Base was easily enough provided. Besides, I wanted to be ready, and it seemed not too soon to begin carrying loads up to the next camp. There was no occasion for hurry in the event. We were obliged to wait nearly three weeks, until September 19, before moving forward. The delay served no useful purpose, the work of supplying our present needs and providing for the future was sufficiently spread over the long tale of days, but interspersed with more rest and leisure than anyone required.

In some respects life at the Advanced Base compared favourably with our experience at other camps. The place had a charm of its own. The short turf about us, the boulders and little streams reminded me of Welsh hillsides; and these high pastures were often decorated by the brilliant blues of *Gentiana ornata* and by the most exquisite of saxifrages, which, with the yellow and ochre markings on the cream glaze of its tiny bowl, recalls the marginal ornament on some Persian page. Whenever the weather cleared for a few hours we saw down the valley a splendid peak in a scene of romantic beauty, and by walking up to a stony shoulder only 2,000 feet above us, we had amazing views of Everest and Makalu. And it was an advantage during these days of waiting to be a larger party, as we soon became.

Bury and Wollaston, and also Raeburn whom we rejoiced to see again, had come up on the 6th, Morshead and Wheeler on the 11th, and for two nights Heron was of our company. We made little excursions to keep ourselves fit, and on one occasion enjoyed some rock-climbing. But it amused nobody to watch the procession of clouds which precipitated sleet by day and snow by night, and our appetite for adventure could not be stimulated by making time pass in some endurable fashion and counting the unhopeful signs.

Under these circumstances I became more than ever observant of the party's physical condition. I find a passage in one of my letters written during this period of waiting in which I boast of finding myself " still able to go up about 1,500 feet in an hour—not bad going at these altitudes "—a reassuring statement enough but for the one word " still," which betrays all my anxiety. In fact there was too much cause to be anxious. Three of our strongest coolies were ill at this camp; others seemed to be tired more easily than they should be. And what of the Sahibs? At least it must be said that several of them were not looking their best. Bullock, though he never complained, seemed no longer to be the fit man he was at the end of July. And for my part I began to experience a certain lack of exuberance when going up hill. I came to realise that all such efforts were unduly exhausting; my reserve of strength had somehow diminished. The whole machine, in fact, was running down; the days continued to pass with their cloud and rain and snow, always postponing our final effort to a later date and a colder season; and with them our chances of success were slowly vanishing.

When at last the weather cleared, it was evident that the fate of our enterprise would be decided by the sun's power to melt the snow. In a subsequent chapter I shall have more to say about the snow's melting; it may suffice to remark here that, before we left the Advanced Base, I had good reason to expect that we should meet adverse conditions, and was resolved at the same time that nothing was to be gained by waiting. The coolies were lightly laden up to the First Advanced Camp and sufficiently unfatigued to proceed next day. On the 20th, therefore, leaving Bullock to accompany Wheeler, Morshead and I set forth to get fourteen loads up to Lhakpa La. We had one spare coolie who carried no load, and Sanglu, who was now our acting Sirdar, four of us in all, to break the trail for the loaded men. Snow-shoes were not carried because there were not enough to go round. Though our prospects of reaching a high point on Everest were already sufficiently dim, I intended to carry out the original plan until obliged by circumstances to modify it; it might prove necessary to spend an extra day in reaching Chang La, and in that case we could perhaps afford to stop short of Lhakpa La and establish our camp below its final slopes. But if the strain on this first day was likely to be severe, I argued that the coolies could rest to-morrow, and that the second journey in frozen tracks would be easy enough. That we should be passing the night a few hundred feet higher (at 22,500 feet) was a relatively unimportant consideration. The great matter was to put heart into the coolies; it would be infinitely more encouraging to reach the crest with a sense of complete achievement, to see the clear prospect ahead and to proceed downwards on the other side.

Our start at an early hour on the 20th was propitious enough. It was the same moonlit glacier of our expedition a month before as we made good our approach to its surface. But the conditions were altered. For the first time since we had come to these mountains we experienced the wonderful delight of treading snow that is both crisp and solid. We walked briskly over it, directly towards Mount Everest, with all the hope such a performance might inspire. The night was exceedingly cold and there was no untoward delay. In less than an hour we were at the foot of the icefall. We were determined on this occasion not to avoid it by the rocks of the left bank, but to find a quicker way through the tumbled ice. At first all went well. A smooth-floored corridor took us helpfully upwards. And then, in the dim light, we were among the crevasses. To be seriously held up here might well be fatal to our object, and in the most exciting kind of mountaineering adventures we had the stimulus of this thought. We plunged into the maze and struggled for a little time, crossing frail bridges over fantastic depths and making steps up steep little walls, until it seemed we were in serious trouble. One leap proposed by the leader proved too much for some of the laden coolies and a good deal of pushing and pulling was required to bring them over the formidable gap. We had begun to waste time. Halted on a sharp little crest between two monstrous chasms Morshead and I discussed the situation, and thereafter gravely proceeded to reconnoitre the ground to our left. In ten minutes we came to another corridor like the first, which brought us out above the icefall.

We were well satisfied with our progress as we halted at sunrise, and it was a pleasant change to get our feet out of the snow and knock a little warmth into chilled toes. But our confidence had ebbed. Even as we entered the icefall our feet had occasionally broken the crust; as we came out of it we were stamping a trail.

Dorji Gompa, our unladen coolie, and perhaps the strongest man of all, took the lead when we went on, and plugged manfully upwards. But already the party was showing signs of fatigue. One coolie, and then two others, fell out and could not be induced to come further. I sent Dorji Gompa back to bring on one of their loads. Morshead, Sanglu and I took turns ahead and soon came to the worst snow we had encountered anywhere. In it no firm steps could be stamped by the leaders to save the coolies behind, and each man in turn had to contend with the shifting substance of fine powder. The party straggled badly. It was necessary for some of us to press on and prove that the goal could be reached. Many of the men were obliged to halt at frequent intervals. But time was on our side. Gradually the party fought its way up the final slopes. As we approached the pass I looked back with Morshead over the little groups along our track and saw some distance below the last moving figure another lying huddled up on the snow. I soon learnt the meaning of this: it was Dorji Gompa who lay there. He had carried on not one load as I had asked him, but two, until he had fallen there dazed and exhausted.

At length eleven loads reached the pass and two more were only 800 feet lower. If we had not done all we set out to do I was satisfied we had done enough. We had established tracks to Lhakpa La which should serve us well when they had frozen hard, and not too many loads remained below to be brought up two days later.

We now obtained a clear view of Chang La; it was possible to make more exact calculations, and it was evident we must modify our plans. We saw a wall of formidable dimensions, perhaps 1,000 feet high; the surface was unpleasantly broken by insuperable bergschrunds and the general angle was undoubtedly steep. The slopes of Everest to the South were out of the question, and if it were possible to avoid a direct assault by the North side the way here would be long, difficult and exceedingly laborious. The wall itself offered the best chance, and I was in good hopes we could get up. But it would not be work for untrained men, and to have on the rope a number of laden coolies, more or less mountain sick, conducted by so small a nucleus as three Sahibs, who would also presumably be feeling the effects of altitude, was a proposition not to be contemplated for a moment. We must have as strong a party as possible in the first place, simply to reach the col, and afterwards to bring up a camp, if we were able, as a separate operation. With this idea I selected the party. Wollaston felt that his place of duty was not with the van; only Wheeler besides had sufficient mountaineering experience, and it was decided that he alone should accompany Bullock and myself on our first attempt to reach the col. Nevertheless, it seemed undesirable to abandon so early the hope that Bury and Morshead would be of use to us later on; and Wollaston clearly must start with us from the 20,000-foot camp where all had gathered on the 20th.

I had hoped we should have a full complement of coolies on the 22nd, but when morning came it was found that three, including two of the best men, were too ill to start. Consequently some of the loads were rather heavier than I intended. But all arrived safely at Lhakpa La before midday. Visited by malicious gusts from the North-west, the pass was cheerless and chilly; however, the rim afforded us some protection, and we decided to pitch our tents there rather than descend on the other side with the whole party, a move which I felt might complicate the return. I was not very happy about the prospects for the morrow. For my own part I had been excessively and unaccountably tired in coming up to the col; I observed no great sparkle of energy or enthusiasm among my companions; Sanglu was practically *hors de combat*; some of the coolies had with difficulty been brought to the col and were more or less exhausted; and many complaints of headache, even from the best of them, were a bad sign.

There was no question of bustling off before dawn on

the 23rd, but we rose early enough, as I supposed, to push on to Chang La if we were sufficiently strong. Morshead and I in a Mummery tent had slept well and I congratulated myself on an act of mutilation in cutting two large slits in its roof. The rest had not fared so well, but seemed fit enough, and the wonderful prospect from our camp at sunrise was a cheering sight. With the coolies, however, the case was different. Those who had been unwell overnight had not recovered, and it was evident that only a comparatively small number would be able to come on; eventually I gathered ten, two men who both protested they were ill casting lots for the last place; and of these ten it was evident that none were unaffected by the height and several were more seriously mountain-sick.* Under these circumstances it was necessary to consider which loads should be carried on. Bury, Wollaston and Morshead suggested that they should go back at once so as not to burden the party with the extra weight of their belongings, and it seemed the wisest plan that they should return. Certain stores were left behind at Lhakpa La as reserve supplies for the climbing party. I decided at an early hour that our best chance was to take an easy day; after a late start and a very slow march we pitched our tents on the open snow up towards the col.

It might have been supposed that in so deep a cwm and sheltered on three sides by steep mountain slopes, we should find a tranquil air and the soothing, though chilly calm of undisturbed frost. Night came clearly indeed, but with no gentle intentions. Fierce squalls of wind visited our tents and shook and worried them with the disagreeable threat of tearing them away from their moorings, and then scurried off, leaving us in wonder at the change and asking what next to expect. It was a cold wind at an altitude of 22,000 feet, and however little one may have suffered, the atmosphere discouraged sleep. Again I believe I was more

* I use this expression to denote not a state of intermittent vomiting, but simply one in which physical exertion exhausts the body abnormally and causes a remarkable disinclination to further exertion.

fortunate than my companions, but Bullock and Wheeler fared badly. Lack of sleep, since it makes one sleepy, always discourages an early start, and hot drinks take time to brew; in any case, it was wise to start rather late so as to have the benefit of warm sun whenever our feet should be obliged to linger in cold snow or ice steps. It was an hour or so after sunrise when we left the camp and half an hour later we were breaking the crust on the first slopes under the wall. We had taken three coolies who were sufficiently fit and competent, and now proceeded to use them for the hardest work. Apart from one brief spell of cutting when we passed the corner of a bergschrund it was a matter of straightforward plugging, firstly slanting up to the right on partially frozen avalanche snow and then left in one long upward traverse to the summit. Only one passage shortly below the col caused either anxiety or trouble; here the snow was lying at a very steep angle and was deep enough to be disagreeable. About 500 steps of very hard work covered all the worst of the traverse and we were on the col shortly before 11.30 a.m. By this time two coolies were distinctly tired, though by no means incapable of coming on; the third, who had been in front, was comparatively fresh. Wheeler thought he might be good for some further effort, but had lost all feeling in his feet. Bullock was tired, but by sheer will power would evidently come on—how far, one couldn't say. For my part I had had the wonderful good fortune of sleeping tolerably well at both high camps and now finding my best form; I supposed I might be capable of another 2,000 feet, and there would be no time for more. But what lay ahead of us? My eyes had often strayed, as we came up, to the rounded edge above the col and the final rocks below the North-east arête. If ever we had doubted whether the arête were accessible, it was impossible to doubt any longer. For a long way up those easy rock and snow slopes was neither danger nor difficulty. But at present there was wind. Even where we stood under the lee of a little ice cliff it came in fierce gusts at frequent intervals, blowing up the powdery snow in a suffocating tourbillon. On the col beyond it was blowing a gale. And higher was a more fearful sight. The powdery fresh snow on the great face of Everest was being swept along in unbroken spindrift and the very ridge where our route lay was marked out to receive its unmitigated fury. We could see the blown snow deflected upwards for a moment where the wind met the ridge, only to rush violently down in a frightful blizzard on the leeward side. To see, in fact, was enough; the wind had settled the question; it would have been folly to go on. Nevertheless, some little discussion took place as to what might be possible, and we struggled a few steps further to put the matter to the test. For a few moments we exposed ourselves on the col to feel the full strength of the blast, then struggled back to shelter. Nothing more was said about pushing our assault any further.

It remained to take a final decision on the morning of the 25th. We were evidently too weak a party to play a waiting game at this altitude. We must either take our camp to the col or go back. A serious objection to going forward lay in the shortage of coolies' rations. Had the men been fit it would not have been too much for them to return, as I had planned, unladen to Lhakpa La and reach Chang La again the same day. I doubted whether any two could be found to do that now; and to subtract two was to leave only eight, of whom two were unfit to go on, so that six would remain to carry seven loads. However, the distance to the col was so short that I was confident such difficulties could be overcome one way or another.

A more unpleasant consideration was the thought of requiring a party which already felt the height too much to sleep at least a 1,000 feet higher. We might well find it more than we could do to get back over Lhakpa La, and be forced to make a hungry descent down the Rongbuk Valley. There would be no disaster in that event. The crucial matter was the condition of the climbers. Were we fit to push the adventure further? The situation, if any one of the whole party collapsed, would be extremely disagreeable, and all the worse if he should be one of the Sahibs, who were none too many to look after the coolies in case of mountaineering difficulties. Such a collapse I judged might well be the fate of one or other of us if we were to push our assault above Chang La to the limit of our strength. And what more were we likely to accomplish from a camp on Chang La? The second night had been no less windy than the first. Soon after the weather cleared the wind had been strong from North-west, and seemed each day to become more violent. The only signs of a change now pointed to no improvement, but rather to a heavy fall of snow—by no means an improbable event according to local lore. The arguments, in fact, were all on one side; it would be bad heroics to take wrong risks; and fairly facing the situation one could only admit the necessity of retreat.

It may be added that the real weakness of the party became only too apparent in the course of our return journey over Lhakpa La on this final day; and it must be safe to say that none of the three climbers has ever felt a spasm of regret about the decision to go back or a moment's doubt as to its rightness. It was imposed upon us by circumstances without a reasonable alternative.

CHAPTER XVI

WEATHER AND CONDITION OF SNOW

Without consulting the meteorologist at Simla it is difficult to accept assertions about the monsoon as ultimate truth. Beyond a general, rather vague, agreement as to what should normally be expected, opinions differ not a little as to the measure and frequency of divergences from the norm. And individuals who observe in one locality more or less than they hope or expect are apt to forget that their dearth or plenty may be elsewhere compensated by capricious incidence. Nevertheless it seems certain that this year's rainfall in North-east India was above the normal both in amount and duration. "We had good rain," people said, and I was tempted to reply, "We had bad snow." Travelling through India I frequently asked questions on this point, and almost invariably heard of an unusually bountiful rainfall, seldom of one which was merely sufficient. Inhabitants of Darjeeling, who have observed the hills in the changing seasons for many years, told me that it was almost unheard of that so much snow should fall in September and lie so low. The general tenor of such remarks may probably be applied to an area including not only Mount Everest itself and the great peaks in its neighbourhood, but also a considerable tract of country to the North. The monsoon, according to Tibetan information, started perhaps a little later than usual, but was still more late in coming to an end; the Tibetans ordinarily lie with an object, and there could be no object in deceiving us about the weather. It may be concluded the year was abnormally wet, though to what extent on Everest itself can hardly be divined.

During our outward journey through Sikkim we saw nothing of the high peaks. It was not until the day of our march to Phari Dzong (May 28) that we had a clear view of the snows, and we had then the good fortune to see Chomolhari late in the morning. But Chomolhari and the range to the North of it were less visited by clouds than the peaks further South. Pawhunri, Kanchenjunga, Chomiomo were less often visible, and even at this early season we began to observe the usual habit of clouds to rise from the valleys or to form about the summits at an early hour, to be dissipated not before evening. The weather was not necessarily bad because the peaks were veiled. When we first saw Everest from Kampa Dzong on June 6, it was obscured some three hours after sunrise, but the weather seemed fine: and on two subsequent days we made the same observation. On June 13, from the hills above Shiling, Bullock and I were trying to make out the Everest group through glasses for about three hours. When first we looked in that direction, it appeared that a storm was in progress, with dark clouds drifting up from the West; but Kanchenjunga at the same time was a glorious sight, and all the mountains were clear before sunset. The most splendid of the distant views was from Ponglet on June 19: we were up our hill half an hour after sunrise and half an hour later there was nothing to be seen. There may have been malice in the clouds that day. It was radiantly fine where we were; but in the afternoon we came under the edge of a thunderstorm which drenched the main body of the Expedition as they were approaching Tingri; and there was a definite break in the weather at this time.

I suppose this break may be taken as the forerunner of the monsoon on Mount Everest. Storms there may have been before; but, generally speaking, it had been fine over the mountains since the beginning of June, and though the evidence is slight enough it seems probable that Everest received little or no snow before June 20. When first we saw it, a few days later, from the Rongbuk

Glacier, it was still comparatively black. It appeared a rocky mass with a white arm to the right, some permanent snow on the ledges and in the gullies of the face turned Northwards in our direction and some snow again on the high North-east arête; but with no pretensions to be a snow-mountain, a real sugar-cake as it seemed afterwards to become. We were lucky in having a few fine days at the outset of our reconnaissance. The conditions then were very different from those which obtained later. The recent snow must have melted quickly; we found clean ice on an East-facing slope at 21,000 feet and also at a gentler angle on one facing West. On Ri-ring the slopes were generally covered with snow near the crest, thinly but sufficiently, or we should never have got up; near the summit we found ice on both sides, North and South. It is impossible to say up to what height one might have found ice in June. Appearances suggested that on all but the steepest slopes above 23,000 feet the surface was hard snow rather than ice.

It was on the day following our ascent of Ri-ring, July 6, that we first experienced a real snowfall; and we woke next morning to find 3 or 4 inches covering the ground. In so far as an exact date can be ascribed to what is hardly a single event, July 6–7 may be taken as the beginning of the monsoon. We imagined at first that this snowfall was an important matter, sufficient to prevent climbing at any considerable height for several days. But from subsequent observations we came to treat such snowfalls with a certain degree of contempt. It was more often than not the case during the whole of July until the date of our departure that snow fell during the day—sometimes perhaps for a comparatively short period between noon and sunset, not seldom for many hours, intermittently during the day from the middle of the morning, and continuing into the night. But it was often so far as we were concerned a harmless phenomenon. Snow was precipitated from clouds so thin that they were easily penetrated by the sun's heat; it melted where it lay, and the moisture so readily evaporated that the snow had hardly stopped falling before the ground was dry. One might suppose that a few hundred feet higher, where the snow could be seen to lie where it fell, the effects would be more severe; but it was remarkable after half a day's unceasing precipitation of this fine granular snow that one might go up early next morning, perhaps to 20,000 feet, and find no more than a thin covering of 2 or 3 inches on the stones.

In saying that this sort of weather was harmless, I am not denying that it hindered our operations; but from the point of view merely of the climber it was remarkably innocuous. A case in point is our ascent of Ri-ring. As we were nearing the summit a thunderstorm gathered to the North and dark clouds came up on every hand, threatening a violent disturbance. I have related in an earlier chapter how we hurried down, expecting at the least a cold unpleasant wind and some nasty snow showers; but the air remained calm and the temperature warm and such grains of snow as fell were hardly remarked in our flight. A more disagreeable experience was our first journey to the col from which we afterwards looked into the West Cwm of Everest; we reached the pass in the teeth of a wind which drove the snow into our faces; but the weather had no real sting, and the wind, though cold, seemed to touch us lightly. Wind, in fact, was never an enemy to be feared during the whole period of the monsoon, and snowstorms, though they prevented more than one expedition, never turned us back. The delays in our reconnaissance caused by bad weather were of course considerable; we were forced to push our camps higher than would have otherwise been necessary, and often found ourselves hurrying after a start before dawn in a desperate race with the clouds to reach a view-point before the view had disappeared. And the precipitation of snow on the glaciers forced us invariably to wear snow-shoes on nevé, and consequently limited the numbers in our parties.

I have already alluded to a more serious snowfall which took place from July 20 to 25. Another occurred during the first days of August and another again on August 20 and 21, when snow came down below 16,000 feet. In September, towards the end of the monsoon, the weather was more monotonously malicious and the snowfall tended to be heavier; I find two heavy falls noted particularly in my diary. But on the whole it was the habit of snow to fall lightly. It is remarkable, when one calls to mind such a big snowfall as may occur during the climbing season in the Alps before the weather is resolved to be fine, how little snow by comparison fell on any one day in the region of Mount Everest. And perhaps in the end the slopes were more laden by the smaller precipitations which deposited a daily accretion.

We naturally sought an answer to the interminable query as to how much melting took place at the highest altitudes. Melting of course was always quicker on rocks. But even on the glaciers it was remarkably rapid whenever the sun shone brightly, and we were more than once surprised after a period of cloudy weather with constant snow showers to find how much the snow had consolidated. It seemed to us on more than one occasion that while snow had been falling at our camps and on the lower peaks, Everest itself must have escaped. But, generally speaking, after July 6 the mountain was remarkably white and became increasingly whiter, and only at the least two perfectly fine days, which rarely came together, made any perceptible difference. It was remarkable how little ice was ever observable on the steep Eastern face, where one would expect to see icicles hanging about the rocks. It is my own impression for what it is worth, and its value I fear is small, that though snow will melt readily enough low down, at least up to 23,000 feet during the warmer weather even on cloudy days, at greater altitudes, perhaps above 25,000 feet, it rarely melts even in bright sunshine. In September this year I doubt if it melted at all above 23,000 feet after the weather cleared.

At lower elevations the direction and angle of the slope made all the difference. After one fine day the snow on a steep East slope had solidified to a remarkable degree at about 20,000 feet; on a North-facing slope at a similar elevation it had been quite unaffected; on flat surfaces 1,000 feet higher a perceptible crust had formed, but the snow remained powdery below it as on the day when it fell. After three and four fine days the snowy surface of a glacier was absolutely hard at about 20,000 feet and remained solid in the afternoon. Fifteen hundred feet higher we were breaking a hard crust and sinking in a foot or more. This condition may have been partly due to the local behaviour of clouds, which were apt to cling about a ridge overlooking the glacier and cast a shadow on this part of it. But higher, on more open ground, we met the same condition; and again the slopes facing North preserved a powdery snow which never changed before it was blown down in avalanches. Perhaps the most convincing phenomena were the powdery snow high up on the Eastern slopes under the North col and the snow on the Western slopes at a similar elevation under Lhakpa La, which was hardly more solid, while 1,000 feet lower we found excellent snow. It is difficult to resist the conclusion that altitude is a determining factor in the sun's power of melting. It is possible that a line might always be drawn on any given day above which the temperature of the air is too cold for snow to melt where it has fallen on snow, and another to meet the case where it covers rocks. From our all too limited observations in June I should judge that in the middle of summer such imaginary lines would be above the height of Everest, but in other and cooler seasons we should quickly find them lower and a long way below the summit.

In close connection with the snow's melting we had to consider the possibility of avalanches. Our observations on this head were so meagre that I can only make with the greatest diffidence a few statements about them. It is astonishing to reflect how seldom we either saw or heard an avalanche, or even noticed the débris of one under steep slopes which had been laden with snow. Only on two occasions, I believe, were we confronted in practice with the question as to whether a slope could safely be crossed. The first was on August 7 in ascending the peak Carpo-ri, of which I have previously made mention. The heavy snowfall at the beginning of the month had ceased during the night August 4–5; the following days had been warm but cloudy, and on both there had been prolonged snow showers of the lighter sort in the afternoon and evening. On the night of August 6 we had hard frost at 17,500 feet, and there was a considerable sprinkling of fresh snow on the stones of the moraine. Between the col and the summit we met some very steep snow slopes on the South side: we carried no clinometer and I shall not venture to estimate their angles of inclination. It was on this occasion, as I have narrated, that in crossing a shallow scoop I was very much afraid of an avalanche, but was able to choose a safe line where we were protected and helped by an island of rocks. The snow here was inclined to be powdery; but it had solidified in some degree and, where we had to tread it, adhered sufficiently to the slope so as to give one a distinct confidence that it would not slide off wherever it might be crossed. Above this place we were able to avoid danger by following an edge where the snow was not so deep; but here again I noticed with surprise the adhesion between new snow and old. The ice below was not solid and smooth, but frothy and rough, and easily penetrated by a strong blow of the axe; it seemed to have been formed very quickly. The snow showed no inclination to slide off, though it was not of the substance in which a secure step could be made: and I concluded that the process of assimilation between the old surface and the new snow must proceed very rapidly whenever the temperature was warm enough. On the final slope, which was even steeper, more snow was lying—it was a more powdery substance: I was able again to escape danger on an edge dividing two faces; but it was surprising that no avalanche had already taken place and that the snow contrived to stay where it was.

The other occasion when we had to face and determine the possibility of an avalanche was in traversing the slopes to the North Col. Here our feet undoubtedly found a solid bed to tread upon, but the substance above it was dubiously loose. It was my conviction at the time that with axes well driven in above us we were perfectly safe here. But on the way down we observed a space of 5 yards or so where the surface snow had slid away below our tracks. The disquieting thoughts that necessarily followed this discovery left and still leave me in some doubt as to how great a risk, if any, we were actually taking. But it is natural to suppose that at a higher elevation or in a cooler season, because the snow adheres less rapidly to the slopes on which it lies, an avalanche of new snow is more likely to occur.

Temperature

Before attempting to draw conclusions as to the relative chances of finding favourable conditions between one month and another, a few words must be said about temperature.

So far as the temperature of the air was concerned, we experienced no severe cold and suffered no hardships from first to last. I do not mean to affirm that it was always warm. We welcomed frost at nights as one does in the Alps. One night so early as July 18, in a camp above 19,000 feet, was exceptionally cold. At our two last camps in September the thermometer went down to two or three degrees below zero (Fahr.) and the wind at the final camp made it more difficult to keep warm ; with as little protection as the coolies had, I should no doubt have shivered in my tent. The air also seemed very cold before sunrise on September 20, though we were walking fast ; but it did not bite the tip of my nose or ears or cause any disagreeable result. In general it may be said that there could be no difficulty in providing equipment against any cold we encountered. Heat was a much more dangerous enemy, as I indicated in describing our first ascent to Lhakpa La. Personally I never felt the sun's power on my head, but I felt it on my back so early as 8 a.m. as a definite attack on my energy and vital power, and more than once, though the sun was not shining, in crossing a glacier late in the day I was reduced from a state of alert activity to one of heavy lassitude.

The temperature of the snow is another consideration of very great importance. Even in July I felt the snow to be cold in the middle of the day towards the summit of Ri-ring, and when wearing snow-shoes in fresh snow under 20,000 feet coolies and all felt the cold in their feet. Later I apprehended a real danger from this source. The coolies were encouraged to anoint their feet with whale oil, and we avoided accident and even complaint: but I always admired their resistance to cold. Personally, though I am not particularly a cold-footed person, I took the precaution of wearing two pairs of long socks which were both new and thick, and a third from which, unfortunately, the toes had to be amputated owing to the timid miscalculation of my bootmaker: this equipment sufficed and I found my feet perfectly warm, while one of my companions was obliged to pull off a boot in order to restore circulation, and the other went on with numb feet and barely escaped frost-bite. And I must again emphasise the fact that this was on an Eastern slope well warmed by the sun in the middle of the morning and at an altitude no higher than about 22,500 feet. It may readily be concluded that forethought and care are in no respect more necessary than in guarding against frozen feet among a large party at the highest altitudes. And the difficulty of guarding against this danger might well determine the limits at either end of the warmest weather within which an assault should be launched on Everest itself or any one of the half-dozen or so highest peaks.

The Best Season for Climbing

It will hardly be doubtful from the whole tendency of my preceding remarks about weather and conditions that my opinion inclines decisively to the earlier rather than the later season as offering the best chances of climbing Mount Everest. We cannot of course assume that because September was a bad month this year it will always be a bad month. But supposing the monsoon were to end punctually and a fair spell to have set in by the first day of September—even then it appears to me improbable that the fresh snow fallen during the monsoon would sufficiently melt near the top of the mountain two and a half months after midsummer. As to the prospects of wind, we can only be content with the statement that in this particular year the wind after the end of the monsoon would alone have defeated even the most determined attempt to reach the summit. A wind strong enough to blow up the snow must always, I believe, prevent an ascent. A superman might perhaps be found, but never a party of men whose endurance at high altitudes would warrant the risk of exhaustion in struggling for long hours against such adverse circumstances. For the earlier season it may be said again, as a simple observation upon which little enough can be built, that the appearance of the clouds before the monsoon did not suggest wind, but rather a calm air on the summit. What precisely the conditions may be, for instance, in May and June, 1922, or what we ought normally to expect, cannot be determined with certainty. Will the whole of the snow fallen during the monsoon of 1921 have melted before the next moonsoon, and if so by what date ? Will the amount of snow on the mountain be the same in June, 1922, as twelve months before ? Or will black and white appear in altered proportions ? And if the snow has melted, where will ice be found ? It might well be that under the North Col all the steeper slopes will have lost their snow. And what of thc final arête ? One conjecture seems as good as another, and tho experience of more travelled mountaineers will suggest the most probable answer to these questions with an instinct less fallible than mine. Nevertheless, I think it may bo said that the chances are all in favour of the earlier season. We know, for instance, about this year that snow must have melted since the last monsoon and actually was melting fast in June, but the summer's snow does not always melt before the winter—not this year, for instance: the chances, therefore, of finding it melted in June are better than those of finding it melted in September. It may be contended that it might then have melted too much so that a party would find ice where they would wish to find snow. But one must prefer the lesser of two evils. Ice is far from an insuperable obstacle on Mount Everest; almost anywhere above Chang La crampons would overcome it: but powdery snow, in case the snow has melted too little, is a deadly handicap. Finally, the earlier is the warmer season with less danger to vulnerable feet and requiring a lighter equipment.

CHAPTER XVII

THE ROUTE TO THE SUMMIT

The reader who has carefully followed the preceding story will hardly have failed to notice that the route which has been chosen as the only one offering reasonable chances of success remains still very largely a matter of speculation. But the reconnaissance, unless it were actually to reach the summit, was obliged to leave much unproved, and its value must depend upon observations in various sorts and not merely upon the practice of treading the snow and rocks. Speculation in this case is founded upon experience of certain phenomena and a study of the mountain's features; and it is by relating what has been only seen with known facts that inferences have been drawn.

It may perhaps be accounted a misfortune that the party of 1921 did not approach Chang La by the East Rongbuk Glacier. The Lhakpa La proved a bigger obstacle than was expected. But in conditions such as we hope to find before the monsoon, this way would have much to recommend it. It avoids all laborious walking on a dry glacier, and with hard snow the walk up to the pass from the camp on stones at 20,000 feet should not be unduly fatiguing. Still the fact remains that the descent from the Lhakpa La on to the East Rongbuk Glacier is not less than 1,200 feet. Would it not be better to follow up this glacier from the Rongbuk Valley? The absence of wood on this side need not deter the party of 1922. For them plenty of time will be available sufficiently to provide their base with fuel, and the sole consideration should be the easiest line of approach; and though no one has traversed the whole length of the East Rongbuk Glacier, enough is known to choose this way with confidence. Here, as on other glaciers which we saw, the difficulties clearly lie below the limit of perpetual snow, and the greater part of them were avoided or solved by Major Wheeler, who found a practicable way on to the middle of the glacier at about 19,000 feet, and felt certain that the medial moraine ahead of him would serve for an ascent and be no more arduous than the moraines of the West Rongbuk Glacier had proved to be. The view of this way from the Lhakpa La confirmed his opinion, and though it may be called a speculation to choose it, whereas the way from the East has been established by experiment, it is a fair inference from experience to conclude that the untraversed section of the East Rongbuk Glacier, a distance which could be accomplished very easily in one march if all went well, will afford a simple approach to Chang La.

The Eastern wall, about 1,000 feet high, by which the gap itself must be reached, can never be lightly esteemed. Here reconnaissance has forged a link. But those who reached the col were not laden with tents and stores; and on another occasion the conditions may be different. There may be the danger of an avalanche or the difficulty of ice. From what we saw this year before the monsoon had brought a heavy snowfall it is by no means improbable that ice will be found at the end of May on the steepest slope below Chang La. In that case much labour will be required to hew and keep in repair a staircase, and perhaps fix a banister, so that the laden coolies, not all of whom will be competent ice-men, may be brought up in safety.

The summit of Mount Everest is about 6,000 feet above Chang La; the distance is something like 2½ miles and the whole of it is unexplored. What grounds have we for thinking that the mountaineering difficulties will not prove insuperable, that in so far as mere climbing is concerned the route is practicable? Two factors, generally speaking, have to be considered: the nature of the ground and the general angle of inclination. Where the climber is confined to a narrow crest and can find no way to circumvent an obstacle, a very small tower or wall, a matter of 20 feet, may bar his progress. There the general angle may be what it likes: the important matter for him is that the angle is too steep in a particular place. But on a mountain's face where his choice is not limited to a strict and narrow way, the general angle is of primary importance: if it is sufficiently gentle, the climber will find that he may wander almost where he will to avoid the steeper places. Long before we reached Chang La Mr. Bullock and I were fairly well convinced that the slope from here to the North-east Shoulder was sufficiently gentle and that the nature of the ill-defined ridge connecting these two points was not such as to limit the choice of route to a narrow line. Looking up from the North Col, we learnt nothing more about the angles. The view, however, was not without value ; it amply confirmed our opinion as to the character of what lay ahead of us. The ridge is not a crest; its section is a wide and rounded angle. It is not decorated by pinnacles, it does not rise in steps. It presents a smooth continuous way, and whether the rocks are still covered with powdery snow, or only slightly sprinkled and for the most part bare, the party of 1922 should be able to go up a long way at all events without meeting any serious obstacle. It may not prove a perfectly simple matter actually to reach the North-east arête above the shoulder at about 28,000 feet. The angle becomes steeper towards this arête. But even in the last section below it, the choice of a way should not be inconveniently restricted. On the right of the ascending party will be permanent snow on various sloping ledges, an easy alternative to rocks if the snow is found in good condition, and always offering a détour by which to avoid an obstacle.

From the North-east Shoulder to the summit of the mountain the way is not so smooth. The rise is only 1,000 feet in a distance of half a mile, but the first part of the crest is distinctly jagged by several towers and the last part is steep. Much will depend upon the possibility of escaping from the crest to avoid the obstacles and of regaining it easily. The South-east side (left going up) is terribly steep, and it will almost certainly be out of the question to traverse there. But the sloping snow-covered ledges on the North-west may serve very well; the difficulty about them is their tendency to be horizontal in direction and to diverge from the arête where it slopes upwards, so that a party which had followed one in preference to the crest might find themselves cut off by a cliff running across the face above them. But one way or another I think it should be possible with the help of such ledges to reach the final obstacle. The summit itself is like the thin end of a wedge thrust up from the mass in which it is embedded. The edge of it, with the highest point at the far end, can only be reached from the North-east by climbing a steep blunt edge of snow. The height of this final obstacle must be fully 200 feet. Mr. Bullock and I examined it often through our field-glasses, and though it did not appear insuperable, whatever our point of view, it never looked anything but steep.

* * * * *

To determine whether it is humanly possible to climb to the summit of Mount Everest or what may be the chances of success in such an undertaking, other factors besides the mere mountaineering difficulties have to be considered. It is at least probable that the obstacles presented by this mountain could be overcome by any competent party if they met them in the Alps. But it is a very different matter to be confronted with such obstacles at elevations between 23,000 and 29,000 feet. We do not know that it is physiologically possible at such high altitudes for the human body to make the efforts required to lift itself up even on the simplest ground. The condition of the party of 1921 in September during the days of the Assault cannot be taken as evidence that the feat is impossible. The long periods spent in high camps and the tax of many exhausting expeditions had undoubtedly reduced the physical efficiency of Sahibs and coolies alike. The party of 1922, on the other hand, will presumably choose for their attempt a time when the climbers are at the top of their form and their powers will depend on the extent of their adaptability to the condition of high altitude. Nothing perhaps was so astonishing in the party of reconnaissance as the rapidity with which they became acclimatised and capable of great exertions between 18,000 and 21,000 feet. Where is the limit of this process? Will the multiplication of red corpuscles continue so that men may become acclimatised much higher? There is evidence enough to show that they may exist comfortably enough, eating and digesting hearty meals and retaining a feeling of vitality and energy up to 23,000 feet. It may be that, after two or three days quietly spent at this height, the body would sufficiently adjust itself to endure the still greater difference from normal atmospheric pressure 6,000 feet higher. At all events, a practical test can alone provide the proof in such a case. Experiments carried out in a laboratory by putting a man into a sealed chamber and reducing the pressure say to half an atmosphere, valuable as they may be when related to the experiences of airmen, can establish nothing for mountaineers; for they leave out of account the all-important physiological factor of acclimatisation. But in any case it is to be expected that efforts above 23,000 feet will be more exhausting than those at lower elevations; and it may well be that the nature of the ground will turn the scale against the climber. For him it is all important that he should be able to breathe regularly, the demand upon his lungs along the final arête cannot fail to be a terrible strain, and anything like a tussle up some steep obstacle which would interfere with the regularity of his breathing might prove to be an ordeal beyond his strength.

As a way out of these difficulties of breathing, the use of oxygen has often been recommended and experiments were made by Dr. Kellas,* which will be continued in 1922.

* See *Geographical Journal*.

Even so there will remain the difficulty of establishing one or perhaps two camps above Chang La (23,000 feet). It is by no means certain that any place exists above this point on which tents could be pitched. Perhaps the party will manage without tents, but no great economy of weight will be effected that way; those who sleep out at an elevation of 25,000 or 26,000 feet will have to be bountifully provided with warm things. Probably about fifteen, or at least twelve loads will have to be carried up from Chang La. It is not expected that oxygen will be available for this purpose, and the task, whatever organisation is provided, will be severe, possibly beyond the limits of human strength.

Further, another sort of difficulty will jeopardise the chances of success. It might be possible for two men to struggle somehow to the summit, disregarding every other consideration. It is a different matter to climb the mountain as mountaineers would have it climbed. Principles, time-honoured in the Alpine Club, must of course be respected in the ascent of Mount Everest. The party must keep a margin of safety. It is not to be a mad enterprise rashly pushed on regardless of danger. The ill-considered acceptance of any and every risk has no part in the essence of persevering courage. A mountaineering enterprise may keep sanity and sound judgment and remain an adventure. And of all principles by which we hold the first is that of mutual help. What is to be done for a man who is sick or abnormally exhausted at these high altitudes? His companions must see to it that he is taken down at the first opportunity and with an adequate escort; and the obligation is the same whether he be Sahib or coolie; if we ask a man to carry our loads up the mountain we must care for his welfare at need. It may be taken for granted that such need will arise and will interfere very seriously with any organisation however ingeniously and carefully it may be arranged.

In all it may be said that one factor beyond all others is required for success. Too many chances are against the

Mount Everest
from the 20,000 foot camp—wind blowing snow off the mountain.

climbers; too many contingencies may turn against them. Anything like a breakdown of the transport will be fatal; soft snow on the mountain will be an impregnable defence; a big wind will send back the strongest; even so small a matter as a boot fitting a shade too tight may endanger one man's foot and involve the whole party in retreat. The climbers must have above all things, if they are to win through, good fortune, and the greatest good fortune of all for mountaineers, some constant spirit of kindness in Mount Everest itself, the forgetfulness for long enough of its more cruel moods; for we must remember that the highest of mountains is capable of severity, a severity so awful and so fatal that the wiser sort of men do well to think and tremble even on the threshold of their high endeavour.

NATURAL HISTORY

By A. F. R. WOLLASTON

CHAPTER XVIII

AN EXCURSION TO NYENYAM AND LAPCHE KANG

By a liberal interpretation of the expression "Mount Everest" we considered it necessary to explore the surrounding country as far as a hundred miles or more from the mountain, East, North and South; in all directions, that is, excepting toward the forbidden territory of Nepal. So it happened one day in July that Major Morshead and I, already nearly fifty miles from Everest, set out in a South-westerly direction, he anxious to add a few hundred square miles of new country to his map, and I intent on animals and plants. Our way lay across the Tingri Plain to Langkor, both names famous in the annals of Tibetan Buddhism. The following story was told us by an old monk in the monastery at Langkor:—

Many generations ago there was born in the Indian village of Pulahari a child named Tamba Sangay. When he grew into a youth he became restless and dissatisfied with his native place, so he went to visit the Lord Buddha and asked him what he should do. The Lord Buddha told him that he must take a stone and throw it far, and where the stone fell there he should spend his life. So Tamba Sangay took a rounded stone and threw it far, so that no one saw where it fell. Many months he sought in vain until he passed over the Hills into Tibet, and there he came to a place where, although it was winter, was a large black space bare of snow.

The people told him that the cattle walked round and round in that space to keep it clear from snow, and in the middle of it was a rounded stone. So Tamba Sangay knew that the stone was his, and there he made a cell and dwelt until he was taken on wings to Heaven. And the place is called Langkor, which means " the cattle go round," to this day. The people for many miles about had heard the stone as it came flying over the Hills from India ; it made a whistling sound like *Ting*, so the country came to be called Tingri, the Hill of the Ting.

We visited the Langkor monastery and saw the casket in which the stone of Tamba Sangay is kept, only to be opened once a year by a high dignitary from Lhasa. Close by was a fair-sized river, the bridge over which had been carried away by a recent flood. The greater part of the population was busily engaged in repairing the bridge, to the accompaniment at frequent intervals of hideous blasts on a large conch-shell : this, we were told, was to keep the rain away and stop the floods. Rain fell heavily in spite of the noise, but the bridge was finished before nightfall.

On the following day we had a long pull of many miles up to the Thung La, a pass of 18,000 feet, from which we had hoped for fine views over the surrounding country. A driving storm of snow blotted out the views and covered the ground, so that nothing was to be seen but little clumps, a few inches high, of poppies of the most heavenly blue. Going down the steep track beyond the pass I was stopped by hearing the unfamiliar note of a bird, so it seemed : the cry was almost exactly that of a female peregrine when its eyrie has been disturbed, but coming from a labyrinth of fallen rocks it could not be. Tracking the note from one rock to another, I came suddenly within a few yards of a large marmot, which sat up and waved her tail at me ; she called again and two half-grown young ones appeared close by ; then all dived into a burrow. These marmots are larger and far less timid of mankind than the marmots of the Alps.

A few miles below the pass the valley widened into an almost level bottom of half a mile or more, with steep bare limestone hills on either side. Here and there were small hamlets, where the inhabitants used the water of the river to irrigate their fields of barley and of blazing golden mustard, whose sweetness scented the valley in the sunshine. Like most of the butter, which is made in vast quantities in Southern Tibet, the mustard seed produces oil for monastery lamps. At one place we came across a spring, almost a fountain, bubbling out of the foothill, of clearest sparkling mineral water that would be the envy of Bath or of Marienbad; in a few yards it had become a racing stream a dozen feet in width.

Four days of leisurely walking down the valley brought us to the village of Nyenyam, where the whole population, a most unpleasant-looking crowd of four or five hundred people, came out to stare at us. A few only were Tibetans; the majority were obviously of Indian origin, calling themselves Nepalese, but without any of the distinctive features of that race. We had received some weeks earlier a cordial invitation from the Jongpens of Nyenyam to visit the place, and we were accordingly much disappointed to find that no person of authority came out to welcome us. A Jongpen, it should be said, is an official appointed by the Lhasa authorities to administer a district and collect revenues: in a place of any importance, as at Nyenyam, there are often two, the idea being that one will keep an eye on the other and prevent him from over-enriching himself. We visited these worthies, whom we found dressed in priceless Chinese silk gowns and cultivating the extreme fashion of long nails on all their fingers, in strange contrast to the squalor and dilapidation of their dwelling, and were annoyed to find that they denied all knowledge of the invitation. The bearer of the message was produced and lied manfully in their cause; the name of Nyenyam was not, as it happened, mentioned in our passport, and we were made to look somewhat foolish. Finally the Jongpens said (with their tongues in their cheeks and reminding us of a vulgar song) that they were very glad to see us, but they hoped that we would go. They then went out of their way to give us false information about the local passes and made our prolonged stay in the place impossible by discouraging the traders from dealing with us.*

Nyenyam, though more squalid and evil-smelling than any place in my experience, is of some importance as being the last Tibetan town before the frontier of Nepal is reached. It is well placed on a level terrace above the junction of the Pö Chu with an almost equally big river flowing from the glaciers of the great mountain mass of Gosainthan. Immediately below the town the river enters the stupendous gorge that cuts through the heart of the Himalaya to the more open country of Nepal, 8,000 feet below. To the West of Nyenyam rises a great range of mountains culminating in the beautiful peaks of Gosainthan, which we had hoped to visit, and somewhere to the East lay the mysterious sacred mountain of Lapche Kang. Our friends the Jongpens assured us that there was no direct route to Lapche, that we must go back the way by which we had come, and so on; but we were weary of their obstructions and made up our minds to find a way to the holy places.

So far our transport animals had been the yak, or the cross-bred ox-yak, a stronger beast; we were now going through country where only coolies could carry loads. We retraced our steps a few miles up the valley to a village ruled over by a friendly woman, the widow of the late headman. True, she demanded for the coolies an exorbitant wage, which we cut down by about a half, but she pressed into our service every able-bodied person in the neighbourhood, young and old, men and women. They have a fair and simple way of apportioning the loads. All Tibetans, men and women alike, wear long rope-soled boots with woollen cloth tops extending toward the knee, where they are secured by garters,

* In fairness it must be said that this was the only occasion on which we met with anything but help and civility from Tibetan officials.

long strips of narrow woven cloth. When all the loads are ready, each person takes off one garter and gives it to the headman, who shuffles them well and in his turn hands them over to some neutral person who knows not the ownership of the garters. He lays one on the top of each load, and whose garter it is must carry the load without any further talk. It is amusing to watch the excitement in their faces as the garters are dealt out, and to hear the shrieks of delight of the lucky ones and the groans of the less fortunate. It makes one feel weak and ashamed to see a small girl of apparently no more than fourteen years shouldering a huge tent or an unwieldy box, until one remembers that they begin to carry almost as soon as they can walk and are accustomed to far heavier loads than ever they carry for us.

Our path led us up a steep side-valley from the Pö Chu, ascending over a vast moraine to the foot of a small glacier about two miles in length. Here I saw a rare sight: a Lämmergeier (bearded vulture) came sailing down in wide circles and settled on the ice barely a hundred paces from us, where he began to peck at something—a dead hare perhaps, but it was impossible to see or to approach nearer over the crevasses. The Lämmergeier, vulture though it is, is one of the noblest birds in flight that may be seen: hardly a day passes in the high mountains without one or more swooping down to look at you, sometimes so near that you can see his beard and gleaming eye; but to see one on the ground is rare indeed. The long-tailed aeroplane at a very great height resembles the Lämmergeier more than any other bird.

We struggled up the glacier, inches deep in soft new snow, crossed crevasses by means of rotten planks which gravely offended our mountaineering sense, and came through dense fog to our pass at its head. Here began the sacred mountain of Lapche Kang, and on the rocks beside the pass, and on many of the pinnacles high up above the pass as well, were cairns of stones supporting little reed-stemmed flags of prayers. Some of our party had brought up from below such little flags, which they planted where their fancy prompted. As we went down on the other side we came to countless little "chortens," miniature temples, and, where the ground was level for a space, to long walls of stones, each one inscribed with the universal Buddhist prayer OM MANI PADME HUM.

Yaks are most satisfactory beasts of burden; if their pace is slow—it is seldom more than two miles an hour—they go with hardly a halt, cropping a tuft of grass here and there, until daylight fails. But the Tibetan coolie is of quite another nature; he (or she) starts off gaily enough in the morning, but very soon he is glad to stop for a gossip or to alter the trim of his load, and then it is time to drink tea, and again at every convenient halting-place more tea, not the liquid that we are accustomed to drink, but a curious mixture of powdered brick-tea, salt, soda and butter, of a better taste than one would suppose. So on this occasion it was long after noon when we had crossed the pass, and when the day began to fade in a drenching cloud of rain, the Tibetans found shelter in some caves, and persuaded us to camp. An uneven space among rocks just held our tents; we dined off the fragrant smoke of green rhododendron and soaking juniper, and we slept (if at all) to the roar of boulders rolling in the torrent-bed a few feet from where we lay.

But it was well that we had not stumbled on in the dark. In the morning light we walked over grassy "alps" still yellow with sweet-scented primulas, and the steep sides of the narrowing valley below were bright with roses, pink and white spiræas, yellow berberis and many other flowers. Soon it became evident that we were approaching a place of more than ordinary holiness; every stone had its prayer-flag, and the tops of trees, which began to appear here, were also decorated. Great boulders were defaced with the familiar words engraven on them in letters many feet in height. In a little while we came to a small wooden hut filled from floor to roof with thousands of little flags brought there by pilgrims; the posts and lintel of the door were smeared with

Temple at Lapche Kang.

dabs of butter, and the crevices of the walls were filled with little bunches of fresh-cut flowers. Outside was a rude altar made of stones from the river-bed, where a Lama was burning incense and chanting prayers.

We passed through the village, a tiny hamlet of a dozen houses, and came to the celebrated temple of Lapche. A square stone wall, about 60 yards each way, on the inner side of which are sheds to shelter pilgrims, encloses a roughly paved courtyard where stands the temple, a plain square building of stone with a pagoda-like roof surmounted by a burnished copper ornament. There is nothing remarkable about the temple excepting the hundred and more prayer wheels set in the wall at a convenient height for the pilgrims to turn as they walk round the building. Inside are countless Buddhas, the usual smell of smoky butter-lamps, and an effigy of the saint. The whole place is dirty and dishevelled, in the supposed care of one old woman and a monk, and nobody would believe that this is one of the most famous places in the country and that every year hundreds of Buddhists from India and from all parts of Tibet make pilgrimage to it.

Mila Respa, poet and saint and (it is said) a Tibetan incarnation of Buddha, spent his earthly life in this mountain valley, living under rocks and in caves, where the faithful may see his footprints even now. He seems to have been not lacking in a sense of humour. He was walking with a disciple on the mountain one day, when they found an old yak's horn lying in the path. Mila Respa told the disciple to pick it up and take it with him. The disciple refused, saying that it was useless, and passed on without noticing that the saint himself had picked up the horn and put it under his cloak. Soon afterwards a mighty storm descended on them—whether or not it was caused by the saint is not known. He took the horn from under his cloak and crept inside it. "Now," said he, when he was safely sheltered from the rain, "you see that nothing in the world is useless."

We stayed for two days at Lapche Kang, picking flowers

and enjoying the beauty of the place, in spite of the clouds which swept up from the South and filled the valley from early morning onwards. To a naturalist it was a tantalizing place; there were many unfamiliar birds that we had not seen in Tibet, but in such a sacred place I dared not offend the people by taking life, and I even had some qualms in catching butterflies. One of the prettiest sights I saw was a wall-creeper, like a big crimson-winged moth, fluttering over the temple buildings in search for insects.

Having found Lapche Kang, where no European had before penetrated, and having placed it on the map, our next object was to go over the ranges Eastward to the Rongshar Valley, the head of which had been visited by members of the Expedition a few weeks earlier. This was accomplished in two long days of rather confused climbing over two passes of about 17,000 feet, crossing sundry glaciers and stumbling over moraines, and nearly always in an impenetrable fog. Our views of mountains were none at all, but the beauty of the flowers at our feet was almost compensation for that. Among many stand out two in particular, both of them primulas. One was ivory-white, about the bigness of a cowslip, with wide open bells and the most delicate primrose scent: the other carried from four to six bells, each as big as a lady's thimble, of deep azure blue and lined inside with frosted silver.*

As we went down the last steep slope into the Rongshar Valley, the clouds parted for a few moments, and across the valley and incredibly high above our heads appeared the summit of Gauri-Sankar,† one of the most beautiful of Himalayan peaks, blazing in the afternoon sun. It was a glorious vision, but it rather added to our regret for the views of peaks that we might have seen. The next morning at daybreak the whole mountain was clear from its foot in the

* Both of these are new species; the former has been described as *Primula Buryana*, the latter as *P. Wollastonii*.

† Gauri-Sankar (23,440 ft.) was for many years confused with Mount Everest, which is still misnamed Gauri-Sankar in German maps.

Gauri-Sankar.

Rongshar River (10,000 feet) up through woods of pine and birch, to rhododendrons and rocks, and so by a knife-edged ridge of ice to its glistening summit. It recalled to me the Bietsch-horn more than any other Alpine peak, a Bietsch-horn on the giant scale and seemingly impassable to man.

The valley of the Rongshar, like the Nyenyam and other valleys we had visited, though within the Tibetan border, is really more Nepalese in character. The climate is much damper than in Tibet, as one can see by the wisps of lichen on the trees and the greenness of the vegetation far up the mountain sides, especially at this season of monsoon, when the South wind blows dense clouds of drenching moisture through the gorges. Like those valleys the Rongshar is sacred, which is inconvenient when the question of food supply is pressing. The people had cattle and flocks of goats; they would sell us an ox or a goat, but we must not kill it within the valley, or ill-luck would come to them. They were a friendly and good-tempered people, much given to religion. In many places we had seen prayer wheels worked by water, but here for the first time we saw one driven by the wind. Though it does not do much work at night, it probably steals a march on the water wheels in winter, when the streams are frozen.

We walked up the valley of Rongshar, which in July should be called the Valley of Roses; on all sides were bushes, trees almost, of the deep red single rose in bloom, and the air was filled with the scent of them. After a journey of about 150 miles through unknown country we came to the village of Tazang, which had been visited by some of us before. Thence over the Phüse La (the Pass of Small Rats) we came into real Tibet again, and so in a few days to the Eastern side of Mount Everest.

CHAPTER XIX

NATURAL HISTORY NOTES

To a naturalist Tibet offers considerable difficulties: it is true that in some places animals are so tame that they will almost eat out of your hand; for instance, in the Rongbuk Valley the burrhel (wild sheep) come to the cells of the hermits for food, and in every village the ravens and rock-doves are as fearless as the sparrows in London. But against this tameness must be set the Buddhist religion, which forbids the people from taking life, so that, whereas in most countries the native children are the best friends of the naturalist, in Tibet we got no help from them whatever. Also, in order to avoid giving possible offence, we were careful to refrain from shooting in the neighbourhood of monasteries and villages, and that was a very severe drawback, as birds congregated principally about the cultivated lands near villages. Another difficulty we found was in catching small mammals, which showed the greatest reluctance to enter our traps, whatever the bait might be. One species only, a vole (*Phaiomys leucurus*), was trapped; all the others were shot, and that involved a considerable expenditure of time in waiting motionless beside burrows. In spite of these disadvantages we made considerable collections of mammals and birds, and we brought back a large number of dried plants and seeds, many of which it is hoped will live in the gardens of this country.

Crossing over the Jelep La from Sikkim into Tibet in the latter part of May we found the country at 12,000 feet and upwards at the height of spring. The open level spaces were carpeted with a dark purple and yellow primula (*P. gammieana*), a delicate little yellow flower (*Lloydia tibetica*)

Lower Kama-chu.

and many saxifrages. The steep hillsides were ablaze with the flowers of the large rhododendrons (*R. thomsoni, R. falconeri, R. aucklandi*) and the smaller *Rhododendron campylocarpum,* an almost infinite variety of colours.* A descent through woods of pines, oaks and walnuts brought us to the picturesque village of Richengong, in the Chumbi Valley, where we found house-martins nesting under the eaves of the houses. Following up the Ammo Chu, in its lower course between 9,000 and 12,000 feet, we found the valley gay with pink and white spiræas and cotoneasters, red and white roses, yellow berberis, a fragrant white-flowered bog-myrtle, anemones and white clematis. Dippers, wagtails and the white-capped redstart were the commonest birds along the river-banks. From Yatung we made an excursion of a few miles up the Kambu Valley, and there found a very beautiful Enkianthus (*Enkianthus himalaicus*), a small tree about 15 feet high, with clusters of pink and white flowers; in the autumn the leaves turn to a deep copper red.

At about 11,000 feet is a level terrace, the plain of Lingmatang, where the stream meanders for two or three miles through a lovely meadow covered in the spring with a tiny pink primula (*P. minutissima*): it looks a perfect trout stream, but what fish there are (*Schizopygopsis stoliczae*) are small and few in number.

Between 11,000 and 13,000 feet you ascend through mixed woods of pine, larch, birch and juniper with an undergrowth of rhododendrons and mountain ash. The larches here have a much less formal habit of growth than those of this country, and in the autumn they turn to a brilliant golden colour. The berries of the mountain ash, when ripe, are white and very conspicuous. At this altitude *Rhododendron cinnabarinum* reaches its best growth, in

* We marked many of the best-flowering specimens with the intention of collecting their seeds on our return in the autumn. Unfortunately when we came over the Jelep La in October it was in a heavy snowstorm which made collecting impossible.

bushes of from 8 to 10 feet in height, and the flowers have a very wide range of colour. In the woods hereabouts may often be heard and sometimes seen the blood pheasant, and here lives also—but we did not see it—the Tibetan stag.

At about 13,000 feet at the end of May you find a yellow primula covering the ground more thickly than cowslips in this country; the air is laden with the scent of it, and growing with it is a pretty little heath-like flower (*Cassiope fastigiata*) with snow-white bells. Here and there is seen the large blue poppy (*Meconopsis* sp.) and a white anemone with five or six flowers on one stem. Soon the trees get scantier and scantier, pines disappear altogether and then birches and willows and junipers, until only dwarf rhododendrons (*R. setosum*) are left, covering the hillsides like purple heather.

In a few miles the country changes in character completely, and you come out on to the open plain of Phari. Here at 14,000 feet we saw the common cuckoo sitting on a telegraph wire and calling vigorously. This is Tibet proper, and henceforward you may travel for scores of miles and hardly see any plant more than a few inches high. In some places a little trumpet-shaped purple flower (*Incarvillea younghusbandii*) is fairly common, it lies prone on the sand with its leaves usually buried out of sight; and as we went Westward we found a dwarf blue iris (*I. tenuifolia*). Animals are few and far between: the Kiang, the wild ass of Tibet, is occasionally seen in small parties; they are very conspicuous on the open plains in full daylight, but almost invisible at dusk. The Tibetan gazelle is fairly numerous, and it is not uncommon to see one or two in company with a flock of native sheep and taking no notice of the shepherd, but when a stranger tries to approach they are off like a flash. Another animal of the plains is the Tibetan antelope (*Pantholops*), which is found in large numbers a little to the North of the region we visited, but the only signs of it we saw were the horns used as supporting prongs for the long muzzle-loading guns of the Tibetans. The Tibetan antelope was probably the Unicorn described by the French priest Huc in 1845.

The only mammals that are commonly seen on the plains are the small mouse-hares or pikas (*Ochotona*), which live in colonies on the less stony parts of the plain, where their burrows often caused our ponies to stumble; they scurry off to their holes at your approach, but if you wait a few moments you will see heads peeping out at you from all sides. These engaging little creatures have been called "Whistling Hares," but of the three species which we found none was ever heard to utter a sound of any kind. The Tibetan name for them is Phüse. It is interesting to record that from one specimen I took three fleas of two species, both of them new to science.

Birds are few on these stony wastes, larks, wheatears and snow-finches being the commonest. Elwes' shore-lark was found feeding young birds at the beginning of June, when the ground was not yet free from snow, and the song of the Tibetan skylark, remarkably like that of our own skylark, was heard over every patch of native cultivation.

A small spiny lizard (*Phrynocephalus theobaldi*) is common on the plains and on the lower hills up to 17,000 feet; it lives in shallow burrows on the sand and under stones.

Rising out of the plain North of the Himalayas are ranges of rounded limestone hills, 18,000 to 19,000 feet high, running roughly East and West. The hills between Phari and Khamba Dzong are the home of the big sheep (*Ovis hodgsoni*), which are occasionally seen in small companies. There are many ranges to the West of Khamba Dzong, apparently well suited to this animal, but it was never seen. On the slopes of these hills are found partridges (*Perdix hodgsoniæ*), and in the ravines are seen Alpine choughs, rock-doves (*Columba rupestris*) and crag-martins. Once or twice at night we heard the shriek of the great eagle-owl, but the bird was not seen.

At rare intervals on these plains one meets with small

rivers, tributaries of the Arun River; along their banks is usually more grass than elsewhere, and here the wandering Tibetan herdsmen bring their yaks to graze. The wild yak is not found anywhere in this region. It might be supposed that so hairy an animal as the yak would become dirty and unkempt. Actually they are among the cleanest of creatures, and they may often be seen scraping holes in soft banks where they roll and kick and comb themselves into silky condition. The usual colour of the domesticated yak is black, more rarely a yellowish brown. A common variety has a white face and white tail. The calves are born in the spring, late April or early May.

Here and there the rivers overflow their banks and form lakes or meres, which in the summer are the haunt of innumerable wild-fowl: bar-headed geese and redshanks nest here, families of ruddy shelducks (the Brahminy duck of India) and garganey teal are seen swimming on the pools. Overhead fly sand-martins, brown-headed gulls, common terns and white-tailed eagles. Near one of these lakes one day I watched at close distance a red fox stalking a pair of bar-headed geese, a most interesting sight, and had the satisfaction of saving the birds by firing a shot in the air with my small collecting gun just as the fox was about to pounce on his intended victim.

Tinki Dzong is a veritable bird sanctuary. The Dzong itself is a rambling fort covering a dozen or so of acres, and about its walls nest hundreds of birds—ravens, magpies, red-billed choughs, tree-sparrows, hoopoes, Indian redstarts, Hodgson's pied wagtails and rock-doves. In the shallow pool outside the Dzong were swimming bar-headed geese and ruddy shelducks, with families of young birds, all as tame as domestic poultry. A pair of white storks was seen here in June, but they did not appear to be breeding. In the autumn the lakes in this neighbourhood are the resort of large packs of widgeon, gadwall and pochard. The Jongpen explained to us that it was the particular wish of the Dalai Lama that no birds should be molested here, and for several

Junipers in the Kama Valley.

years two lamas lived at Tinki, whose special business it was to protect the birds.

Crossing over a pass of about 17,000 feet (Tinki La), the slopes gay with a little purple and white daphne (*Stellera*), said by the natives to be poisonous to animals, we came to a plain of a different character, miles of blown sand heaped here and there into enormous dunes, on which grows a yellow-flowering gorse. Here, near Chushar, we first met with rose-finches (Severtzoff's and Przjewalsk's) and the brown ground-chough (*Podoces humilis*): the last-named is a remarkable-looking bird, which progresses by a series of apparently top-heavy bounds, at the end of which it turns round to steady itself; in the middle of June it was feeding its young in nests at the bottom of deep holes in sand or old mud walls.

Following up the valley of the Bhong-chu we crossed the river by a stone bridge near Shekar Dzong. Here we found a colony of white-rumped swifts nesting high up in cliffs and ruddy shelducks nesting in holes among the loose boulders below. Occasionally we saw a pair of black-necked cranes, which are said by the natives to breed near lakes a little to the North, but we had no opportunity of visiting them. The slopes of the hills facing South were covered with a very pretty shrub (*Sophora*) with blue and white flowers and delicate silvery grey leaves, and among the loose stones a small clematis (*C. orientalis*) was just beginning to appear. Groups of small trees, like a sea buckthorn, growing 15 to 20 feet high, indicate a gradual change in the climate as you go Westwards. Here also for the first time we began to find a few butterflies, of the genera *Lycæna* and *Colias*.

At Tingri we found ourselves in a large plain about 20 miles long by 12 wide; a large part of the plain is saturated with soda and is almost uninhabited by bird or beast. In our three weeks' stay at Tingri we collected several mammals, including a new subspecies of hamster (*Cricetulus alticola tibetanus*) and a number of birds. This was the only place where we ever received any natural history specimen from a Tibetan.

A woman came into our camp one day and, after making certain that she was not observed by any of the villagers, produced from a sack a well-worn domestic cat's skin stuffed with grass and a freshly killed stoat (*Mustela longstaffi*). The skin of the stoat is highly prized by the Tibetans, who say that it has the property of restoring faded turquoises to their former beauty. About the houses of the village were nesting tree-sparrows, hoopoes, rock-doves and ravens, the latter so tame that they hardly troubled to get out of the way of passers-by. In a tower of the old fort lived a pair of the Eastern little owl (*Athene bactriana*), which appeared to live principally on voles. On the plain the commonest birds were the long-billed calandra lark, Brook's short-toed lark, the Tibetan skylark, and Elwes' shore-lark, all of which were found with eggs, probably the second brood of the season, at the beginning of July. The nest of the yellow-headed wagtail, rare at Tingri, was found with eggs, and Blanford's snow-finch was found feeding its young more than 2 feet down the burrow of a pika (*Ochotona curzoniæ*). The common tern and the greater sand-plover nested on the shingly islands in the river.

Plants at Tingri were few and inconspicuous: a small yellow cistus, the dwarf blue iris, a small aster and a curious hairy, claret-coloured flower (*Thermopsis*) were the most noticeable. Along the rivers which traverse the plain is very good grazing for the large flocks of sheep and goats of the Tibetans; the sheep are small and are grown entirely for wool. By a simple system of irrigation a large area of land near Tingri has been brought into cultivation. The principal crop here is barley, which constitutes the chief food of the people; they also grow a large radish or small turnip, the young leaves of which are excellent food. The animals usually used for ploughing are a cross between the yak and ordinary domestic cattle, called by the Tibetans "zoh"; they are more powerful than the yak and are excellent transport animals. We found barley grown in many districts up to 15,000 feet—it does not always ripen—and in the valley of the Dzakar Chu near its junction with the Arun River is a small area where wheat is grown at an altitude of about 12,800 feet. Peas are grown in the Arun Valley near Kharta, where they ripen in September and are pounded into meal for winter food of cattle as well as of the Tibetans themselves. Mustard is grown in the lower valleys below 14,000 feet. It is to be regretted that we did not bring back specimens of these hardy cereals.

During the course of an excursion of about three weeks in July to the West and South of Tingri we covered a large tract of unexplored country, much of which is more Nepalese than Tibetan in character. Going over the Thung La we found numerous butterflies of the genus *Parnassus*, and near the top of the pass (18,000 feet) we found for the first time the beautiful little blue *Gentiana amœna*; it is not easy to see until you are right over it, when it looks like a little square blue china cup; some of the flowers are as much as an inch in diameter. Here also was just beginning to flower the dwarf blue poppy (*Meconopsis horridula*), which grows in a small compact clump, 6 to 8 inches high, with as many as sixteen flowers and buds on one plant; the flowers are nearly 2 inches across and of a heavenly blue. In this region, too, we met for the first time marmots, which live in large colonies at about 16,000 feet; the Himalayan is larger than the Alpine marmot, and it has a longish tail which it whisks sharply from side to side when it is alarmed; it has a twittering cry, curiously like that of a bird of prey.

Continuing down the valley of the Pö Chu to Nyenyam, we found several birds that we had not met hitherto, notably the brown accentor, Himalayan tree-pipit, Adams's snow-finch, the Himalayan greenfinch and Tickell's willow-warbler. At about 12,500 feet we first found the white-backed dove (*Columba leuconota*), which inhabits the deep gorges of the Himalayas but does not extend out on to the Tibetan plain. Beside the big torrent that flows South from Gosainthan we saw a pair of that curious curlew-like bird, the ibis-bill (*Ibidorhynchus struthersi*); it was evident that they had eggs or young on an island in the torrent, at about 13,800 feet, but unfortunately it was impossible to reach it.

The most conspicuous flowers in this region were a little bushy cistus with golden flowers the size of a half-crown, a dwarf rhododendron (*R. lanatum*) with hairy leaves, a white potentilla with red centre, which carpeted the drier hillsides, a white gentian (*G. robusta*), and a very remarkable louse-wort (*Pedicularis megalantha*) with two quite distinct forms—one purple, the other yellow.

Crossing a pass to the East of Nyenyam, we camped on a level spot covered densely with white primulas (*P. Buryana*) six to eight inches high; an inch or two of snow fell during the night, and so white are these flowers that it was difficult to see them against the snow. Near the top of another pass we found at about the same altitude, 15,000 feet, another primula (*P. Wollastonii*) with three to six bells on each stem, the size of a small thimble, of a deep blue colour, and lined inside with frosted silver. In the moister valleys hereabouts a pretty pink-flowered polygonum (*P. vacciniifolium*) rambled everywhere over the rocks and boulders. The Rongshar Valley in July was chiefly notable for the large gooseberry bushes, 10 to 12 feet high, and for the profusion of red and white roses. A wall-creeper, the only one we saw in Tibet, was seen creeping about the temple at Lapche, a few miles to the West of Rongshar.

From the beginning of August our headquarters were at Kharta in the Arun Valley, about 20 miles East of Mount Everest, and from there we made excursions South to the Kama Valley, and West up the Kharta Valley in the direction of Everest. Kharta itself is curiously situated as regards climate: the wide dry valley of the Arun narrows abruptly and the river passes into a deep gorge, where it falls rapidly at a rate of about 200 feet to the mile on its way to Nepal. The heavy monsoon clouds roll up the gorge to its mouth, where they are cut off sharply, so that within a mile you may pass from the dry climate of Tibet to the moist, steamy air of a Nepalese character, with its luxuriant vegetation.

In the immediate neighbourhood of Kharta were several birds we had not met elsewhere, notably Prince Henry's laughing thrush (*Trochalopterum henrici*), which is very much venerated as a sacred bird by the Tibetans, the Central Asian blackbird, almost indistinguishable from our blackbird except by its voice, the solitary thrush, Indian brown turtle-dove, and a meadow-bunting (*Emberiza godlewskii*), probably a migrant from the North.

Several species of small gentians and two very fragrant onosmas were flowering in August, and in this place *Clematis orientalis* attains its best growth, clambering over the trees and the houses of the natives; the flower of this clematis has a very wide range of colour from an apricot yellow to almost black. About the houses are often planted junipers and poplars, and it was about 10 miles from Kharta that we saw a poplar nearly 40 feet in girth, which we were informed was five hundred years old.

A few miles to the south of Kharta is a valley filled with a dozen or so of small lakes or tarns, inhabited apparently only by tadpoles (*Rana pleskei*); no fish could be seen. Not far from here was discovered an interesting toad of a new species (*Cophophryne alticola*). Growing about the lakes were large beds of purple and yellow iris (*I. sibirica*, near); the steeper banks were blue with a very striking campanula (*Cyananthus pedunculatus*); growing out from among the dwarf rhododendrons in dry places were tall spikes of a claret-coloured meconopsis, now going to seed—some spikes had as many as twenty seed-pods; and in the moist places beside the lakes and streams was the tall yellow primula (*P. elongata*), growing to a height of over 30 inches.

Ascending from the lakes to the Chog La we saw a small black rat amongst the huge boulders of a moraine; it appeared to be a very active little animal, and though four or five were seen at different times in similar situations we failed to secure a specimen. Near the Chog La we found the snow-partridge (*Lerwa lerwa*), and one was shot out of a flock of very beautiful blue birds—Hodgson's grandala. Another very handsome bird in this region is the red-breasted rose-finch, which is found up to 18,000 feet. Descending from the Chog La towards the Kama Valley we found at 16,000 feet the giant rhubarb (*Rheum nobile*), and at 14,000 feet we picked quantities of the wild edible rhubarb. A little lower down we came to large blue scabius, 3 to 4 feet high, a dark blue monkshood and quantities of the tall yellow poppy. Rhododendrons, birches and junipers begin at about 13,500 feet, and at 12,000 feet the junipers are the predominating tree; they are of immense size, upwards of 20 feet in girth and from 120 to 150 feet in height and of a very even and perfect growth. Here we met with the Sikkim black tit (*Parus beavani*), and a little lower down among the firs (*Abies webbiana*) we came upon bullfinches (*Pyrrhula erythrocephala*). At 11,000 feet I saw a langur monkey (*Semnopithecus entellus*), the only monkey I saw in Tibet. Excepting one solitary bat, the only other mammal we saw in this valley was another species of pika (*Ochotona roylei nepalensis*), which appears here to be confined to a zone between the altitudes of 12,000 and 14,000 feet; it is not found in dry valleys.

Among the trees in the lower Kama Valley grow many parnassias, a tall green fritillaria, a handsome red swertia and a very sweet-scented pink orchis. We found the tubers (but not the flowers) of an arum, which the Tibetans collect and make of it a very unpalatable bread. We went down through large rhododendrons, magnolias, bamboos, alders, sycamores, all draped in long wisps of lichen (*Usnea*), to the junction of the Kama with the Arun River, where we found ourselves in the region of the blue pine. The lower part of the Kama Valley is unpleasantly full of leeches, and in the course of an excursion to the Popti La (14,000 feet), one of the principal passes from Tibet to Sikkim, we were astonished to find them very numerous and active at an altitude of 12,000 feet. At our low-altitude camps in this valley hundreds of moths were attracted by the light of our

FOREST IN THE KAMA VALLEY.

camp fire, and a few came to the dim candle lamps in our tents. A collector who came here with a proper equipment could not fail to make a large collection of moths.

Proceeding up the Kharta Valley in the beginning of September we found that most of the roses and rhododendrons had gone to seed, but some of the gentians, particularly *Gentiana ornata*, were at their best. Near our camp at 17,000 feet, along the edges of streams, a very handsome gentian (*G. nubigena*) with half a dozen flowers growing on a single stem was very conspicuous, and growing with it was an aromatic little purple and yellow aster (*A. heterochæta*); in the same place was a bright yellow senecio (*S. arnicoides*) with shining, glossy leaves. A curious dark blue dead-nettle (*Dracocephalum speciosum*) was found on dry ground at the same altitude. In the stony places grew up to 19,000 feet the dwarf blue meconopsis mentioned above, and many saxifrages, notably a very small white one (*S. umbellulata*). On the steeper rocks from 16,000 feet to the snow-line (roughly 20,000 feet) were found edelweiss (*Leontopodium*) of three species. Very noticeable at these altitudes are the curious saussureas, large composites packed with cotton wool; if you open one of them on the coldest day, even when it is covered with snow, you find it quite warm inside, and often a bumble bee will come buzzing out.

Another very interesting plant at 17,000 to 18,000 feet is a dwarf blue hairy delphinium (*D. brunnoneanum*) with a strong smell. The Tibetans dry the flowers of this plant and use them as a preventive against lice. This has its disadvantages, for when a Tibetan dies his body is undertaken by the professional butcher, who cuts it up and exposes it on the hills to be disposed of by the vultures and wolves. A body tainted with the delphinium flowers is unpalatable to the scavengers, and it is known that a man must have been wicked in life whose body is rejected by the vultures and wolves.

The smallest rhododendrons (*R. setosum* and *R. lepidotum*) disappear before 19,000 feet, after which vegetation is almost non-existent. A few grasses and mosses are still found to 20,000 feet, and the highest plant we found was a small arenaria (*A. musciformis*), which grows in flat cushions a few inches wide up to 20,100 feet.

Mammals in the upper Kharta Valley are not numerous. A pika of a new species (*Ochotona wollastoni*) is found from 15,000 to 20,000 feet, and a new vole (*Phaiomys everesti*) was found at 17,000 feet. The small black rat previously seen was here too, and an unseen mouse entered our tents and ate our food at 20,000 feet. Fox and hare were both seen above 18,000 feet, and undoubted tracks of them on the Kharta Glacier at 21,000 feet. Wolves were seen about 19,000 feet, and those tracks seen in snow at 21,500 feet, which gave rise to so much discussion, were almost certainly those of a wolf. Burrhel were fairly common between 17,000 and 19,000 feet, and we found their droppings on stones at 20,000 feet.

Birds of several species were found from 17,000 feet upwards. The Tibetan snow-partridge (*Tetraogallus tibetanus*) is common in large parties up to the snow-line. Dippers (*Cinclus cashmiriensis*) are found in the streams up to 17,000 feet, and at about the same altitude lives in the big boulders of moraines a small and very dark wren, which is almost certainly new, but only one immature bird was brought home. Snow-finches and the Eastern alpine accentor appeared to be resident up to the snow-line. Several migrating birds were seen in September at 17,000 feet and above, among them Temminck's stint, painted snipe, pin-tailed snipe, house-martin and several pipits. More than once at night the cry of migrating waders was heard, curlew being unmistakable, and (I think) bar-tailed godwit.

Our camps at 17,000 feet and at 20,000 feet were visited daily by lammergeier, raven, red-billed chough, alpine chough and black-eared kite, and I saw twice a hoopoe fly over the Kharta Glacier at about 21,000 feet; a small pale hawk flew overhead at the same time. The highest bird seen was a lammergeier (bearded vulture); when I was taking photographs from our camp on the Lhakpa La (22,350 feet) I saw one of these birds come sailing over the top of the North peak of Everest and apparently high above the peak, probably at an altitude of not less than 25,000 feet.*

* Detailed accounts of the collections made will be found: Mammals, *Annals and Magazine of Nat. Hist.*, Feb. 1922. Birds, *Ibis.*, July, 1922. Insects, *Annals and Magazine of Nat. Hist.*, May and June, 1922.

CHAPTER XX

AN APPRECIATION OF THE RECONNAISSANCE

By Professor NORMAN COLLIE, F.R.S.
President of the Alpine Club

The chance of wandering into the wild places of the earth is given to few. But those who have once visited the Himalaya will never forget either the magnificence or the beauty of that immense mountain land, whether it be the valley country that lies between the great snow-covered ranges and the plains, where wonderful forests, flowers, clear streams and lesser peaks form a fitting guard to the mighty snow-peaks that lie beyond, or the great peaks themselves, that can be seen far away to the North, as one approaches through the foot-hills that lead up to them. The huge snow-covered giants may be a week's journey away, they may be far more, yet when seen through the clear air of the hills, perhaps 100 miles distant, they look immense, inaccessible, remote and lonely. But as one approaches nearer and nearer to them, they ever grow more splendid, glistening white in the mid-day sun, rose-red at dawn, or a golden orange at sunset, with faint opalescent green shadows that deepen as the daylight fails, till when night comes they stand far up in the sky, pale and ghostly against the glittering stars. Those who have been fortunate enough to see these things, know the fascination they exert. It is the call of the great spaces and of the great mountains. It is a call that mocks at the song of the Lotus-eaters of old, it is more insidious than the Siren's call, and it is a call that, once heard, is never forgotten.

One may be contented and busy with the multitudinous

little events of ordinary civilised life, but a chance phrase or some allusion wakes the memory of the wild mountain lands, and one feels sick with desire for the open spaces and the old trails. The dreams of the wanderer are far more real than most of the happenings that make up the average man's life. It may be the memory of some desolate peaks set against an angry sky, or of islands set in summer seas, or some grim fight with deserts of endless sands, or with tropical forests that have held their growth for a thousand years; it may be the memory of rushing rivers, or lakes set in wild woods where the beavers build their houses, or sunsets over great oceans—the spell binds one, the present does not exist, one is back again on the old trail—" The Red Gods have called us out, and we must go."

There is no part of the world where lofty mountains exist at all comparable with the Himalaya. Elsewhere the highest is Aconcagua, 23,060 feet. But in the Himalaya there are over eighty peaks that tower above 24,000 feet, probably twenty above 26,000 feet, six above 27,000 feet, and the highest of all, Mount Everest, is 29,141 feet.

The huge range of mountains, of which the Himalaya forms the chief part, is by far the greatest mountain range in the world. Starting to the North of Afghanistan, it sweeps Eastwards, without a break, to the confines of China, over 2,000 miles away. Yet in this vast world of mountains, very few have been climbed. For many years to come the Himalaya will provide sport for the mountaineer when most of the other mountain ranges of the world will have been exhausted, as far as exploration and new ascents are concerned.

Mountaineering is a sport of which Englishmen should be proud; for they were the first really to pursue it as a pastime. The Alpine Club was the first mountaineering club, and if one inquires into the records of climbing and discovery amongst the mountains of the world, one usually finds that it was an Englishman who led the way. It is the Englishman's love of sport for its own sake that has enticed him on to battle with the dangers and difficulties that are offered with such a lavish hand by the great mountains.

As a sport, mountaineering is second to none. It is the finest mental and physical tonic that a man can take. Whether it be the grim determination of desperate struggles with difficult rocks, or with ice, or whether it be the sight of range after range of splendid peaks basking in the sunshine, or of mists half hiding the black precipices, or the changing fairy colours of a sunrise, or the subtle curves of the wind-blown snow, all these are good for one. They produce a sane mind in a sane body. The joy of living becomes a real and a great joy, all is right with the world, and life flies on golden wings. It is, of course, true that there are many other beautiful and health-giving places besides the mountains. The great expanses of the prairie lands, the forests, the seas set with lonely islands, and in England the downs and the homely lanes and villages nestling amongst woods, with clear streams wandering through the pastures where the cattle feed—all these are good; but the mountains give something more. There things are larger, man is more alone, one feels that one is much nearer to Nature, one is not held down by an artificial civilisation. And although the life may be more strenuous (for Nature can be savage at times, as well as beautiful), and the struggle may be hard, yet the battle is the more worth winning.

Nowhere in any mountain land does Nature offer the good things of the wilds with more prodigal hand than in the Himalaya. On the Southern slopes, coming down from the great snow-peaks, are the finest river gorges in the world, wonderful forests of mighty trees, open alps nestling high up at the head of the valleys, that look out over great expanses of the lesser ranges; and as one ascends higher and higher, the views of the great peaks draped in everlasting snow, changing perpetually as the clouds and mists form and re-form over them, astonish one by their magnificence.

All things that the Himalaya gives are big things, and

now that the mountaineer has conquered the lesser ranges, he turns to the Himalaya, where the peaks stand head and shoulders above all others. Up to the present, however, owing to the difficulties of distance and size, none of the greater peaks have been climbed.

In climbing the great peaks of the Himalaya, the difficulties are far greater than those of less lofty ranges. On most of the highest the mere climbing presents such difficulties that it would be foolish to attempt their ascent. Thousands of feet of steep rock or ice guard their summits. Unless climbing above 24,000 feet is moderately easy, and no strenuous work is required, it could not be accomplished. For in the rarefied air at high altitudes there is insufficient oxygen to promote the normal oxidation of bodily tissue. Above 20,000 feet a cubic foot of air contains less than half the amount of oxygen that it does at sea-level. As the whole metabolism of the body is kept in working order by the oxygen supplied through the lungs, the obvious result of high altitudes is to interfere with the various processes occurring in the system. The combustion of bodily material is less, the amount of energy produced is therefore less also, and so capacity for work is diminished progressively as one ascends.

But that one is able still to work, and work hard, at these altitudes is evident by the experiences of Dr. Longstaff and Mr. Meade. On Trisul, 23,360 feet, Dr. Longstaff in ten and a half hours ascended from 17,450 feet to the summit. Whilst on Kamet, Mr. Meade's coolies carried a camp up to 23,600 feet. Dr. Kellas also in 1920 found his ascent on moderately easy snow above 21,000 feet approximated to 600 feet per hour. All these climbers were, however, acclimatised to high altitudes. The effect on anyone making a balloon or aeroplane ascent from sea-level would be different. Tissaudier in a balloon ascent fainted at 26,500 feet and on regaining consciousness found both his companions dead. Even on Pike's Peak, 14,109 feet, in the United States, many of those who go up in the railway suffer from faintness, sickness, breathlessness and general lassitude. Yet there are places on the earth,—the Pamirs,—where people live their lives at higher altitudes than Pike's Peak, without any effects of the diminished pressure being felt. They are acclimatised; their bodies, being accustomed to their surroundings, are good working machines.

Although it is true that at high altitudes there is less oxygen to breathe, the body rapidly protects itself by increasing the number of red blood corpuscles. These red corpuscles are the carriers of oxygen from the air to the various parts of the body. An increased number of carriers means an increase of oxygen to the body. It is just possible, therefore, that anyone properly acclimatised to, say, 23,000 feet would be able to ascend the remaining 6,000 feet, to the summit of Mount Everest. Moreover, if oxygen could be continuously supplied to the climbers by adventitious aid there is little doubt that 29,000 feet could be reached.

The physiological difficulties met with in ascending to high altitudes are doubtless of a very high order, but can to a certain extent be eliminated by ascending gradually, day after day, so as to allow the body to accommodate itself by degrees to the new surroundings.

There are, however, other difficulties that must be reckoned with, such as intense cold and frequent high winds. In any engine where loss of heat occurs, there is a corresponding loss of available energy. A bitterly cold wind not only robs one of much heat, but lowers the vitality as well. At altitudes above 24,000 feet, the temperature is often arctic, and the thermometer may fall far below zero. On the other hand, the rays of the sun are intense. The ultra-violet rays, that are mostly cut off by the air at sea-level, are a real source of danger where there is only one-third of an atmosphere pressure, as in the case at the summit of Mount Everest.

The mountaineer also encounters dangers in the Himalaya, on the same scale as the difficulties. A snow-slide on a British mountain or in the Alps is an avalanche; often in the Himalaya it becomes almost a convulsion of nature. The huge ice-fields and glaciers that hang on the upper slopes of the mountains, when let loose, have not hundreds of feet to fall, but thousands, and the wind that is thereby produced spreads with hurricane force over the glaciers below, on to which the main body of the avalanche has fallen. Sometimes even the broken debris will rush across a wide glacier.

Rock falls also assume gigantic proportions in the Himalaya. But all these dangers can be largely avoided by the skilled mountaineer, and he can choose routes up a mountain where they are not likely to occur. Some risks, however, must be always run, but they can be reduced to a minimum.

On Mount Everest, as we now know, most of these dangers will be less than on any of the other very high mountains in the Himalaya. Also there are no difficulties in the approach to Mount Everest from India. In this respect it differs from such peaks as K² and others. As a rule the highest mountains in the Himalaya always lie far back from the plains in the main chain, beyond the foot-hills and the intervening ranges. To approach them from the South in India, weeks of travel are often necessary, up deep gorges, and over rivers, where it is next to impossible to take baggage animals. Fortunately the approach to Mount Everest by the route from Darjeeling to Phari Dzong and thence over an easy pass into Tibet avoids all these difficulties. In Tibet a high tableland, averaging 13,000 feet, is reached.

Travelling in Tibet, North of the main range of the Himalaya, is entirely different from that on the South of the range. Instead of deep-cut gorges, a rolling, bare, stone-covered country exists, over which it is easy to take baggage animals, the only obstacle being the rivers that sometimes are not bridged, and are often swollen by the melting snow. From Kampa Dzong to Tingri Dzong, the base of operations for the Expedition, is an open country. Mount Everest lies 40 to 50 miles South of Tingri Dzong; the approach also is without difficulty.

The ascent of Mount Everest was not the primary object of the Expedition of 1921. A mountain the size of Mount Everest cannot be climbed by simply getting to it and starting the ascent immediately.

A reasonable route has to be discovered to the summit; which usually can only be done by a complete reconnaissance of the mountain. This has been admirably done, and a most magnificent series of photographs has been brought back by the members of the Expedition.

Mount Everest consists of a huge pyramid, having three main arêtes, the West, the South-east, and the North-east. It is the last, the North-east arête, that is obviously the easiest, being snow-covered along most of its length. Nowhere is it excessively steep, and nowhere are there precipices of rock to stop the climber. We now know that it can be reached, by means of a subsidiary ridge, from a col 23,000 feet, the Chang La, that lies to the north of the North-east arête. This col was the highest point on Mount Everest reached by the Expedition, and had it not been for savage weather a considerably higher altitude would have been attained; for above the col for several thousand feet lay an unbroken snow-slope.

It was only after much hard work, and over two months' exploration, that a route to this col was discovered. As is usually the case even with mountains far smaller than Mount Everest, it can be seen that if a point, often a long way below the summit, can be reached, not much farther difficulty will be encountered. But the puzzle is, how can that point be arrived at from below?

Quite early in the exploration of Mount Everest it was obvious that if the 23,000-foot col could be reached, most of the physical difficulties of the approach to the mountain would have been surmounted. But it was not so obvious how to win to the col. It lies on the South-east at the head of the main Rongbuk Glacier; it was therefore to this glacier that the mountaineers, Messrs. Mallory and Bullock, went from Tingri Dzong on June 23. They spent a month exploring the country to the North and the West of Mount Everest from the Rongbuk Glacier. Much valuable information was accumulated. A peak, Ri-Ring, 22,520 feet, was climbed and a pass on the West ridge of Mount Everest was visited, from which were seen views of the South-west face of the great mountain and also many high peaks in Nepal. Unfortunately, however, no feasible route from the main Rongbuk Glacier to the 23,000-foot col could be found. The next attempt was made by leaving the Rongbuk Glacier and exploring the Kama Valley that flows South-east from Mount Everest. Here a most magnificent ice-world was discovered. For a chain of giant peaks running South-east from Mount Everest to Makalu, 27,790 feet, guards the whole of the South-west side of the valley. But as an approach to the North-east arête of Mount Everest this valley was found to be useless. From the point of view, however, of exploration it was most fortunate that this valley was visited. The photographs of Makalu and its satellite Chomo-Lönzo, N.[63], 25,413 feet, are superb; moreover the lower reaches of the Kama Valley, as it dips down to the deep Arun Valley, was full of luxuriant vegetation, totally different from the wind-swept wilderness of Tibet.

The Kharta Valley, that runs North-east from Mount Everest, was the next exploited, to see whether from it an easy approach to the North-east arête existed. But by this time the monsoon weather was at its worst. Days of rain and mist, with snow higher up, succeeded one another, making climbing impossible. However, towards the end of September a high camp at 22,500 feet was made at the head of the Kharta Valley. From this camp the 23,000-foot col, Chang La, was finally reached, by crossing the head of a glacier that ran to the North. Higher climbing was out of the question; a furious North-west gale lasting for four days drove the party off the mountain.

The glacier mentioned above, running to the North, was found to be a tributary of the main Rongbuk Glacier, and has been named the East Rongbuk Glacier. There is no doubt that the easiest route to Chang La, the North Col, will not be all the way round by the Kharta Valley, but up this East Rongbuk Glacier.

Several other interesting expeditions were carried out by other members of the party. Colonel Howard Bury visited the group of five great peaks (25,202 to 26,867 feet), that lie about 15 miles North-west of Mount Everest. He explored the Kyetrak Glacier to its summit the Khombu La, also crossed the Phüse La with the Rongshar Valley that drains down into Nepal. Later he visited another pass on the ridge that connects Mount Everest with Makalu. From this pass most interesting views of the country South of Mount Everest were obtained.

Major Wheeler's and Major Morshead's map of the country that lies between the Himalaya and the Bramapootra River will be of the highest value, and the results of Dr. Heron's geological survey and Mr. Wollaston's collections of birds, beasts, insects and flowers, when they have been thoroughly examined, will certainly yield much new scientific information. The Expedition therefore has accomplished all that was expected of it, and has brought back material of the greatest interest, from a part of the world about which almost nothing was known, and into which Europeans had never been.

The attempt to ascend Mount Everest itself necessarily had to be postponed, but this year the Expedition that is being sent out will have for its primary object the ascent of the mountain. There will be easy access to the base of the peak from Chöbuk, where a base camp will be established, and from thence a feasible route on to the summit of the great North-east arête has been discovered.

Most fortunately this year General Bruce was able to undertake the leadership of the Expedition. His unrivalled experience of climbing in the Himalaya and particularly his special capacity for handling Himalayan people will be invaluable to the Expedition. Not only will he be able to organise and instil the right spirit into the coolie corps upon whom so much will depend for ultimate success, but he will also be able to give much wise advice to the actual climbers who are to take part in the ascent of the mountain.

Moreover, with his long experience of dealing with Asiatics he can be trusted to deal with the Tibetan people and officials in such a way as to retain their present good-will.

As the main object of the Expedition this year is to make a definite attempt to reach the summit of Mount Everest, it has been decided that the actual climbing party should be as strong as possible. But a limit to the size of the Expedition was imposed by the necessity of respect for the feelings of the Tibetans, and a warning had been received from Lhasa to keep the numbers as small as possible. For, although the authorities at Lhasa might be friendly enough, and although there might be no difficulty in obtaining transport from the district round Tingri Dzong, where animals were plentiful, yet a large party might press hardly on the inhabitants in the matter of food, such as wheat and barley. This consideration had therefore to be regarded. Still it was thought that the district would not be unduly pressed by a party of twelve Europeans. This number will include a climbing party of six chosen mountaineers, with two in reserve, making eight in all. With General Bruce, a doctor (who would also be a naturalist), a photographer and a painter, the expeditionary force of Europeans will be complete.

Colonel E. L. Strutt, C.M.G., has been chosen as second in command. He possesses first-rate mountaineering experience, and has been Vice-President of the Alpine Club.

Mr. Mallory fortunately has been able to accept the invitation of the Committee to return to Mount Everest again this year. The remainder of the climbing party are: Captain George Finch, who was unable to join the Expedition last year on account of his health; Mr. T. H. Somervell, a surgeon, a member of the Alpine Club and an extremely energetic climber; Major E. F. Norton (Royal Artillery); and Dr. A. W. Wakefield, renowned for his strenuous climbing in the Lake District and work in Labrador. Besides these six mountaineers, Captain Geoffrey Bruce and Captain C. J. Morris, both of Gurkha Regiments, and able to speak the language of the Himalayan coolies, will assist General Bruce both in looking after and encouraging the coolies, and also help in the general arrangement and organisation of the Expedition as a whole. They also are accustomed to mountaineering and will act as a reserve to the six climbers.

As doctor and naturalist Dr. T. G. Longstaff has been invited to join the Expedition. He has made many climbs in the Himalaya and other mountain regions, including the ascent of Trisul, 23,360 feet. He is not expected to join the climbing party, but his experience will be of great benefit to the Expedition generally.

As photographer, Captain J. B. L. Noel has been selected. He had reconnoitred in the direction of Mount Everest in 1913. For several years he has made a special study of photography in all its various branches.

But besides photographs of the mountains, the Expedition is anxious to bring back pictures which would alone be able not only to serve as a record of the infinitely delicate colouring of that lofty region, but at the same time would show how probably some of the grandest scenery of mighty mountains should be represented from the point of view of an artist.

Difficulty was experienced in finding a suitable painter, for painters capable of doing justice to mountain scenery, and who are also physically fit to travel amongst them at such altitudes as those round Mount Everest, are few. We have, therefore, to depend on Mr. Somervell to paint us pictures.

In the meantime communications were also passing between Colonel Bailey, the Political Agent in Sikkim, and the Mount Everest Committee regarding the enlistment of coolies for the special corps, and the engagement of the very best headman obtainable to look after them. Many of the coolies who were with the Expedition in 1921 had volunteered to rejoin this year. But a stronger corps and more carefully selected men were needed. The Maharaja of Nepal has been asked to allow some of the most famous Gurkha mountain climbers to join the Expedition, and the Government of India has been asked to put two or three non-commissioned Gurkha officers at the service of General Bruce, to assist him generally in looking after the coolies, and seeing that they were properly fed and paid, and that they behaved themselves properly.

The members of last year's Expedition on their return were freely and fully consulted as to equipment and provisioning of this year's party; the experience gained last year has been therefore made use of in every way possible. Suggestions for the improvement of the Mummery-Meade tents have been adopted. Better clothing has been provided for the coolies. General Bruce has purchased leather coats, waistcoats, socks, jerseys and boots from the equipment provided for our troops in North Russia during the war, which will be admirably suited for the majority of the coolies, whilst for the few chosen for high climbing on Mount Everest itself, clothing precisely similar to that worn by the British climbers has been provided.

Captain Farrar and the equipment committee have provided a most varied and ample supply of provisions which was despatched to India in January. The Primus-stoves have been overhauled and retested by Captain Finch.

Colonel Jack and Mr. Hinks have carefully examined all the instruments brought back. The aneroids have been retested, and all broken instruments replaced.

The photographic outfit has been considerably enlarged, including a cinematograph instrument. The question of supplying oxygen has been most thoroughly gone into. All flyers in aeroplanes at high altitudes find oxygen absolutely necessary. In mountain climbing, however, the almost insuperable difficulty is the weight of the apparatus supplying the oxygen. As far as possible, this weight has been reduced to a minimum. A large number of cylinders, the lightest and smallest obtainable, have been sent out full of compressed oxygen, and it is hoped that they will be capable of being used by the party that will attempt to climb to the summit of Mount Everest. If the climbers are capable of carrying them, and so getting a continuous supply of oxygen during the whole of the climb, there is little doubt that climbing up to 29,000 feet is possible. In aeroplanes considerably higher altitudes have been reached with the help of oxygen. Moreover, there is this fact in favour of the climbers on Mount Everest, they will be acclimatised to altitudes of 20,000 feet, whilst anyone in an aeroplane is not so acclimatised, having risen from sea-level. The climbers will have to accommodate themselves only to an increased height of 9,000 feet, whilst those in an aeroplane have to suffer a diminution in pressure equivalent to 29,000 feet.

Finally, arrangements have been made with the Press for the publication of telegrams and photographs from the Expedition. Full information of the progress of the Expedition will therefore be available for the public, and it will be possible to follow the climbing party, after they leave the base camp, which will be somewhere near Chöbuk, as they ascend the East Rongbuk Glacier to the advanced base under the North col. Afterwards all the preliminary arrangements will be reported, and finally there will be an account of the great attempt to reach the summit.

The Expedition will be starting nearly two months earlier than in 1921. The weather in May and June, before the monsoon breaks in July, apparently is more or less settled, and so the most must be made of it. In 1921 from the end of July till September high climbing was impossible. It is therefore obvious that a determined attempt to climb Mount Everest should be made before the monsoon sets in.

The ascent from the North col, Changa La, 23,000 feet, to the summit of Mount Everest, 29,000 feet, is only 6,000 feet, and the distance to traverse is about 2 miles. As far as can be judged from the numerous photographs of Mount Everest, the climbing is straightforward with no insurmountable difficulties in the form of steep rock precipices. There

Mount Everest at Sunset
from the 20,000 foot camp, Kharta Valley.

will be no glaciers overhanging the route which might send down avalanches, and no excessively steep ice-slopes.

But the final ascent will test the endurance of the climbers to the utmost. Many people have found the last 1,000 feet of Mont Blanc more than they could accomplish. The last 1,000 feet of Mount Everest will only be conquered by men whose physique is perfect, and who are trained and acclimatised to the last possible limit, and who have the determination to struggle on when every fibre of their body is calling out—Hold ! enough !

The struggle will be a great one, but it will be worth the while. To do some new thing beyond anything that has been previously accomplished, and not to be dominated by his environment, has made man what he is, and has raised him above the beasts. He always has been seeking new worlds to conquer. He has penetrated into the forbidding ice-worlds at the two poles, and many are the secrets he has wrested from Nature. There remains yet the highest spot on the world's surface. No doubt he will win there also, and in the winning will add one more victory over the guarded secrets of things as they are.

APPENDIX I

THE SURVEY

BY MAJOR H. T. MORSHEAD, D.S.O.

The personnel selected to form the Survey Detachment under my charge were as follows: Brevet-Major E. O. Wheeler, M.C., R.E., Mr. Lalbir Singh Thapa, Surveyors Gujjar Singh and Turubaz Khan, Photographer Abdul Jalil Khan, sixteen khalasis, etc.

The tasks allotted to the detachment were :—

(1) A general survey of the whole unmapped area covered by the Expedition, on a scale of 1 inch to 4 miles.

(2) A detailed survey of the immediate environs of Mount Everest on the scale of 1 inch to 1 mile.

(3) A complete revision of the existing ¼-inch map of Sikkim.

With the exception of a few rough notes and sketches by early travellers and missionaries in the seventeenth and eighteenth centuries, our first knowledge of the Southern portion of the Tibetan province of Tsang dated from the epoch of the Survey of India by trained native explorers in the middle of the nineteenth century. Thus, much of the area visited by the Expedition in 1921 was traversed by the explorer Hari Ram during the course of his two journeys in 1871–2 and 1885 respectively. At that time, however, foreign surveyors were not regarded with favour in Tibet; work could only be carried on surreptitiously, and the resulting map merely consisted of a small-scale route traverse which gave no indication of the surface features beyond the explorer's actual route.

The first rigorous survey undertaken in the neighbourhood was that carried out by Captain C. H. D. Ryder, R.E. (now Colonel Ryder, C.I.E., D.S.O., Surveyor-General of India), during the Tibet Mission of 1903–1904. During the stay of the Mission at Kampa, the ¼-inch survey was carried as far West as longitude 88°; while, on the subsequent return march up the Tsangpo Valley, surveys were extended as far as the Southern watershed of the great river—the so-called Ladak Range—in latitude 29° approximately,

West of longitude 88° there thus remained a stretch of unsurveyed country some 14,000 square miles in area, between the Ladak Range on the North and the Great Himalaya Range on the South—the latter forming the Northern frontier of Nepal. The Mount Everest Expedition provided an opportunity of making good the whole of this area, with the exception of some 2,000 square miles at the extreme Western end, into which, in view of the restrictions of the Indian Foreign Department, I did not feel justified in penetrating.

Fortunately, Colonel Bury's plans contemplated an outward Northerly journey via Shekar and Tingri to the Western flanks of Mount Everest, whence the reconnaissance of the mountain was to be carried out from West to East, parallel to the Northern frontier of Nepal. This rendered feasible the mapping of the whole unsurveyed area between the Southern watershed of the Tsangpo and the Great Himalaya Range, as far West as longitude 85° 30′, without in any way infringing the Foreign Department's orders and restrictions.

For the purpose of the detailed survey of the Mount Everest regions, it was arranged for my Assistant, Major Wheeler, to make a thorough test of the Canadian pattern of photo-survey apparatus, of which he had had previous experience in the Canadian Rocky Mountains. This method of survey, which had not hitherto been employed in India, is particularly adapted for use in high mountain regions. Fortunately, the experimental outfit, which had recently been ordered from England, was delivered just in time to accompany the Expedition. Wheeler's account of his season's work will be found in Appendix II.

With a view to carrying out the revision survey of Sikkim while awaiting the arrival of the members of the Expedition from England, the Survey Detachment was authorised to assemble at Darjeeling early in April, six weeks before the date fixed for the start of the Expedition. In spite of an unusually wet and cloudy spring, the three surveyors made such good use of their time that 2,500 square miles of country were completed before the advance of the Expedition necessitated the temporary abandonment of this work.

After completing the necessary preliminaries with Colonel Bury, I myself left Darjeeling on May 13, intending to rejoin the remainder of the Expedition in Sikkim. Continuous rain, however, rendered the latter task impossible; the Sikkim roads were, moreover, blocked in several places by severe landslips, so that I was only with difficulty able to reach Kampa by the 28th. It transpired, however, that there was no cause for hurry, since the main body of the Expedition, travelling via the Chumbi Valley, had encountered greater difficulties than mine, and did not arrive at Kampa until June 5. While awaiting their arrival, I filled in the time by occupying and re-observing from Colonel Ryder's old triangulation stations of 1903, overlooking the Kampa Plain.

I had received no news whatever of the Expedition or of the outside world since leaving Darjeeling three-and-a-half weeks previously. Consequently the death of my old friend Dr. Kellas on the very day of their arrival at Kampa came to me as a very severe shock.

The Sikkim revision-survey having been so much hampered by bad weather, I decided to take only two of the three surveyors with the Expedition into Tibet, leaving Surveyor Turabaz Khan to complete the comparatively dry areas of Northern Sikkim before the arrival of the monsoon. This he succeeded in doing at the cost of considerable personal discomfort, returning to Darjeeling in July.

It was not until we reached the summit of the Tinki Pass on June 11 that we found ourselves for the first time looking into unsurveyed country. From here onwards as far as Tingri the survey was kept up by Lalbir Singh, whose unflagging energy alone enabled him to keep pace with the long marches of the Expedition. Each morning he was away with his plane-table and squad of coolies long before our breakfast was served, seldom reaching camp before nightfall. The gathering clouds and other ominous signs of a rapidly approaching monsoon, however, forbade any respite.

On arrival at Tingri, after spending a week in fruitless efforts to observe the triangulated peaks of the main Himalayan Range through the dense monsoon clouds which were daily piling up more and more thickly from the South, I departed on June 26 with Surveyor Gujjar Singh on a short trip to explore and map the upper valley of the Bhong Chu.

Our first march led across the wide Tingri Plain, past the hot spring village of Tsamda, to the hamlet of Dokcho, at the Southern extremity of the Sutso Plain. This plain is covered with the ruins of numerous villages and watch-towers, the haunt of countless rock-pigeons. They are all of loftier and more substantial construction than the miserable hovels which form the scattered hamlets of to-day—indicating, apparently, the former presence of a large and warlike population. It is impossible even to hazard a guess at the age of these ruins, which may have preserved their present state for generations in the comparatively arid climate of Tibet. Many of the towers are 60 feet or more in height; roofs and floors have all disappeared, but the massive mud walls in many instances still bear the marks of the wooden shuttering used in their erection. This method of construction is unknown, I believe, in Tibet at the present day.

The next day's march, skirting the Western edge of the plain, brought us to the village of Phuri, where the river flows in a flat-bottomed, cultivated valley, between bare brown hills. On the 28th we camped at Menkhap-to, the highest village in the valley. The headman, a sort of local "warden of the marches," refused to see me and shut himself up in his house, guarding his door with three huge mastiffs who effectively frustrated the efforts of my messengers to establish communications. Evidently he feared the subsequent results to himself of harbouring strangers. The remaining villagers were quite friendly, however, and supplied all my requirements. One man, the owner of a gun, surprised me by a request for 12-bore cartridges just after I had greatly shocked his neighbour's Buddhist susceptibilities by killing a butterfly for my collection! Much snow is reported to fall at Menkhap-to, which is deserted during the winter months, when the inhabitants descend to Menkhap-me ("lower Menkhap") and the Sutso Plain.

Above Menkhap-to the road leaves the main valley and proceeds Westwards over a spur known as the Lungchen La (17,700 feet). This spur commands an extensive view across the wide, uninhabited Pekhu Plain, with its three lakes, as far as the snowy range running North-west from the summit of Gosainthan. On a fine day, the whole panorama can be sketched in from a couple of fixings on either side of the pass; unfortunately, at the time of our arrival bad weather had set in, and the whole snow-range was hidden in cloud. I had therefore to leave Gujjar Singh camped near the summit of the pass to await a fine day for the completion of his surveys, and myself returned at the end of the month to Tingri, where I rejoined Mr. Wollaston, who had been detained at headquarters by an outbreak of enteric fever amongst the Expedition servants.

Wild game is plentiful in the Upper Bhong Valley. I shot numerous hares, some ram-chakor and a bar-headed goose during the trip; while Gujjar Singh caught a young, week-old barhal lamb on the summit of the Lungchen Pass, which, however, died after three weeks in captivity. Gazelle are common on the Sutso Plain.

By the end of June, Lalbir Singh had finished the inking of his previous surveys, and was ready for fresh work. Accordingly, after spending a couple of days in examining his board, and checking the spelling of his village names with the aid of the local Tibetan officials,

I despatched him on a lengthy programme of work in Pharuk and Kharta. It was three months before I saw him again.

About this time a messenger arrived from the Dzongpen of Nyenyam, inviting us to visit his district, which lay four marches to the South-west, in the valley of the Po Chu or Bhotia Kosi R. Although Nyenyam was not one of the districts specifically mentioned in our passport, Wollaston and I decided, with the concurrence of Colonel Bury, to avail ourselves of the opportunity of visiting this little-known area.

Leaving Tingri on July 13, with the interpreter Gyaldzan Kazi and Surveyor Gujjar Singh, who had now returned after completing his work on the Lungchen Pass, we camped that evening at Langkor, a small village at the Western edge of the Tingri Plain. A cantilever bridge which spans the Gya Chu opposite the village had been carried away by floods shortly before our arrival, and the whole population of the hamlet, male and female, were busily engaged in its reconstruction, working in relays to the accompaniment of prolonged and vigorous blasts on a "conch" which a monk was diligently blowing in order—as it was explained to us—to avert further rainfall until the bridge should be completed. His efforts were rewarded with tolerable success, as the rain held off all day in spite of the threatening storm-clouds which loomed up from the South-west.

The most interesting feature of Langkor is an ancient temple, an appanage of the great Drophung monastery of Lhasa. This building, which is said to be over 1,000 years old, contains a sacred stone alleged to have been hurled across the Himalayan Range from India, and to have pitched in the Tingri Plains. The name Tingri is said to be derived from the noise ("ting") made by the falling stone. The stone is carefully preserved inside a wooden box, which is opened with much ceremony on the first day of the Tibetan new year. The temple, which is managed by a committee of fifteen civilian monks (nyakchang), also contains a library of 4,400 books, and an image of the Indian saint Tamba Sanye which is popularly believed to have grown by itself from the ground *in situ.*

Crossing the Tang La (17,980 feet) in a driving snowstorm, a long march of 22 miles brought us next day to the bleak village of Tulung, in the upper valley of the Po Chu. As we descended the Western side of the pass the snow-clouds gradually dispersed, disclosing glimpses of the magnificent twin summits of Gosainthan (26,290 feet), 30 miles to the West. Several of our coolies succumbed to mountain sickness on the pass, with the result that my bedding and the kitchen box only reached camp at 9 p.m.

On July 15 our road lay for 8 miles along the flat valley of the Po Chu; the river then turns sharply Southwards, passing for 3 miles through a gorge of granite and schist. Bushes of wild currant, gooseberry, berberis and dog-rose here begin to appear, and around the village of Targyeling, where we camped, were smiling fields of mustard and buckwheat, in addition to the usual Tibetan crops of barley and dwarf pea. After a month spent in the bleak Tibetan uplands, it was a relief to pitch our tents in a homely green field, alongside a rippling brook lined with familiar ranunculus, cow parsley, forget-me-not, and a singularly beautiful pale mauve cranesbill, and to feast our eyes on the glorious purple of the wild thyme which clothed the hillsides in great patches of colour.

The next day, still following the course of the Po Chu, we reached Nyenyam, a large and very insanitary village which is known under the name of Kuti by the Nepalis who constitute the majority of its inhabitants. These Nepali traders (Newars) have their own Hindu temple in the village. There is also a Nepalese chauki (court-house) with a haqim (magistrate) invested with summary powers of jurisdiction over Nepali subjects; he is specially charged with the settlement of trade disputes, and with the encouragement of Tibeto-Nepalese trade and commerce.

As is customary in all important districts of Tibet, there are here two Dzongpens, who by a polite fiction are known as "Eastern" and "Western" (Dzongshar and Dzongnup) respectively. Actually, the functions of the two Dzongpens are identical; the *raison d'être* of the double regime being an attempt to protect the peasants from extortion by the device of providing two administrators, who, in theory at least, act as a check upon each other's peculations. At the time of our arrival, those two worthies were so busy preparing a joint picnic that we had considerable difficulty in getting their attention.

I spent three days in exploring the neighbourhood of Nyenyam, while Wollaston was engaged in his botanical and zoological pursuits. Gujjar Singh, with the plane-table, was detained by bad weather higher up the valley. Below Nyenyam the river enters a very deep, narrow gorge; pines and other forest trees begin to appear. The road, which here becomes impassable for animals, crosses the river four times in 6 miles by cantilever bridges before reaching the village of Choksum, but I could find no trace of the portion described by explorer Hari Ram in 1871 as consisting of slabs of stone 9 to 18 inches wide supported on iron pegs let into the vertical face of the rock at a height of 1,500 feet above the river. At Choksum (10,500 feet) the river falls at an average rate of 500 feet per mile. The Nepal frontier is crossed near Dram village, some 10 miles further down stream, but owing to the vile state of the weather, which rendered even the roughest attempts at surveying impossible, I abandoned all idea of reaching the spot.

On July 20 we retraced our steps 9 miles up the valley to Tashishong, where we found Dr. Heron encamped, together with Gujjar Singh, whose work had been hung up for a week by continued cloud and rainfall. Heron returned Northwards next day, while we followed a rough easterly track leading over the Lapche Range to the village of the same name in the valley of the Kang Chu. The weather on this day was atrocious, and our last pretence of accurate surveying broke down. We were unable to reach Lapche village by dusk, and spent a somewhat cheerless night on boulders in drenching rain at 14,600 feet, with no fuel except a few green twigs of dwarf rhododendron.

Lapche (La-Rimpoche, "precious hill") is sacred as the home and birthplace of Jetsun Mila Repa, a wandering lama and saint who lived in Southern Tibet in the eleventh century, and who taught by parables and songs, some of which have considerable literary merit. The two principal works ascribed to him are an autobiography, or namtar, and a collection of tracts called Labum, or the "myriad songs." They are still among the most popular books in Tibet.* His hermit-cell still remains under a rock on the hillside, and his memory is preserved by an ancient temple and monastery, the resort of numerous pilgrims, alongside which we pitched our tents.

Lapche village is situated on a spur overlooking the junction of two branches of the Kang stream—the latter being a tributary of the Rongshar River, which, in turn, joins the Bhotia Kosi River in Nepal. The extreme dampness of the local climate is indicated by the trailing streamers of lichen which festoon the trees, and by the pent roofs of the buildings. The village contains some ten or twelve houses, of which half are occupied by Tibetans and half by Nepalese subjects (Sharpas)—each community having its own headman. The inhabitants were very friendly and pleasant, and gave us a good deal of information. The village is deserted during the winter months, when the whole population migrates across the border into Nepal. The Tibetans pay no taxes to Nepal during their half-yearly sojourn

* *Journey to Lhasa and Central Tibet*, by S. C. Dass, C.I.E., page 205, footnote by Hon. W. W. Rockhill.

in the lower valley; conversely, the Nepalis during their summer residence in Lapche are not subject to Tibetan taxation or to the imposition of ulag (forced labour). The Tibetans of Lapche pay their taxes in the form of butter direct to the Lapche monastery, the head lama, or abbot, of which resides at Phuto Gompa near Nyenyam. The Nepal frontier is some 10 miles below Lapche, opposite the snow-peak of Karro Pumri. Katmandu can be reached in eight days, but the track is bad and very little trade passes this way.

Transport arrangements necessitated a day's halt at Lapche, which was fortunately enlivened by the timely arrival of a large parcel of letters and newspapers, which Colonel Bury had thoughtfully sent after us from Tingri—almost the last news of the outside world which we were to receive for over two months.

From Lapche we proceeded to the Rongshar Valley, crossing the Kangchen and Kangchung ("big snow" and "little snow") passes. Descending the hill to Trintang village, where we camped on July 25, the clouds lifted momentarily, disclosing an amazing view of the superb snow summit of Gaurisankar towering magnificently above us just across the valley. This mountain, which is called by the Tibetans Chomo Tsering, or Trashi Tsering, is the westernmost of a group of five very sacred peaks known collectively as Tsering Tse-nga ("Tsering five peaks"). Unfortunately, owing to constant clouds, I was unable to identify with certainty the remaining four peaks of Tingki Shalzang, Miyo Lobzang, Chopen Drinzang and Tekar Drozang. Owing to the sacred nature of the Rongshar Valley, the slaughtering of animals is strictly forbidden; the large flocks and herds of the villagers are only sold for slaughter in the adjoining districts of Tingri and Nepal, and we were only able to buy a sheep on promising not to kill it until after quitting the valley.

Trintang village occupies a plateau 1,750 feet above the level of the river; 1,400 feet below is the village of Tropde, to which the Trintang residents all descend in winter. Rongshar Dzong, which is situated in the lower village, has no importance; at the time of our visit the Dzongpen had gone to his home on leave of absence, leaving his affairs in the hands of a steward.

A day's halt being necessary in order to collect transport, I took the opportunity of descending the Rongshar Valley as far as the Nepal frontier, while Gujjar Singh endeavoured, without much success, to pick up the threads of his survey by identifying the snowy peaks which occasionally afforded brief glimpses through rifts in the clouds. The Rongshar River drops 1,400 feet in 7 miles between Tropde and the Nepal frontier, which is crossed at an altitude of roughly 9,000 feet.

On July 27 we marched 20 miles up the Rongshar Valley to the village of Tazang (Takpa-Santsam, "limit of birch trees"), which, as its name implies, is situated at the extreme upper limit of the forest zone. On the way we passed the village and monastery of Chuphar, whence a track leads South-east over the difficult snow-pass of Menlung ("vale of medicinal herbs") to the villages of Rowaling and Tangpa in the Kangphu Valley of Nepal.

Tazang had already been visited by Colonel Bury, a month previously. The local headman was too drunk, on the evening of our arrival, to send out the necessary messages summoning the village transport-yaks from their grazing grounds. In consequence, our baggage was only got under weigh at 11 a.m. next morning, and we were compelled to pitch our tents at a grazing camp (16,500 feet) after only covering 9 miles. The weather showed signs of improvement in proportion as we receded from the Himalayan gorges, but dense banks of cloud still obscured all the hill-tops. An easy march over the Phuse La (17,850 feet) brought us on the 29th to the bleak village of Kyetrak, situated at the foot of the great Kyetrak Glacier, on the extreme Southern edge of the Tingri plain—an area which we had already surveyed six weeks previously.

From Kyetrak we proceeded via the Lamna La to Chöbuk, thence following the tracks of the Expedition headquarters which Colonel Bury had just transferred from Tingri to Kharta in the lower Bhong Chu Valley. On reaching headquarters on August 2, we found Colonel Bury in sole occupation—Mallory and Bullock having left that very morning on a reconnaissance of the Eastern approaches to Mount Everest.

The weather during the whole of August was such as to render out-of-door survey operations impossible. Gujjar Singh was occupied during the month in adjusting and inking his surveys, while I filled in several days in making tracings of all work so far completed, after which, for the remainder of the season, I joined the mountaineers, whose doings are recorded elsewhere in this book.

On the return journey in October I despatched Gujjar Singh from Gyangkar Nangpa to complete the remaining portions of the Sikkim revision-survey; at the same spot I picked up Lalbir Singh, who, after completing his survey of the Pharuk and Kharta areas, had crossed the Bhong Chu below Lungdo and worked his way back via Tashirakar and Sar. Travelling via Kampa and Lachen Valley, we reached Darjeeling on October 16. Tracings of the new survey were hastily finished and sent to press, with the result that a complete preliminary ¼-inch map in six colours was published before the last members of the Expedition had sailed for England. A ½-inch preliminary sketch-map of the environs of Mount Everest was also prepared by Major Wheeler at the same time for the use of the mountaineers in discussing the details of their next year's climb.

The out-turn of work during the Expedition was as follows :—

¼-inch revision survey	4,000 square miles
¼-inch original survey	12,000 square miles
Detail photo-survey (environs of Mount Everest)	600 square miles

The surveyors all worked splendidly under difficult and trying conditions. Major Wheeler had probably the hardest time of any member of the Expedition, and his success in achieving single-handed the mapping of 600 square miles of some of the most mountainous country in the world is sufficient proof of his determination and grit. It is difficult for those who have not actually had the experience to conceive the degree of mental and physical discomfort which results to the surveyor from prolonged camping at high altitudes during the monsoon, waiting for the fine day which never comes. Such was our fate for four months during the Expedition of 1921, yet on looking back one feels that the results were well worth while. The discomforts soon fade from recollection ; the pleasures alone remain in one's memory, and there is not one of us but would gladly repeat our season's experiences, if so required.

APPENDIX II

THE PHOTOGRAPHIC SURVEY

By Major E. O. WHEELER, M.C.

I had purchased a set of photo-topographical surveying instruments of the Canadian pattern, on behalf of the Survey of India, while on leave in 1920. A trial of this method of surveying mountainous country was to be carried out in Garhwal in 1921; but when Survey of India officers were asked for to accompany the Mount Everest Expedition, I was detailed to carry out the trial there. Possibly a word of explanation of the method used may not be amiss.

The "Canadian" method—if I may call it so; for although it was invented and has been used elsewhere, it has been far more extensively applied in Canada than in any other part of the world—may be briefly described as "plane-tabling by photography." It requires, equally with the plane-table, an accurate framework, on which to base the detailed survey; and simply substitutes a small (3-inch vernier) theodolite and camera for the sight-rule and plane-table. Stations are fixed and photographs oriented by means of the theodolite; the photographs, which are taken so as to be as nearly as possible true perspectives, represent the country as it would be seen by the plane-tabler, and detail on them may be fixed by intersections or sketched in by eye in exactly the same way as on the plane-table.

Angles are read and photographs taken in the field; and, if considered necessary to test exposures or protect photographic plates from deterioration due to climatic conditions, development of plates is also carried out there. Otherwise, the map is made wholly in the office, using either contact prints or enlargements, from the negatives taken in the field. The latter are usually preferable. The main advantages at high altitudes over the plane-table are, that a much larger area can be covered in a given time in the field, that the instruments are more portable for difficult climbing, that there is no necessity to do accurate drawing with numbed fingers, and that the draughtsman may see the country from several points of view at one time. On the other hand, more equipment is necessary, and —a great disadvantage sometimes, as in this case—the map does not come into being as one goes along.

After carrying out various preliminary adjustments and tests at the office of the Trigonometrical Survey at Dehra Dun, I reached Darjeeling on April 30, and Tingri on June 19, travelling with Expedition Headquarters via Phāri Dzong.

En route Tingri, we had caught glimpses of Everest and the neighbouring peaks; so that by the time we arrived there, I was able, with the help of the existing maps and what local information we had obtained, to decide on the area I would attempt to survey. I say "attempt," for little was really known then about the geography, and still less about the weather conditions throughout the summer. As it turned out in the end, the area had to be much curtailed, and certain parts surveyed in considerably less detail than I should have liked: almost wholly on account of the weather. Although it was often fairly clear at 6 a.m. or so, photographs taken before 8, particularly at the latter end of the season, were of little use for surveying purposes.

However, at the outset, I had hoped to map, on the scale of 1 inch = 1 mile, the whole area between the Arun Gorge on the East and the Rā Chu on the West: and from the Nepāl-Tibet boundary Northwards for some 20 miles; i.e. to the point where the various streams, flowing in a Northerly direction from the high boundary ridge, issue from the mountains proper into the more rolling foot-hills on the Southern outskirts of the Tibetan Plateau. This area includes Mount Everest itself near the centre of its Southern side, Makālu and Pk. 25,413 to the South-east, Pks. 23,800 (Khārtaphu), 23,420, and 23,080 to the North-east and North, and Pks. 25,990 (Gyāchung Kang), 25,202, 25,909 and 26,867 (Cho Oyu) to the North-west; and comprises some 1,000 square miles of country: a suitable season's work, given reasonably fine weather. This unfortunately we did not get.

On June 24, the day after Messrs. Mallory and Bullock had started for the Rongbuk Valley, Dr. Heron and I marched South across the plain to the village of Shärto, *en route* Kyetrāk, in the Rā Chu Valley, where I intended to establish my base camp while surveying the Kyetrāk Glacier and West face of the Cho Oyu—Gyachung Kāng group. The next day we moved on to Kyetrāk, 1 mile below the snout of the glacier, and made camp there. This bleak village and the route to it and over the Phüse La have already been described.

June 26 was fine, so after crossing the Rā Chu on local ponies, ourselves and our ice-axes and rucksacks perched on Tibetan saddles —a cold and uncomfortable proceeding in the early morning—we ascended the 18,000-foot hill immediately West of the village. Up to 1 p.m. we had excellent views across and up the Kyetrāk Valley; but only a glimpse of Gauri Sankar (Chomo Tsering) to the South-west, where heavy clouds soon began to roll up. Cho Oyu and Pk. 25,909 and their spurs unfortunately cut out all distant views to the South-east, as they did everywhere in the upper part of this valley; so that my first view of Everest was from Tingri a month later. Next day, we started shortly after daylight for a spur on the East side of the valley; unfortunately—and this happened in the case of almost every peak I started for until mid-September—clouds began to roll up, and we were forced to stop to take the photographs before we had reached a really good view-point.

Colonel Bury arrived at Kyetrāk shortly after we got back to camp. On the 28th he and Heron started off early for a flying visit to the Kyetrāk Glacier and Nangba La; I started later, after getting kit together, for a camp half-way up the glacier, and about 6 miles from Kyetrāk. About 2 p.m. I found a comparatively dry spot on shale at 18,000 feet, and pitched my tents there, the last of the coolies arriving only at 6 p.m. The place was bleak enough, but was as far as I could get that day, and seemed suitable for two climbs—one on either side of the glacier.

My equipment consisted of the camera, theodolite, and a small plane-table—to help in identifying triangulated points—by way of instruments, which were carried by three coolies who remained with me. Ten other coolies slept at the base camp at Kyetrāk, and carried stores up to me or moved the camp, as required; the camp consisted of a Whymper tent for the three coolies and a Meade for myself; bedding, food, a Primus stove and tin of kerosene for my own cooking, and yak dung fuel for the coolies. My servant remained at the base camp and sent up cooked meat and vegetables; otherwise I cooked for myself.

June 29 and 30 were useless days; but on July 1 the weather cleared a bit, and after crossing the glacier, I went up a sharp rock shoulder of Cho Rapzang. The peak was mainly loose granite blocks at a steep angle, so that progress was slow: it was noon when I reached the top (about 19,500 feet), and as I did so the clouds settled down, and it began to snow. However, at 4 p.m. it cleared sufficiently for some work to be done; after that we came down as quickly as possible in another blinding snowstorm, and reached camp just after dark; I for one very tired. I found the coolies exceedingly slow in coming down the loose blocks, I think because their balance was bad—they had to use their hands far more than I did.

I had a good view of the glacier from here: the East side is very steep and broken, with several tributary glaciers flowing down from Cho Oyu and Pk. 25,909, and from a 23,000-foot Peak (not triangulated) to the North of the latter. The West side, except for Cho Rapzang, round which the glacier flows, is a snowfield falling more or less gently from a low ridge running from the pass to the West of Cho Rapzang. The glacier itself is like many others in this region, moraine covered for 3 or 4 miles above its snout, "pinnacled" for another mile, and finally practically flat. But this flat portion gives by no means good going; when frozen it is very irregular and trying to walk over; and when thawed, is slushy and water soaked. There are two large water channels in the ice which are unpleasant to cross; these are from 10 to 15 feet wide and 20 feet deep, and carry a large volume of water in the afternoon. Crossing without a rope is distinctly dangerous, for although one can find places easy enough to jump, a slip would be certain death, for once in the channel it would be quite impossible to get out, or even to stop oneself on its smooth ice floor and sides.

Cloudy weather then set in; but on the 3rd I got a few photographs from a shoulder near by, and moved camp 2 or 3 miles farther up the glacier (at about 18,500 feet). I was in this camp for nine days and only succeeded in taking two low stations, one on either side of the glacier and each about 1½ miles from the pass (Nangba La) to Nepāl; but the valley on the South side, leading down to Khungphu, turns sharply to the East just below the pass, and little could be seen of the Nepalese side. Each of these stations I went up twice—to wait all day long the first time, in each case, for weather which never came. To reach the station on the East side of the glacier I had the only comparatively difficult rock climbing which I met with during the course of the Expedition; and on the way down watched my theodolite coolie, whom I had left behind exhausted in the morning, tumble off a steep rock arête, theodolite and all; fortunately he jammed in a crack a few feet below, and was unhurt. During the day he had started up after us on his own, and had lost his way in the clouds.

On July 12—another wet day—I moved camp some distance down the main glacier and up a tributary flowing from Pk. 25,909 and Cho Oyu, and next day ascended a shoulder whence a good view into the cirque below these two peaks was obtained—or should have been obtained! But again I sat till dusk and saw little or nothing. Early the following day, however, it was fairly clear, so I got my photographs and then moved camp back to the base at Kyetrāk.

The next three days were spent in moving my base camp to the bridge across the Rā Chu, 6 miles below Kyetrāk; taking a light camp up to about 18,000 feet on the prominent hill immediately East of the bridge, climbing the latter, sitting through the usual storms without doing any work, and returning to the bridge. Time was getting on, and the weather was still bad, so I then decided to leave my camp at the bridge and move into Headquarters myself to get developing, etc., up to date, and have a short rest. I walked into Tingri, with two coolies, on July 18, and found Colonel Bury there alone: and the Headquarters house felt very comfortable indeed after a Meade tent, in spite of nightly pilgrimages from one dry spot to another, as the roof leaked!

Five busy days were spent at Tingri developing and printing; and as the weather showed little sign of improvement, I decided to go on with Headquarters to Chöbuk, in the Rongbuk Valley and work on that side, so as to make sure of completing the most important part, in the vicinity of Everest, and return to the Kyetrāk Valley if there should be time. So on the 24th Colonel Bury and I left Tingri and reached Chöbuk on the 25th, where we met Mallory and Bullock, just in from their reconnaissance of the North and North-west sides of Everest. A talk with them gave me some idea of the country, and the view from an 18,000-foot hill above Chöbuk enabled me to make a plan of campaign: far more extensive, as always, than the weather eventually allowed.

Colonel Bury, Mallory and Bullock had gone on to Khārta on July 26; on the 27th I moved up the right bank of the Rongbuk Valley some 10 miles, to the monastery, above which I took a 20,000-foot tation the next day. The weather was dreadful, but at 6 p.m. I got a round of photographs, which really turned out very well considering the time of day at which they were taken: it took me four and a half hours to get up this peak—fresh snow and scree—and although I had no glissades, only half an hour to come down.

On the 27th I moved camp to a grassy hollow near the snout of the glacier—Mallory and Bullock's base—and next day occupied another hill overlooking the main glacier and valley, and looking up the side valley on the East, which joins the Dzākar Chu just below the glacier snout. The next three days were spent in establishing a light camp on the left bank of the East branch of the Rongbuk Glacier, about 3 miles from its snout, and taking a station on its left bank to overlook both the East and main glaciers.

The Rongbuk Glacier is made up of two large branches, one flowing from the snow basin immediately below the great North wall of Everest, and the other, the "West Rongbuk" which joins the main stream about 4 miles above the snout of the glacier, flowing East in the basin between the high North-west ridge of Everest and the South-east slopes of Pk. 25,990 (Gyăchung Kang). At one time there was a third branch, the "East Rongbuk," which must have also joined the main stream, but this has receded until its snout is now a mile or more East of the main glacier, and only its torrent pours into a large cave in the latter. The East Rongbuk itself consists of two branches: one, the more southerly, flows from the great snow basin (which we eventually crossed to reach the North Col) between Everest, its North Peak and Col, and Pk. 23,800 (Khărtaphu); and the other, which joins the South branch about 2 miles from its snout, from between Pks. 23,800 and 23,420. The former gives a 20,000-foot pass, very steep on the South side, to the Kāma Valley; and the latter, an easy pass of about the same height to the head of one branch of the Khărta Valley.

I camped, at about 19,500 feet, on the moraine-covered glacier opposite the junction of the northerly branch from Pks. 23,800 and 23,420. On the way up I followed the watercourse between the ice of the Main Rongbuk Glacier and the scree and conglomerate slopes to the East of it, as far as the mouth of the East Rongbuk stream (3 miles), which gave good though boulder-strewn going. Thence a short scramble up "cut-bank" on the right bank of the East Rongbuk stream to the shelf of an old lateral moraine of that glacier, and along the latter—excellent going—to near its snout. The stream is pretty big in the evening; but quite easy to cross—except for iced rocks—in the early morning: and from there I followed up a series of lateral moraines on the left bank, to my camp. It was not till I was coming down that I discovered that the moraine-covered glacier itself—here covered with shale instead of boulders and scree as in the case of the main glacier—gave comfortable walking.

A little distance below my camp site, the moraine-covered snout gives place to pinnacled ice, divided into three sections by two broad, shaly medial moraines. Either of the latter would be very suitable for a camp, and would give an excellent route to our 21,500-foot camp below the Chang La. The latter might, I think, be reached by this route in three days from the base camp at the snout of the main glacier, camping the first night at 19,000 feet at the start of the medial moraine, the second at 20,000 feet on the medial moraine some 2 miles above the junction of the Northern and Southern branches of the East Rongbuk, and the third night on snow at 21,500 feet below the North Col. The better moraine to ascend would require reconnaissance ; for the pinnacles between them are difficult and slow to cross. The valley sides are steep in the lower reaches of the glacier, but more shaly and gentle on both branches, above their junction.

August 3 broke clear ; and I started up a likely looking peak behind (South of) camp, which appeared to be on the ridge between the East and main glaciers. I afterwards found that this was not the case ; at the time I had to stop on a lower point as the clouds settled down. From here I had a glimpse of a big peak—Makālu, I thought—over the pass at the head of the southerly branch of the glacier : and this gave me the idea that there must be a comparatively low pass from here to the Kāma Valley. But clouds prevented me seeing more and studying the topography more carefully. There were heavy snowstorms on August 4 and 5, but the 6th looked better, and after four hours' most strenuous step-cutting up and slithering down pinnacles, I crossed the glacier and ascended a 21,000-foot station on the other side, from which I obtained good, if cloudy, views of the East Rongbuk Glacier. Snow in the night and a dull morning made me decide to abandon this area—I could get my camp no farther up owing to having insufficient warm clothes to camp all my coolies at this height—and I returned to the base camp, preparatory to tackling the West side of the Rongbuk Valley. Six hours' easy going took me to my base camp.

After two days' rest and office work, I crossed the glacier and put a light camp at about 19,000 feet in a small hanging valley below the "Finger," a black rock gendarme which is a very prominent landmark on the left bank of the Rongbuk Valley. On August 11 it snowed heavily, and I found my bed, in which I spent the day, very hard indeed—the camp being pitched on large boulders on top of the moraine. On the 12th, 13th, and 14th, I started for the "Finger," the first time by the ridge immediately above camp, which gave some nice climbing with the rocks partly snow covered as they were, and the other two days, by a much quicker but less interesting route up soft snow and scree. Each day the clouds came down, and although I waited till nearly dark at about 20,500 feet on the ridge, it was not till the third day that I got a round of indifferent photographs.

Time was getting on, so on the 15th I called my "Finger" station "good enough" and moved camp up the left bank of the main glacier to a point on the old lateral moraine, opposite the entrance of the stream from the East Rongbuk; and the next day round the corner to the West, some distance up the West Rongbuk Glacier, and about 1,000 feet above it. *En route,* I tried to get some photographs from the high moraine at the junction of the West with the main glacier; but again the weather defeated me, and I got into camp—another uncomfortable one—soaked to the skin.

I was in this camp for five days; most of them spent huddled under rocks waiting for the clouds to lift. I had one beautiful day, my only one in six weeks, and got some very nice photographs of Mount Everest and its West ridge. It is surprising how a little good weather and the feeling of having really done some work affects one's spirits!

On August 21 I moved back to my base camp at the glacier snout, again trying for a station at the corner—and failing. I had not done nearly as much as I wanted to do; but there seemed to be no end to the bad weather, and only a month or a bit more remained in which to map the whole of the East side of the mountain: and I had heard from Colonel Bury that there would be a considerable amount of work on that side. Originally, I had hoped not only to return to the bridge over the Rā Chu to complete the work in the Kyetrāk Valley, but also to take several stations in the valleys running North from the 23,000-foot group North of Everest. But again apart from shortage of time, the weather made it out of the question, and I went through to Khārta, via the Doya La, arriving there on August 27.

The change in scenery immediately one crosses the Doya La is most marked, both as regards rock and vegetation. The former—mostly gneiss—is far more rugged and interesting, and there is infinitely more of the latter. The Headquarters camp at Khārta, in a little poplar grove, was pleasant indeed after the bleak, uninteresting Rongbuk Valley; and I thoroughly enjoyed my five days there, developing and printing; busy days, but very different from lying on one's back on the sharp boulders of the Rongbuk moraines. Mallory, Bullock and Morshead were in Khārta when I arrived; Colonel Bury and Wollaston returned from their excursion to the Popti La soon after, and Raeburn arrived on September 1. It was a great treat to me to be able to "swap lies" with so many people, after two months almost wholly alone!

On September 3 Morshead and I started up the Khārta Chu in

the wake of Mallory and Bullock, who had gone up to get the "bundobust" for the final fling going. As usual, bad weather dogged my footsteps, and although the weather while I was in Khārta had been glorious, Morshead and I spent seven days in taking two very indifferent stations in the lower part of the Khārta Valley, before joining the remainder of the expedition at the "Advanced Base" on September 11. A further eight days were spent there, waiting for the weather; but in that time I was able to get two very useful stations, one on either side of the valley.

On September 19 I moved up to "No. 1 Camp" with Mallory, Bullock and Morshead; and shared the fortunes of the rest of the Expedition as far as Kampa Dzong on the way back to Darjeeling, where Raeburn, Heron and I left Headquarters to return to Darjeeling via Lachen and the Teesta Valley. I was delighted to get into the "final push," and enjoyed the few days' change from surveying to climbing, enormously; except that I felt the cold very much in my feet, and had it not been for Mallory's good offices—he rubbed my feet for a solid hour after we came down from Chang La—I feel sure that the result might have been much more serious than the slight discomfort I afterwards experienced.

I took three stations in the neighbourhood of No. 1 Camp—one on either side of the Kharta Glacier, and one at 22,300 feet on the "Lhakpa La." This was on snow, with my instrument resting on, and steadied by, bags of "tsampa"; which proved to be a most excellent substitute for rock!

On September 26 I crossed with Colonel Bury and Wollaston to the Kāma Valley; unfortunately, we only had two clear days there, and I had to leave it without covering as much ground as I should have liked, though—as usual—I spent my days in snowstorms, hoping for breaks in the clouds.

The return to Darjeeling via the Serpo La, Lāchen, and the Teesta Valley, made a pleasant change from the Phāri route; but again bad weather spoiled our views, and we saw nothing at all of Kangchenjunga and its neighbours. Raeburn went in by the usual road via Gangtok; Heron and I followed the river—an excellent route in spite of the prevalence of leeches—and reached Pashok on October 19. Heron went on to Darjeeling, a further 18 miles, the same day. I followed on the 20th.

I enjoyed the Expedition and my work with it, thoroughly; but in my opinion, Tibet, at any rate that portion of it in which we were, is a place to have *been*, rather than one to go to!

APPENDIX III

A NOTE ON THE GEOLOGICAL RESULTS OF THE EXPEDITION

BY A. M. HERON, D.Sc., F.G.S., Geological Survey of India.

The area geologically examined is somewhat over 8,000 square miles, comprising the Tibetan portion of the Arun drainage area, with, in the West, the headwaters of the Bhotia Kosi and its tributaries.

The circumstances of the Expedition were not favourable for work in any detail, but an endeavour was made to traverse and map as large an area as possible on a scale of $\frac{1}{4}$-inch to the mile, on skeleton maps very kindly furnished by Major Morshead and his surveyors as their plane-tabling proceeded; my work must therefore be considered as a geological reconnaissance pure and simple.

If I am accorded the privilege of accompanying the second Expedition, by which time Major Wheeler's map on a scale of 1-inch to the mile will be available, I hope to be able to make a detailed survey of the vicinity of Mount Everest and investigate the complicated inter-relationships of the metamorphosed sedimentaries and the associated gneisses and granites.

My survey continues to the Westward Sir Henry Hayden's work during the Tibet Expedition in 1903–4.

Geologically this area is divided into two broad divisions: (*a*) Tibetan and sedimentary, (*b*) Himalayan and crystalline, a distinction which is clearly displayed in the topography resulting from the underlying geological structure, for to the North we have the somewhat tame and lumpy mountains of Tibet contrasting with the higher, steeper and more rugged Himalayas on the South.

The Tibetan zone consists of an intensely folded succession of shales and limestones, with subordinate sandstone quartzites, the folds striking East–West and mainly lying over towards the South, showing that the movements which produced them came from the North.

The uppermost rocks consist of the Kampa system of Hayden, a great thickness of limestones, which, where the rocks have escaped alteration, yield an assemblage of fossils which determine their age as Cretaceous and Eocene.

Below these is a monotonous succession of shales, practically unfossiliferous, with occasional quartzites and limestones representing the Upper and Middle Jurassic with at the base beds probably belonging to the Lias.

These Jurassic shales are by far the most conspicuous formation in this part of Tibet, being repeated many times in complicated folds.

The Cretaceous-Eocene limestones form comparatively narrow bands, occurring as compressed synclines caught up in the folded complex of Jurassic shales.

Along the Southern border of the Tibetan zone, below the base of the Jurassic shales, is a great thickness (2,000 feet–3,000 feet) of thinly bedded limestones in which the fossils have been destroyed and the rocks themselves converted over considerable areas into crystalline limestones and calc-gneisses containing tremolite, epidote, tourmaline, etc., but still retaining their original bedded structure in the banding of the altered rock.

The absence of determinable fossils makes it impossible to determine the age of these with certainty, but from their lithological character and position in the sequence, it is possible that they correspond with the Tso Lhamo limestone in Sikhim (Lias) and the Kioto limestone of the Zangskar range (Lower Jurassic and Upper Trias).

The Himalayan and crystalline zone is essentially composed of foliated and banded biotite-gneiss, usually garnetiferous, on which lie, at comparatively low angles and with a general Northerly dip, the above-mentioned calc-gneisses.

These occur most abundantly to the North and West of Everest, in the Keprak, Rongbu, Hlalung and Rebu Valleys. The group of high peaks to the North-west of Everest (overlooking the Khumbu Pass) is made up of these and intrusive schorl granite, and it would seem that the precipitous North-western face and spurs of Everest are the same.

The Eastern and North-eastern valleys, Chongphu, Kharta and Kama, which are in general at a lower level than the North-western valleys, are excavated in the biotite-gneiss. On the North-eastern face of Everest fresh snow was too abundant at the time of my visit to make out what the rocks were.

Associated with the limestones and calc-gneisses are quartzites and tourmaline-biotite schists which probably represent the lowest portions of the shales immediately overlying the limestones.

It is probable that the biotite-gneiss is an igneous rock intrusive in the calc-gneisses and schists, but this and many other puzzling features of the crystallines require more detailed study than I was able to give this year.

Both biotite-gneiss and metamorphosed sedimentaries are crowded with dykes and sills, of all dimensions, of schorl granite or pegmatite to such an extent that this granite is frequently the predominant rock. It is highly resistant to weathering and it is doubtless due to its presence in large amount that such comparatively soft rocks as the calc-gneisses take part in forming some of the highest summits.

In the same way the scattered peaks of over 20,000 feet on the watershed between the Arun and the Tsangpo owe their prominence to their being groups of veins of a very similar granite, differing in that it contains biotite in place of schorl. Around these separate centres of intrusion are areoles of metamorphism in which the Jurassic shales have been converted into slates and phyllites.

Economically the area traversed by the Expedition is devoid of interest. Barring a little copper staining on a few boulders on moraines no traces of ore were seen.

APPENDIX IV

THE SCIENTIFIC EQUIPMENT

By A. R. HINKS, F.R.S., Secretary of the Royal Geographical Society.

The most important scientific work of the first year's expedition should have been the study of the physiological effects of high altitude that Dr. Kellas had undertaken, with the support of Professor Haldane, F.R.S., and of the Oxygen Research Committee of the Department of Scientific and Industrial Research. In his work on Kamet in 1920, Dr. Kellas had tried, and provisionally decided against, the use of oxygen compressed in cylinders: but he laboured under the grave disadvantage that the light cylinders he hoped to obtain had been, after his departure for India, pronounced unsafe; and the cylinders sent out were clearly too heavy for effective use in climbing. Dr. Kellas had therefore fallen back on the use of oxygen prepared from the reaction between water and oxylith in an apparatus which included a kind of gas mask. He was prepared also to make several difficult researches into the physiological processes of adaptation to low oxygen pressure; and some delicate apparatus was prepared and sent out to him by the Oxygen Research Committee. Unhappily these interesting and important enquiries came to nought, for there was no one competent to carry them on after his lamented death at Kampa Dzong; and the Expedition of 1922 was thereby deprived of much information that should have been at its disposal in studying the use of oxygen for the grand assault.

The scientific equipment for which the Mount Everest Committee were directly responsible was not ambitious: the Survey of India were responsible for the whole of the survey and brought their own equipment, which is described elsewhere in this book. It was necessary to provide the climbing party only with aneroids, compasses, reserve field-glasses, thermometers and cameras, with subsidiary apparatus for checking the aneroids at the base camps, and heavier cameras for work at lower levels.

The aneroids by Cary, Porter & Co. and by Short & Mason were constructed in pairs, to operate from 15,000 to 23,000, and 22,000 to 30,000 feet respectively. They seem to have performed well on the whole, and tests made at the National Physical Laboratory since their return show that they have changed very little; but it cannot be said that their performances were very effectively controlled in the field, for until late in the season there were no trigonometrical heights available, and the climbers had little opportunity in their rather isolated circumstances of employing their aneroids to the best advantage, for purely differential work. Nor is there much to be said as yet on the value of the shortened form of George mercurial barometer, to come into action only at 15,000 feet (Cary, Porter & Co.). These instruments will find effective use only in the second season, when the reference points of the trigonometrical survey will be available as fundamental data.

The climbers carried "Magnapole" compasses with luminous points, and sometimes a Mark VIII prismatic; these all worked well. The simpler compass is the more convenient for use on snow when goggles must be worn. A luminous liquid compass (Short & Mason) was found very useful on long reconnaissance rides.

For the record of temperatures in camps Messrs. Negretti & Zambra had made three small pairs of maximum and minimum thermometers in leather travelling cases. These suffered some casualties, by theft, or being accidentally left out in the sun; and the pattern has been repeated for the second year's work.

The heavier photographic equipment included an old and well-seasoned 7½ × 5 Hare Camera, lent to the Expedition, but newly fitted by Messrs. Dallmeyer with a Stigmatic lens of 9 inches focal length, a negative telephoto lens of 4 inches focal length giving enlargement up to 6 times, and a set of Wratten filters. With this camera Mr. Wollaston secured some of the finest pictures taken on the Expedition.

There were also two quarter-plate cameras for glass plates: a Sinclair Una camera fitted by Messrs. Dallmeyer with a Stigmatic lens of 5·3 inches focal length, and Adon telephoto lens; and a second Sinclair camera lent by Captain Noel.

One or the other of these two was used by Mr. Mallory at many of the high camps, and both the Hare 7½ × 5 and the Sinclair quarter-plate went to the 22,500-foot camp at the Lhakpa La: doubtless the greatest height yet attained by so large a camera as the former. The principal difficulty with these cameras was unsteadiness in a heavy wind when the telephoto lens was in use: and the tripods have been strengthened and the lens supports stiffened before they go out again.

The plates were of two kinds: Imperial Special Rapid and Fine Grain slow. The latter were generally preferred, and could hardly have been better. The Imperial Dry Plate Company, who generously made and presented these plates to the Expedition, deserve special thanks for their skill and for their generosity.

The cameras which used films were a Panoram Kodak of 5 inches focal length, with films 12 × 4 inches; a No. 1 Autograph Kodak, and two Vest Pocket Kodaks, all three fitted with Cooke lenses by Messrs. Taylor, Taylor & Hobson. The Panoram Kodak was used very successfully by Colonel Howard-Bury, and the splendid series of panoramas is the most useful, if not quite the most beautiful, set of photographs brought home. The smaller cameras were used by the climbing party with many good results.

Finally it must be said that a large part of the best photographs were taken by Colonel Howard-Bury with his own 7 × 5 Kodak, and the results very generously placed at the disposal of the Committee.

All the instruments were examined and tested at the National Physical Laboratory, and the thanks of the Committee are due to the Director and his staff, who gave most valuable advice and assistance.

APPENDIX V

MAMMALS, BIRDS AND PLANTS COLLECTED BY THE EXPEDITION

By A. F. R. WOLLASTON

A.—LIST OF MAMMALS COLLECTED

Stoat. *Mustela temon*
Stoat. *Mustela longstaffi*
Marmot. *Marmota himalayana*
Hamster. *Cricetulus alticola tibetanus*, subsp. n.
Vole. *Phaiomys leucurus*
Vole. *Phaiomys everesti*
Vole. *Microtus* (*Alticola*), sp.
Pika. *Ochotona roylei nepalensis*
Pika. *Ochotona wollastoni*, sp. n.
Pika. *Ochotona curzoniæ*

B.—LIST OF BIRDS COLLECTED

Central Asian blackbird. *Turdus maxima*
Solitary thrush. *Monticola solitarius*
White-breasted Asiatic dipper. *Cinclus cashmirensis*
Indian stone-chat. *Saxicola torquata indica*
Gould's desert chat. *Saxicola montana*
Bush chat. *Pratincola prjevalskii*
Indian redstart. *Ruticilla rufiventris*
Guldenstadt's Afghan redstart. *Ruticilla grandis*
White-capped redstart. *Chimarrhornis leucocephalus*
Hodgson's grandala. *Grandala cœlicolor*
Tickell's willow-warbler. *Phylloscopus affinis*
Mandelli's willow-warbler. *Phylloscopus mandellii*
Smoky willow-warbler. *Phylloscopus fulviventris*
Spotted bush-warbler. *Lusciniola thoracica*
Prince Henry's laughing thrush. *Trochalopterum henrici*

Eastern alpine accentor. *Accentor rufiliatus*
Red-breasted accentor. *Accentor rubeculoides*
Rufous-breasted accentor. *Accentor strophiatus*
Brown accentor. *Accentor fulvescens*
Sikkim black tit. *Parus beavani*
Wren. *Troglodytes*, sp.
Hodgson's pied wagtail. *Motacilla hodgsoni*
White-faced wagtail. *Motacilla leucopsis*
Yellow-headed wagtail. *Motacilla citreola.*
Blyth's pipit. *Anthus citreola*
Indian tree-pipit. *Anthus maculatus*
Hodgson's pipit. *Anthus rosaceus*
Grey-backed shrike. *Lanius tephronotus*
Slaty-blue flycatcher. *Cyornis leucomelanurus*
Himalayan greenfinch. *Hypacanthis spinoides*
Tree-sparrow. *Passer montanus*
Cinnamon tree-sparrow. *Passer cinnamomeus*
Blanford's snow-finch. *Montifringilla blanfordi*
Adams' snow-finch. *Montifringilla adamsi.*
Hodgson's ground-finch. *Fringilauda nemoricola*
Brandt's ground-linnet. *Leucosticte brandti.*
Walton's twite. *Linota rufostrigata*
Red-breasted rose-finch. *Pyrrhospiza punicea*
Scarlet rose-finch. *Carpodacus erythrinus*
Hodgson's rose-finch. *Carpodacus pulcherrimus*
Severtzoff's rose-finch. *Carpodacus severtzoi*
Prejewalk's rose-finch. *Carpodacus rubicilloides*
Red-headed bullfinch. *Pyrrhula erythrocephala*
Godlevski's meadow bunting. *Emberiza godlevskii*
Elwes' shore-lark. *Otocorys elwesi*
Long-billed calandra lark. *Melanocorpha maxima*
Tibetan skylark. *Alauda inopinata*
Short-toed lark. *Calandrella brachydactyla*
Brook's short-toed lark. *Calandrella acutirostris tibitana*
Chough. *Pyrrhocorax graculus*
Brown ground-chough. *Podoces humilis*
Common hoopoe. *Upupa epops*
Pied crested cuckoo. *Coccystes jacobinus*
Eastern little owl. *Athene bactriana*
White-backed dove. *Columba leuconota*
Snow partridge. *Lerwa lerwa*

Temminck's stint. *Tringa temmincki*
Redshank. *Totanus calidris*
Dusky redshank. *Totanus fuscus*
Greater sand plover. *Aœgialitis mongola*
Common tern. *Sterna fluviatilis*

In addition to the above the following birds were identified, but specimens of them were not obtained :—

Wall-creeper
House martin
Sand martin
Rock martin
Alpine chough
Magpie
Black crow
Raven
Swift
Siberian swift
Cuckoo
Himalayan vulture
Lammergeier
Sea eagle
Pallas' sea eagle
Black-eared kite
Barheaded goose
Ruddy sheldrake
Garganey
Wigeon
Pochard
Gadwall
Hill rock-dove
Chinese turtle dove
Tibetan partridge
Tibetan snow partridge
Blood pheasant
Black-necked crane
White stork
Ibis-bill
Painted snipe
Pin-tailed snipe
Brown-headed gull

C.—LIST OF PLANTS COLLECTED BETWEEN JUNE AND SEPTEMBER, 1921, 12,000–20,400 FT.

Clematis orientalis, L.
Ranunculus pulchellus, C. A. Mey., var. sericeus, Hk. f. & T.
Ranunculus pulchellus, C. A. Mey.
Anemone obtusiloba, Don
Anemone polyanthes, Don
Anemone rivularis, Ham.
Geranium Grevilleanum, Wall.
Caltha scaposa, Hk. f. & T.
Delphinium Brunonianum, Royle
Aconitum gymnandrum, Max.
Aconitum orochryseum, Stapf, sp. nov.
Delphinium Pylzowii, Maxim.
Halenia elliptica, Don
Delphinium grandiflorum, L.
Hypecoum leptocarpum, Hk. f. & T.
Meconopsis horridula, Hk. f. & T.
Meconopsis grandis, Prain ?
Meconopsis, sp.
Corydalis, sp.
Corydalis juncea, Wall.

Corydalis Moorcroftiana, Wall.
Arabis tibetica, Hk. f. & T.
Lepidium ruderale, L.
Arenaria ciliolata, Edgew.
Dilophia salsa, Hk. f. & T.
Cardamine macrophylla, Willd.
Arenaria Stracheyi, Edgew.
Silene Waltoni, F. N. Williams
Silene Moorcroftiana, Wall.
Arenaria musciformis, Wall.
Arenaria melandrioides, Edgew.
Polygonum islandicum, Hk. f.
Geranium collinum, A. DC.
Impatiens sulcatus, Wall.
Thermopsis barbata, Royle
Thermopsis lanceolata, R. Br.
Sophora Moorcroftiana, Benth.
Stracheya tibetica, Benth.
Astragalus strictus, Grah.
Oxytropis microphylla, DC
Gueldenstædtia uniflora, Benth.
Desmodium nutans, Wall.
Potentilla coriandrifolia, Hk. f.
Potentilla multifida, L.
Potentilla sericea, L.
Potentilla microphylla, Don
Potentilla peduncularis, Don
Potentilla Griffithii, Hk. f.
Spiræa arcuata, Hk. f.
Saxifraga Lychnitis, Hk. f. & T.
Saxifraga nutans, Hk. f. & T.
Saxifraga aristulata, Hk. f.
Saxifraga near S. saginoides, Hk. f. & T.
Saxifraga flagellaris, Willd.
Saxifraga Hirculus, L.
Saxifraga Lychnitis, Hk. f. & T.
Saxifraga fimbriata, Wall.
Saxifraga pilifera, Hk. f. & T.
Saxifraga Caveana, W. W. Sm.
Saxifraga microphylla, Royle
Saxifraga pallida, Wall.
Saxifraga umbellulata, Hk. f. & T.
Parnassia ovata, Ledeb.
Parnassia pusilla, Wall.
Eutrema Prewalskii, Hk. f. & T.
Sedum fastigiatum, Hk. f. & T.
Sedum trifidum, Wall.
Sedum crenulatum, Hk. f. & T.
Sedum himalense, Don
Epilobium palustre, L.
Epilobium reticulatum, C. B. Cl.
Pleurospermum Hookeri, C. B. Cl.
Scabiosa Hookeri, C. B. Cl.
Valeriana Hardwickii, Wall.
Aster, sp.
Aster heterochætus, C. B. Cl.
Allardia glabra, Dcne.
Aster tibeticus, Hk. f.
Cremanthodium Decaisnei, C. B. Cl.
Aster diplostephioides, C. B. Cl.
Erigeron, sp.
Leontopodium fimbrilligerum, J. R. Drum. ?
Leontopodium monocephalum, Edgew.
Leontopodium Stracheyi, C. B. Cl.
Anaphalis xylorhiza, Sch. Bip.
Anaphalis cuneifolia, Hook. f.
Tanacetum tibeticum, Hk. f. & T.
Senecio arnicoides, Wall. var. frigida, Hk. f.
Cremanthodium pinnatifidum, Benth.
Chrysanthemum Atkinsoni, C. B. Cl. ?
Artemisia Moorcroftiana, Wall.
Sonchus sp.
Senecio glomerata, Decne.
Senecio (§ Ligularia) sp.

Senecio chrysanthemoides, DC.
Tanacetum khartense, Dunn, sp. nov.
Aster sp.
Lactuca macrantha, C. B. Cl.
Senecio sorocephala, Hemsl.
Saussurea gossypina, Wall.
Saussurea tridactyla, Sch. Bip.
Tanacetum gossypinum, Hk. f. & T.
Saussurea wernerioides, Sch. Bip.
Crepis glomerata, Hk. f. ?
Saussurea graminifolia, Wall.
Senecio arnicoides, Wall.
Saussurea uniflora, Wall.
Morina polyphylla, Wall.
Saussurea glandulifera, Sch. Bip.
Lactuca Dubyæa, C. B. Cl.
Lactuca Lessertiana, C. B. Cl.
Cassiope fastigiata, D. Don
Daphne retusa, Hemsl.
Rhododendron lepidotum, Wall.
Rhododendron setosum, Don
Rhododendron near R. lepidotum, Wall.
Rhododendron campylocarpum, Hk. f.
Rhododendron cinnabarinum, Hk. f.
Rhododendron lanatum, Hk. f.
Rhododendron arboreum, Sm.
Rhododendron Thomsoni, Hk. f.
Cyananthus incanus, Hk. f. & T.
Glossocomia tenera, DC.
Cyananthus pedunculatus, C. B. Cl.
Campanula modesta, Hk. f. & T.
Campanula colorata, Wall.
Campanula aristata, Wall.
Androsace chamæjasme, Hort., var. coronata, Wall.
Androsace villosa, L. var. ?
Androsace strigillosa, Franch.
Primula minutissima, Jacq.
Primula Buryana, Balf. f. sp. nov.
Primula Wollastonii, Balf. f. sp. nov.
Primula pusilla, Wall.
Primula sikkimensis, Hook. microform
Primula capitata, Hook.
Primula capitata, microform.
Primula uniflora, Klatt
Primula Dickieana, Watt.
Primula obliqua, W. W. Sm.
Primula indobella. Balf. f.
Primula minutissima, Jacq.
Primula glabra, Klatt
Primula Younghusbandii, sp. nov.
Primula tibetica, Watt.
Primula denticulata, Sm.
Primula sikkimensis, Hook.
Primula nivalis, Pallas, var. macrocarpa, Pax.
Gentiana amœna, C. B. Cl.
Gentiana ornata, Wall.
Gentiana sp. Probably new but the material is too imperfect to decide this.
Gentiana Elwesii, C. B. Cl.
Gentiana robusta, King
Gentiana micantiformis, Burkill
Gentiana nubigena, Edgew.
Gentiana tubiflora, Wall., var. longiflora, Turrill, var. nov.
Gentiana stellata, Turrill, sp. nov.
Gentiana tenella, Fries
Swertia cuneata, Wall.
Arenaria Stracheyi, Edgew.

Swertia Kingii, Hk. f.
Swertia Younghusbandii, Burkill
Swertia multicaulis, D. Don
Nardostachys grandiflora, DC.
Trigonotis rotundifolia, Benth.
Eritrichium densiflorum, Duthie
Microula sikkimensis, Hemsl.
Onosma Waddellii, Duthie
Onosma Hookeri, C. B. Cl.
Verbascum Thapsus, L.
Lancea tibetica, Hk. f. & T.
Lagotis crassifolia, Prain
Pedicularis trichoglossa, Hk. f.
Pedicularis Elwesii, Hk. f.
Pedicularis megalantha, Don, forma
Pedicularis megalantha, Don, var. pauciflora, Prain
Pedicularis Roylei, Maxim.
Pedicularis siphonantha, Don
Pedicularis cheilanthifolia, Schrank
Pedicularis tubiflora, Fischer
Pedicularis integrifolia, Hk. f.
Pedicularis globifera, Hk. f.
Incarvillea Younghusbandii, Sprague
Escholtzia eriostachya, Benth.
Nardostachys Iatamansi, DC.
Dracocephalum breviflorum, Turrill, sp. nov.
Dracocephalum tanguticum, Maxim.
Dracocephalum heterophyllum, Benth.
Dracocephalum speciosum, Benth.
Veronica lanuginosa, Benth.
Nepeta discolor, Benth.
Nepeta Thomsoni, Benth.
Atriplex rosea, L.
Polygonum vaccinifolium, Wall.
Polygonum viviparum, L.
Polygonum tortuosum, Don
Polygonum affine, Don
Polygonum amphibium, L.
Stellera chamæjasme, L.
Euphorbia Stracheyi, Boiss.
Orchis cylindrostachys, Kränzl.
Liparis sp.
Goodyera fusca, Lindl.
Dendrobium alpestre, Royle
Pleione Hookeriana, S. Moore
Orchis Chusna, Don
Roscoea purpurea, Sm.
Iris nepalensis, Don
Iris goniocarpa, Baker
Iris tenuifolia, Pallas
Lloydia tibetica, Baker
Lloydia sp.
Fritillaria Hookeri, Baker
Fritillaria near F. Stracheyi, Hk. f.
Fritillaria cirrhosa, Don
Allium, sp.
Allium Wallichii, Kunth
Allium Govenianum, Wall. ?
Allium cyaneum, Regel
Larix Griffithii, Hk. f.
Dryopteris Linneana, C. Chr.
Dryopteris Filix-mas, var. serrato-dentata, C. Chr.
Cryptogramma Brunoniana, Wall.
Calophaca crassicaulis, Benth.
Glaux maritima, L.
Androsace sessiliflora, Turrill, sp. nov.
Astragalus oreotrophes, W. W. Sm.
Thamnolia vermicularis, Schær.
Stereocaulon alpinus, Laur.
Thelochistes flavicans, Norm.

NOTE.—The material of some of the numbers was insufficient for accurate determination; in a few cases the material necessary for comparison was on loan, and in the case of one or two genera, such as *Aster*, revision of the North Asian and Indian species will have to be undertaken before certain plants can be definitely named. The numbers in the list coming under these categories are named " ——sp."

ROYAL BOTANIC GARDENS, KEW.

March 7, 1922.

INDEX